THE PARANORMAL AND THE NORMAL

A Historical, Philosophical and Theoretical Perspective

Morton Leeds and Gardner Murphy

The Scarecrow Press, Inc.
Metuchen, N.J., & London 1980

Library of Congress Cataloging in Publication Data

Leeds, Morton.
    The paranormal and the normal.

    Bibliography: p.
    Includes index.
    1. Psychical research. I. Murphy, Gardner, 1895-
joint author. II. Title.
BF1031. L39   133   79-25307
ISBN 0-8108-1278-9

To Lois

Table of Contents

iv

List of Figures

List of Tables

Acknowledgments

First of all, we want to thank our colleagues and friends who have read this manuscript and have provided valuable comments. Montague Ullman and Karlis Osis patiently read it several times in the early stages, and their suggestions were invaluable. Charles Tart and Charles Honorton both added important criticism, while Ian Stevenson and Laura Dale caught innumerable errors. Wendy and Karen Leeds and Linda Christie helped with the typing. Richard T. Davis did yeoman work with the illustrations. To these we want to add those others who encouraged us with help and advice as we struggled along--friends, family and colleagues.

For permission to reprint material from the published sources indicated, we and our publisher gratefully extend thanks to the following.

E. P. Dutton and Co., Inc., and Charles T. Tart, for two figures, 7-1 and 4-6, from States of Consciousness, by Charles T. Tart. Copyright © by Charles T. Tart. Reprinted by permission of the publisher, E. P. Dutton.

John Wiley & Sons, Inc., and Charles T. Tart, for a quotation from his article "Psychedelic Experiences Associated with a Novel Hypnotic Procedure, Mutual Hypnosis," in Altered States of Consciousness, Charles T. Tart, Editor. Copyright © 1969, by John Wiley & Sons.

The Journal of Communication, Winter 1975, v. 25, #1, On Psychical Research, by Gardner Murphy.

Viking Penguin, for the excerpt from The Medium, the Mystic and the Physicist, by Lawrence LeShan. Copyright © 1966, 1973, 1974 by Lawrence LeShan.

Rand McNally & Company and Ronald Rose, for a quotation from Living Magic by Ronald Rose. Copyright © 1956

turbances." JASPR, 1971. 65, 409-454.

Roll, W. G., D. S. Burdick, and W. T. Joines. "Radial and Tangential Forces in the Miami Poltergeist." JASPR, 1973. 67, 267-281.

Stanford, R. G., et al. "Psychokinesis as Psi-Mediated Instrumental Response." JASPR, 1975. 69, 127-133.

Pierce, H. W. "RSPK Phenomena Observed Independently by Two Families." JASPR, 1973. 67, 86-101.

Maher, M., and G. R. Schmeidler. "Quantitative Investigation of a Recurrent Apparition." JASPR, 1975. 69, 341-352.

Grad, B. "Some Biological Effects of the 'Laying on of Hands.' A Review of Experiments with Animals and Plants." JASPR, 1965. 59, 95-129.

White, R. A. "The Influence of Persons Other Than the Experimenter on the Subject's Scores in Psi Experiments." JASPR, 1976. 70, 133-166.

Foreword

Past research in psi has dealt largely with careful study of spontaneous cases and the production of mediums, with descriptive documentation of experimental work. Recently, experimental subjects have been tested more thoroughly, and the statistical treatment has improved considerably. There has, however, been limited serious effort to develop a theory of so-called paranormal functions. We do not in fact know whether what we have been calling paranormal lies outside the boundaries of normal functioning. We have considered it so because it is rare, because it is hard to study with repeatable experiments and because such a wide range of parameters appears to be involved in it.

The present book attempts to deal with this gap. Part I outlines for the reader who is not thoroughly familiar with psi research, important work from the earliest days to the present. It provides a selective historical review aimed at those persons, events and ideas that form a conceptual backdrop to the subsequent materials. Part II deals with the philosophical implications of the basic conceptual issues. Part III then moves into a formulation of the relation between paranormal events and the normal channels that we assume are being utilized. The beginning of a theory of psi is presented, with a suggested induction process of how psi is likely to arise. Part IV continues to develop the theory and presents the psi matrix, with testable hypotheses, quoting relevant research to date, spontaneous instances and related scientific data. These hypotheses are intended to trigger varied research that could bear upon the broad-ranging field of psi. We recognize that future work and other thinkers will have to modify, elaborate or even contradict some of what we have formulated, but in any event, the effort to conceptualize the processes of paranormal functioning is not only necessary but is as important as the demonstration of paranormal events. We do not suggest that what we propose is definitive--rather just the opposite; it is suggestive, tentative, subject to constant revision upon the presentation of new facts and evidence. It offers, however, a kind of framework for a field notably lacking a satisfactory framework related to normal functioning. We hope that it serves our purpose--to enlist the service and serious study of a generation of dedicated, competent, imaginative and unafraid researchers. The cases we have chosen, incidentally, illustrate aspects of the theory, without attempting to prove anything. Part IV concludes with some miscellaneous concepts that are too speculative to include in the initial hypothesis. Part V provides some final reflections on the problem as a whole, emphasizing the issue of repeatability.

A note on the personal pronoun "I," in a book with two authors. Gardner Murphy wrote the initial introduction, Parts I and II (except for "The Psi Scene Today," which includes his role), and Sections C and D of Part V. The rest is the work of Morton Leeds. Interaction, however, continued throughout.

Introduction

Sir Arthur Conan Doyle had a go at the mystery of psi, but in this regard he was no Sherlock Holmes, since it was too great even for him to solve. Instead, it takes the rivals and successors of a Sherlock Holmes to cope with this vast, mysterious, many-niched pyramid of concepts and events.

Telepathy, clairvoyance and precognition aroused the interests of the ancients--Aristotle, for example, in the West and Patanjali in the East. Far back in our prehistory people fretted about the strange quality of dreams that seemed to foretell the future. Priests who could heal mysteriously were revered and feared. Those who could detect events at a great distance when possessed by alien spirits were given special titles and places to stay. From every corner of the earth stories have been gathered, such as those about the Australian Bushmen who clung to their glassy meteoritic tektites, while describing serious illness occurring to members of their families hundreds of miles away.

Until modern science took shape a few centuries ago, reasonable men and women could be found everywhere who took such phenomena seriously, and other reasonable people who doubted or belittled them. Shakespeare, as always, shows us the range of attitudes to be expected: at the beginning of Hamlet, for example, a rough soldier's point of view about the ghost; later, the more thoughtful comments of a student; and finally the deeper efforts at understanding on the part of Hamlet himself help us to feel that these are confrontations with the more challenging aspects of nature. Thus psychic phenomena have been a puzzle to humankind for a very long time.

A very common attitude in most eras was to believe that such events were more than strange; they expressed an especially rich vein of the divine in human life, or perhaps even more commonly, they represented supernatural diabolism.

Macbeth, indeed, tries to wrench from the witches what it was unlawful for him to know, as Saul did from the witch of Endor. To the inherent likelihood of damage from the uncanny and the unearthly was added the possibility of a direct and intelligent malevolence. Men and women could, however, use the "white," rather than the "black," and rely upon God to guide them through the supernatural quicksand. These attitudes are still deep in our culture: if I seem to catch a thought from someone a thousand miles away, this is not ordinarily held to be a simple question of scientific challenge for authentication or rejection; it is held to be "spooky," and there is a faint stigma associated with listening to such marvels. The reports of such happenings studied by psychical research are often classified with the "miraculous."

The Scientific Approach

For many, a plausible, modern physical theory as to the operation of "psychic phenomena" would rid them of their annoying quality and make them almost palatable. For others, with deeper resistance to understanding, it would spoil the appeal lying in that which is intrinsically a superchallenge, a possible path to something new in a very special sense. It will be very difficult, in pursuing our historical approach to research into psi, to remember that men and women of various periods have had varying attitudes toward the nature of scientific inquiry and have devised methods of accumulating accepted evidence in accordance with the thought forms of the era, exactly as the more lucid books on the history of science have made clear. Like all the sciences, presciences and would-be-sciences, psi is a child of its time, and readers will find the data and, indeed, the whole approach credible or incredible largely in terms of what they understand to be the nature of the scientific enterprise. It will be worthwhile, then, to say a few words about the rise of the systematic "materialistic" or "mechanist" conceptions in recent centuries and the alternative interpretations of the universe with which these views have contended. The systematic material atomism and mechanism of the Greek philosopher Democritus was opposed by all philosophies that thought mind and matter to be fundamentally different kinds of things; and to these "dualistic" views the Christian church gave dignity and spiritual approval. The rise of mechanical conceptions of the universe in Copernicus's, Galileo's and Newton's orderly explanations of the movements of celestial bodies and of terrestrial objects subjected to experiments made it appear in the eight-

eenth century that the universe was one great homogeneous
system, allowing no real credibility for mental events independent of physical events. Thomas Hobbes in England, and
La Mettrie a little later in France, made it possible to think
of man as a machine. It was not a question of denying the
reality of the mind, but rather of making the mind an expression of the physical realities of bodily functioning.

The development of a consistent philosophy of nature's
unity, which we may call "naturalism," had made nature so
well articulated, so snugly rolled into a single unified system,
that radical new physical forces were a nuisance and a threat
to the expanding labors of the sciences.

This raises some curious questions. Why did the
naturalism of the seventeenth and eighteenth centuries necessarily entail the end of belief in the traditional phenomena of
telepathy, clairvoyance, precognition, paranormal healing,
and the rest? What was it about the paranormal that had
become "unnatural"? Was it the religious conception of the
phenomena or was it their implied philosophic dualism, or
both? Most of the reported phenomena could in time have
been so stated as to be viewed naturalistically. Perhaps the
deep "materialistic monism" that was creeping through seven-
teenth- and eighteenth-century science was determining in advance how the unexplained phenomena of telepathy and clairvoyance had to be explained, asserting in advance that they
could certainly not be explained at all, whether in physical
or nonphysical terms. From this point of view these newly-
reported phenomena simply had to be interpreted as a threat
to the physical monism of the period.

In our own little study of dowsing for water (see pp.
134-135 below) with twenty-seven ordinary Americans from
Maine, all of our subjects made an attempt to explain dowsing
in simple physical terms, as if we were dealing with batteries, grounds and resistances; not one suggested the possibility that these were "psychic" capacities. "Psychic" matters, to their way of thinking, were something entirely different. There has apparently been a "displacement" in thinking about the "nonphysical" operating in two diametrically opposed directions: (a) in the direction of making the phenomena inherently incredible because nonphysical, and (b) in the
direction of pushing the phenomena into the physical category.

However this may be, the conception of the paranormal
has in the last few decades become pretty clear. Almost

everyone understands with reasonable consistency the concepts of seeing without using the sense organs, or looking
directly into the future, or producing movements of distant
objects without use of the usual muscular energies. This is
what people mean, in fact, by the paranormal; and to keep
close to the community of which we are a part, we may, so
long as no direct logical contradictions or violations of known
fact are involved, use the term psi to indicate all the processes subsumed under this general head. These are the
events that stand out as not belonging to the known, physically interpretable world.

Is this all that the world of psi consists of? Not
really, because for many reasons there is an intermediate
region between the paranormal and the normal. There is a
widespread tendency to regard various altered psychological
states, such as those of ecstasy, trance, prophetic vision,
states of "cosmic consciousness," or samadhi, or satori,
not only as belonging to psi, but as constituting a key to
paranormal process.

The more disciplined adherents to the current scientific world view will usually endeavor to bring this intermediate class of phenomena within the naturalistic physical-
chemical system of explanatory concepts, and will, more
explicitly than with the less sophisticated thinker, gladly re-
pudiate those events that do not belong to the matter-time-
space-energy-force world of the modern physical sciences.

This will mean that our Western scientific outlook will
go quite far in exposing the paradoxes that we noted above,
while the philosophies of Asia will offer no resistance.
Whether various types of paranormal phenomena exist or not
appears to be primarily a question of the validity of the
various reported observations. The phenomena are so evanescent and often uncertain; are intertwined with deep inner
fears and aspirations; and emerge in dreams and other
strange border states, out of the normal. No wonder that
they have an inherent tendency to lead to prejudgments that
"the phenomena must be of such and such a type." Only in
terms that prejudge vast areas of future research can the
phenomena be described so as to sound credible.

Energy and Perception

From an evolutionary point of view it would appear
highly probable that the means of making contact with the

environment would be developed along many different lines, and that these should be investigated by science in an order determined by existing knowledge and research skills. Relatively simple and dependable energies, such as the energies involved in light and sound, touch and temperature, must be investigated as their operation becomes clear. Electromagnetic phenomena come much later. Today, the effects of x-rays and cosmic rays upon living tissue have begun to be investigated. How far these may prove to be models or prototypes of other types of energy relationships used by the living organism in adaptation to its environment is simply unknown today.

Organisms live in an ambience of multiple energies. Tiny particles impinge on mucous membranes and set going messages to higher nerve centers, which activate behavior; we also speak of "chemo-receptors." Sound waves impinge upon delicately specialized receptor surfaces, which trigger a series of inwardly moving messages to "auditory centers." A very considerable number of electromagnetic wave lengths produce triggering action at specialized surfaces, some of which set going the intricate mechanisms of vision. Gross pressures yield messages having to do with position and movement, and from the muscles that are responsible for movement, there are feedback messages that tell us about our ongoing movement. The "five senses" of antiquity have become twenty-odd senses today, the number depending upon the refinement, the specification of what we mean by a "sense." Thus the "vibratory sense," ancillary to the skin pick-up from pressure, must be added to the "vestibular" sensitivities, which report on acceleration in one direction or on rotary movement.

Many of the sensory functions are "unconscious" in the sense that they bring information without bringing into consciousness a specific quality of experience. Ordinarily, vestibular functions, for example, are "unconscious" in this sense, although if there is an overload of energy in the system, it may "spill over" and dizziness or nausea may follow. This is one of the many respects in which modern information theory would differentiate between the sensory qualities conveyed by sensory messages on the one hand, and the information that is imparted with or without the conscious experience specific to the sensory excitation. As J. J. Gibson (1966) has pointed out in The Perception of the Visual World, we may consider the senses as "perceptual systems" from the viewpoint of information theory, and our interest may lie less in the sensory qualities than in the kind of information conceived.

From this viewpoint the critical question constantly arises: can we, once and for all, define the types of energy that mediate information? Do we know all the sources of energy? It may be that there are senses whose receptor organs are not yet discovered. There may be forms of information that are dependent upon direct excitation of the brain by some sort of energies and physical systems not yet understood. The effects of light on the pineal glands of migrating birds are an example of this. We may be leading beyond the compass of today's wise speculation, but there may well be forms of stimulation beyond those currently understood.

Knowing nothing of information theory, or even of sense organs as such, preliterate societies have been quite familiar with forms of communication that they attributed to an immaterial soul capable of making itself known to other immaterial souls at a distance, or exerting physical effects of a sort different from those that they could most directly understand and control. They saw visual apparitions of the deceased, sometimes clear and distinct, sometimes showing in face or posture some emotion that they wished to convey. Often, as a man dreamed, he encountered distant friends or enemies, and returning and awakening he would describe the spirits whom he had thus encountered. This kind of contact of the living with the deceased thus expressed either in the waking hallucination or in the dreaming fantasy were well known to the Homeric era and classical Roman times, as expressed in Aeneas's attempt to grasp the "shade" of his father. The Old Testament and the epic poems of India make real to us the encounter of living with deceased personalities.

Sometimes the need to control leads to the attribution of Satanic or divine attributes to that which is so close to humankind, so needful to life. From this viewpoint, it is not quite correct to say that humans attribute "supernatural" powers to the dead, to the sacred spring, or to the hair and fingernails of the chief. Physical and mental are not sharply separated, and there is in the fingernails as there was in the chief itself, a power that our wishes and our fears inflate to almost omnipotent levels. Often, as one stumbles, one finds a malignant intent on the part of the stone upon which one stumbled, or the diabolical force which caused it to happen. The world is shot through with purposes that are fully natural. The supernatural is thus merely the natural in an inflated form.

Scientific progress has consisted to a considerable degree in withdrawing the purposes and personal qualities from inanimate objects, in ceasing to assign psychological attributes altogether to the raw physical events of nature. This trend, so central in the growth of science, was pushed by Descartes into the thesis that animals are automata, and by implication his followers began to think of people likewise as automata. Instead of two systems--a physical system and a psychological system--hovering over the lives of animal and human, there came about, as with La Mettrie, a conception of one physicalist system, perfectly expressed both in animal life, and even in the life of the individual human. Not all who read La Mettrie found the automaton theory useful, but all thoughtful people of the eighteenth century began to see that the anima, the soul, something added to the physical body, was not a necessary assumption to explain the events of the visible world about us, whether of human or subhuman origin; the physical system, if intelligently stretched to cover all experiences, could result in a coherent system.

However, each science has its stages, beginning with open-minded observations ranging all the way up to systematic testing, rigid internal criteria and canons of proof. Somewhere along the middle of a given science's evolution we may find the experiment, based on assembled knowledge that suggests careful testing to the experimenter who is trying to systematize his or her thoughts amid a bewildering array of apparent facts and artifacts. Here in psi, one complication is the apparently sharp difference in individual abilities among "sensitives." Another is the difficulty in replicating genuine emotional or physical crises that occur in real life. Thus, in any arranging of an experimental setting, we need to recognize the varieties of data and observations that arise spontaneously versus those of the laboratory setting.

The Replicable Experiment

Where would physics be if there were neither a replicable experiment nor a generally received comprehensive theory? The answer is that it would be a proto-science, a collection of observations and concepts on their way toward systematization. This is approximately where psi stands now. Let us look first at the problem of the replicable experiment, and second at the problem of conceptual order.

There are several classes of repeatable experiments, if one means that the phenomena will frequently--or indeed, usually--appear under certain defined experimental conditions. When G. R. Schmeidler (Schmeidler and McConnell, 1958) specifies that those who believe in the possibility of extra-sensory perception under the conditions of the experiment (the "sheep") will score higher than those who do not (the "goats"), she reports over a span of nearly thirty years that the great majority of such experimental tests have come out in the expected direction to a significant degree. We are actually a little bit better off thereby than we should be if relying simply upon a mass trend, for in several of the cases where a closer analysis of the psychology of the situation is possible, there are reasons why the "sheep" should not be expected in fact to surpass the "goats." Of course, we may not for statistical purposes allow ourselves the benefit of such hindsight, but if we are looking for a comprehensive theoretical principle, we may say that it is not negated by the Schmeidler work as a whole. Her work and that which has followed from it does in fact exemplify a major principle --that of motivation, attitude, set--which appears to be emerging both from spontaneous and from experimental data. In the matter of replication by other investigators, Mangan's (1958) and Palmer's (1971) reports indicate that a majority of the efforts in this direction have confirmed the Schmeidler conclusions--again with some debatable instances in which the psychology of the situation was perhaps not of a sort in which we would expect the general principle to hold. We have no certain and undebatable replication here, but we have an interesting trend: replication both by the original investigator and by other investigators, attempting to follow the prescribed method.

This is not, however, replication in the sense in which we look for it in the establishment of science, or even in the confirmation of a principle deemed probably sound. The chemist teaching beginners the nature of combustion does not expect the magnesium strip to catch fire "most of the time," but every time a match is applied. When handling a mixture of hydrogen bubbles and oxygen bubbles, the chemist does not expect H_2O to emerge most of the time, but <u>every</u> time. There is, of course, a world of probability unclear in nuclear physics in which events do not happen all the time, but this is a problem entirely different from that of the introductory principles that we expect to be confirmable in any established science, and are confirmable in point of fact in the sciences of physics and chemistry. In psi, the

basic principles are not vitiated merely because they appear
in situations in which contexts are more complex than those
of elementary physics and chemistry. There are, on the
contrary here, no elementary principles of this sort. There
are principles on which evidence converges, principles that
are very probably sound, but at present they do not give us
uniformly replicable experiments with similar results.

The effort toward generating such experiments is becoming irresistible today. The work for example, of Ullman, Krippner and Honorton, at Maimonides Medical Center
(Ullman and Krippner, with Vaughan, 1973) is in this direction and definite progress is being made. Let us be cautious, however, as to what is to be claimed. The evidence
for telepathy, for clairvoyance, for precognition and for psychokinesis is strong, but there appear to be no replicable
experiments. Converging evidence from many lines of work,
including both spontaneous and experimental studies, does
support the principles given above, but these are not the
elementary cornerstone data that the tougher members of the
scientific fraternity demand.

It is necessary to meet fairly a general class of objection often heard at this point: Why should we expect one
of the most complex phenomena of human personality to appear under standardized, indeed almost mechanized, conditions? Why, when we know so much about individuality in
human respondents, and indeed in experimenters as well as
subjects, should we expect to find the same kind of results
appearing time after time? Do we not know that there are
evanescent factors of attitude and value, and a host of preconscious and unconscious dynamic components, that push
data in one direction or another? Though we want control
enough to produce replication, phenomena strong enough to
overcome all these other factors, must we not wait a very
long time to get the machine-like type of data that are turned
out for us so easily in the laboratories of physics and chemistry?

The argument has a certain charm, but in psi we are
claiming progress toward the development of those classes
of uniformities that regularly appear when we confront the
enterprise known as science. We are not contending that
the only worthwhile human endeavor is science; only that the
study of psi must be concerned with the problem of the nature of science, and its methods and data must be classified
somehow under the tent of science, or else a "local habita-

tion and a name" must be found for its phenomena elsewhere.
Whenever the appeal is actually to the psychological laboratory, there must be some uniformity, some unlawfulness to
which we can point, and these uniformities must specify
working conditions under which the same general classes of
results can be expected to occur; in other words, some replicable methods and confirmatory results are to be expected.
It is hard to know what any of the generalizations of published experiments in psi research mean unless they mean
that under such-and-such conditions, as represented by the
published reports, certain results appear. If the results only
appear with that particular experimenter, with those particular subjects at that particular time, how can they claim the
status of science? Indeed, how can they claim any secure
place within the realm of knowledge?

In point of fact, there has been an implicit debate
throughout the whole history of psi regarding the problem of
basic progress. There is the "replication" school of thought,
which has attempted to determine the working conditions under which particular classes of events occur. There are,
however, likewise the eager, ambitious, nervous and confi-
dent investigators who will have nothing to do with sheer
replication, and who will start off in a new direction to see
what the soil will turn up. They may indeed find pay dirt,
by a lucky hunch. More such investigations, however, have
yielded hosts of unreplicable experimental data. So is it
really useful to scratch the surface in so many directions,
each new generation confidently hoping to "see for itself, "
and turning up so many spadefuls of interesting, but ultimately uninterpretable, data?

There are perhaps two answers here, based upon rather close consideration of the history of physics and of other
sciences based upon physical principles. First, very competent and able students struggled for a long time with physical principles that seemed sound but were not. Physics,
chemistry and astronomy, too, proceeding from "common
sense" assumptions or from explicit Aristotelian formulations, got onto the wrong track over and over again. Astronomers for centuries "knew" that God was perfect, therefore the planets "had" to move in perfect circles. Galileo's
studies of gravity and Newton's studies of the spectrum
emerged after many mistakes had been made, and the failures of replication were to be expected as thrusts into the
unknown were repeatedly made. When, for example, Galileo
tried to explain why a hand pump cannot lift water forty or

fifty feet he supposed that the column of water broke of its
own weight. This was a completely mistaken assumption,
which was displaced both by fresh empirical trials and by
fresh conceptualization. Harvey, in his study of the circula-
tion of the blood, missed some points and went astray on
others, but he did look directly at the movement of heart and
arteries, and the valve structure within veins, and checked
against the water pump to be sure that the mechanics were
feasible. Replication became possible as attention was given
to exact conditions and as theory was clarified.

Second, the same was true, two hundred years later,
when Lyell and his colleagues established a scientific geology.
Nature does not, as a rule, give us replicable experiments
in geography and geology. We have to look for different,
yet comparable, contours of land, patterns of wind and air
erosion, together with the accumulation of strata, hard and
soft, regular and broken. We have to resort to nature's own
kind of replication, which is not the replication of the laboratory, but allows descriptive and mathematical comparison
of the outcomes of various basic physical conditions. Physical conditions found in physics laboratories are fortunately
useful as we turn to the outdoor phenomena of geography and
geology.

Conceptual Order

Perhaps psi is going to prove to be like early geology
in a sense, a proto-science in which many working principles
today are beginning to emerge, but it can become a true science, insofar as we carefully study nature's own orderly and
systematic interrelations, as well as some of those limited
possibilities that the experimental laboratory offers. It may
well be that with spontaneous cases--apparitions, and the
unexplained movements of objects, psychosomatic effects
transcending what we can currently explain in terms of the
kind of physiology known to us, and the experience of mystical and "cosmic" types of consciousness--we may ultimately
find ourselves in a new house, the very foundations of which
are still indistinct and the walls and roofs of which belong
to centuries ahead.

Our task in the book to follow will consist partly of
struggling for the replicable experiment along the lines already noted. It will consist partly, however, of a structural
rearrangement of the better-authenticated typical observa-

tions; it will consist of conceptual strokes, bold indeed from today's point of view, but working, as Henry Margenau (1966) has suggested, toward that kind of rigorous, systematic, architectonically commanding theoretical unity that modern physics is beginning to achieve. It will not be a final or static system, and it will, of course, trail far behind physics in its coherence, its intelligibility and the internal isomorphic pattern of its structure.

Psi phenomena cannot adequately be understood or scientifically studied by the techniques of the physical sciences alone, since they are human events, or more broadly, events produced in living organisms. We shall see that major questions are related to individual differences not only in the external conditions in which given individuals produce psi, but also internal differences as illustrated by differences in sensitivity or temperament, reactivity to extreme stress, depth of empathy, relatedness to selected others, and readiness to enter dissociative states. For all we know the attitudes and beliefs of the experimenter may well be critical variables, too (Kennedy and Taddonio, 1976; White, 1976).

It is possible, therefore, that the plea for the patterning of psi upon contemporary physics is misguided. Even psychology, as an evolutionary science, is going the way of other life sciences in which ecological considerations are often absolutely fundamental; in which open-system relationships require that we emphasize those dynamisms within living things that belong at another level of analysis from those that appear in physics. These may be field dynamisms involving very complex interactions between what is inside the organism and what is outside it. This often means that the laboratory is not big enough, not complex enough, to give the meaningful interactions that the biological sciences want to study. If this should be the case for biology and for psychology, it will certainly prove to be the case for psi. In fact, psi may demand units of greater complexity and research tools even more complex than those that are becoming appropriate in physiological psychology, the psychology of consciousness, or the psychology of altered ego states, which are themselves demanding our utmost discipline, not only in observation, but in the struggle for articulate order and "organized complexity."

Part I

A Brief History of Psi Research

A. TO 1882

Benjamin Franklin, who lived through much of the eighteenth century, will serve as an example of the thinking with which we moderns have come to terms. Familiar as he was with the elements of magnetism and electricity, as scientist and inventor, he found it natural to bring a spark from the skies to his Leyden jar, demonstrating the relation of celestial to terrestrial static electricity. Soon, as scientist, inventor and philosopher, he became a savant, as respected in Europe as he was at home. Thus, when in 1778 Anton Mesmer arrived in Paris to demonstrate "animal magnetism," it was natural that six years later Franklin should be appointed one of a committee of nine to study Mesmer's claims. Time and thought were given to the study of the remarkable cures effected by Mesmer's presence and his passes made over ill persons suffering from many complaints.

It seemed clear to Franklin and the committee that the cures were due not to "magnetism," but to imagination, a part of the normal psychological operations of a normal human individual. No dualism, no double-barreled set of hypotheses--one physical, one mental--was necessary, for the mental was a part of the organic living system of the individual patient.

When the nineteenth century began to capitalize on the new chemistry and the experimental physiology that underlay what we now call modern medicine, students of science rapidly divested themselves of the concept of an independent spiritual system of forces, souls or psychical propensities that could somehow exist independently of the chemical and physiological system observed in the living person. Animism disappeared from the scientific thinking of the medical community, and of all who were oriented to science, at the very time

3

when animism was being discovered by anthropologists as a mainstay in the thinking of preliterate peoples. The story of the decline of animism in modern times has been well told in William McDougall's (1911) Body and Mind.

Another event, however, occurred almost simultaneously with these philosophical changes. Science had come to mean a preoccupation with the systematic and orderly understanding of everything that happened in the world, not just mechanical, chemical, or electrical events. As Sir William Dampier put it, the conception of science applied not only to infrahuman, but to human events. Lawfulness had to be found in the world of heart and mind as much as in the world of physics and chemistry. It was indeed exactly the spirit of radical scientific challenge that was giving rise to experimental psychology at the same moment. Having once appealed to the method of science, one had to ask questions about the kinds of events with which the animistic events had once been associated. How is it that a person reports seeing a fatal accident at a long distance away at the time this accident is occurring? What is the meaning of the testimony regarding the possibility of communication from mind to mind? Is this a farrago of nonsense, a bundle of superstition, obsessing serious as well as childish observers and coloring the thought of men like Goethe, Gladstone and Lincoln as much as the thought of any peasant or hod carrier? It is no less than a scandal, said Henry Sidgwick of Cambridge, that in "our enlightened age" events of these types are not investigated.

It was actually in the third quarter of the nineteenth century that the three historical events just described took place: the systematic infiltration of vigorous monistic "materialistic" ideas into the scientific view of man; the discovery of almost universal preliterate animism; the strong determination to make of alleged psychical phenomena a field of genuine scientific exploration. These practices were thoroughly familiar to the Mediterranean world and were never stamped out by Christianity. When the beginnings of a serious scientific approach took shape, mediumistic phenomena were still a commonplace.

Mediums also represented highly developed instances of two basic kinds of psi: they could perceive that which no ordinary eyes could perceive--deep into the future and faraway in space--and they could control physical events by unknown means. These two classes of psi events help to out-

line first a cognitive psi and second a motor psi; they were
named by Thouless and Wiesner (1947) "psi gamma" and "psi
kappa, " respectively.

The authentication of such phenomena is one of the
first scientific tasks for the field; the second is the discovery of the conditions under which the authenticated phenomena
occur; the third is the attempt to build a more comprehensive theory or schema within which the paranormal may be
in some measure integrated with the normal.

The Trance

Forty years after the discredited Mesmer left Paris
a fresh wave of enthusiasm and a fresh wave of cures resulted, involving this time both England and France. In India
the British surgeon James Esdaile (1846) had conducted successful surgery (e. g. scrotal tumors) when men were in a
"mesmeric" state of anesthesia, and the Manchester surgeon
John Elliotson endlessly tried to persuade the British medical
public of the value of the sleep-like state.

While in "mesmeric trance" many patients showed
awareness of activities and thoughts that were hard to explain
in normal terms. Telepathy came to be one of the regular
marvels associated with the mesmeric state. Numerous
cases were reported of "transposition of the senses, " in
which, for example, the tips of the fingers would yield information ordinarily obtainable only through the eyes. Another British surgeon, James Braid, determined to show up all
this nonsense about mesmerism. He did in fact observe
some of the phenomena, and decided that it was a type of
"nervous sleep" on a psychological basis, invoking a Greek
term, neurypnology to describe it. In his struggles to understand the process, Briad succeeded in drawing the attention
of reputable physicians and surgeons to the reality of some
unusual sleep-like states.

For the next few decades, until the phenomena were
widely demonstrated and applied to psychiatric purposes by
the French physician, J. M. Charcot, the separation of reputable or creditable phenomena from the occult byproducts,
which had been associated with mesmerism, was effective.
When, however, formal psychical research was organized in
1882, the phenomena that had accumulated for a hundred years
in the form of telepathy and related processes were deemed

worthy of investigation, and the hypnotic trance as a major modality leading to these strange phenomena became a significant area of research.

The evolutionary approach, however, poses a specific challenge: beginning with celestial or astronomical evolution and passing over the bridge to the life sciences, can we not imagine types of receptivity to the environment that dispense with the sense organs as we know them, and allow for direct communication between organisms in non-sensory contact with one another--even contact between organisms and events far removed from them in space? Is it not possible to imagine in this sense a "naturalistic" approach to the question of telepathy and clairvoyance? <u>Improbable</u> such responses might be regarded, but <u>impossible,</u> no.

From the point of view of another kind of evolution, the evolution of stable forms of interdependent relations between human beings, as shown in anthropology, might we not expect a progressive elaboration of forms of communication much more complex than those expected at a biological level? Actually, it is in the form of interpersonal relations and response to culturally significant objects and artifacts that the world of psi first draws our attention. While to the biologically and physically oriented scientist it is utterly inconceivable that the personality or individuality of a human being could literally continue to exist after death, the cultural material that draws our attention to psi is very frequently and very intimately related to intense belief in the continuity of personality beyond death. This is not a special feature of Western civilization as such, although there is no break from Homer's ghosts or the ghosts of Seneca to those of Shakespeare, either. Throughout Chinese, Indian and other Asian civilizations intervention by the deceased in the affairs of the living is a well-organized institution.

The Swedenborg who, in his celebrated announcement of the fire raging in Stockholm long before word could physically be brought to describe the event, was the same Swedenborg who dealt constantly with spirits among the living (as when he settled an argument by announcing that St. Paul had been speaking with him expressly on the point at issue). What we have then in the world of belief in matters "psychical" is not simply the evolutionary proposition of a new type of sensitivity mixed up historically with the conception of traffic with the spirits. The resistance is not only to the rather intangible nature of psi communications. It is mixed up culturally with mind-body dualism and is loaded, almost to the point of sinking, with cultural freight of this type of concept.

Mediumship

When there is a demand for any given kind of personality to perform a function within a given society, there is usually a technique, a skill, for cultivating this kind of personality. Bali provides an outstanding relevant example. Little girls are early identified as capable of falling into trance. The men set up a dance pattern among a group of puppets: "Two little girls ... come and sit beside the men with the sticks. They hold the lower end of the sticks tightly with both hands and are thus shaken by the movements of the sticks. Each child sits in the lap of an older girl who is ready to catch her when she falls into trance" (Bateson and Mead, 1942, vol. 2, p. 91).

Here, and in many other societies, one may grow into the part to become a doorway, in act and word, between another world and the world of the senses. In general, the "medium" is simply an intermediary between the deceased and the living, or between supernatural non-human forces, such as gods, angels and devils on the one hand, and humankind on the other.

B. THE SOCIETY FOR PSYCHICAL RESEARCH

The physical sciences were making extraordinary headway through the whole era of Lavoisier, Franklin, Dalton and Helmholtz, and a systematic and monistic approach to the life sciences, based upon the concepts of physics and chemistry, became everywhere the standard approach to psychological reality. Psychological processes that appeared to be independent of a physiological and physical basis were confidently rejected. When Sir William Barrett, Professor of Physics at the Royal College of Science, Dublin, told Hermann Helmholtz in 1876 that he had observed some telepathic phenomena in the course of his own experiments, Helmholtz replied: "Neither the testimony of all the Fellows of the Royal Society, nor even the evidence of my own senses, would lead me to believe in the transmission of thought from one person to another independently of the recognized channels of sensation. It is clearly impossible. " (Barrett, 1904, p. 329). When, therefore, Henry Sidgwick, Professor of Philosophy at Cambridge, and his associates determined to investigate the world of telepathy, clairvoyance, hauntings, premonitions and the like, they knew that they were breaking through the bounds established by reasonable and reputable scientists. The assumption was that the phenomena could not exist. Many took a middle ground: investigation was commendable, but on an ultra-cautious basis.

Sidgwick, well-known author of The Methods of Ethics (1874), a man whom everyone trusted, agreed to become president of a new organization, the Society for Psychical Research (SPR). Barrett played a large part; so did a student of classics, Frederic W. H. Myers, who was at the time an inspector of schools; W. Stainton Moses, a clergyman, who himself apparently had had many types of psychic experiences, was likewise highly active in forming the organization. In 1882 the "Articles of Agreement" were signed and investigations begun. From the vantage point of today it is extraordinary how many able and active people suddenly appeared and how much thorough investigation was soon undertaken.

Studies of spontaneous telepathy were systematically planned and carried out in large scale by a committee headed at first by Professor Sidgwick, notably assisted by his wife, Eleanor Mildred Sidgwick, Principal of Newnham College (for women), Cambridge University; by Myers; and by a young scientist, Edmund Gurney, a Fellow of Trinity College, Cambridge. Another prominent figure in this group was Frank Podmore, who was also active in collecting and authenticating many reported cases of telepathy. For several decades his careful research acted as a brake upon what he regarded as overconfidence and premature generalizations on the part of other investigators. Within four years the three main organizers of the study of spontaneous telepathy-- Gurney, Podmore and Myers--had completed a two-volume study, Phantasms of the Living (1886), dealing mostly with spontaneous instances. The cases were analyzed in terms of the social, psychological and physiological conditions under which the experiences occurred: the characteristics of the "agents" (senders) and the "percipients" (receivers), and with special attention to the state of consciousness--waking, drowsy or sleeping--of the percipient at the time. Face-to-face interviews plus correspondence were regularly employed. Cases were usually not included unless there was strong first-hand authentication available with testimony from other persons in a position to know the facts.

This concept of authentication became a standard for subsequent research into psi, and with few exceptions has been characteristic of all attempts to get at the modus operandi of paranormal communication; unless there was reasonable certainty as to what happened both to the agent and the percipient, generalizations of all sorts became shaky.

The hundreds of cases analyzed, authenticated and published in Phantasms of the Living permitted a few generalizations. First, the sleeping state in the percipient is particularly rich in telepathic impressions, and the state between waking and sleeping seems to be very rich indeed. Second, though there may be some evidence of certain individuals having a telepathic gift, most of the percipients with striking experiences had no other such experience to report. Third, tragedies or serious accidents were especially numerous as instigators of the agent's experiences even when allowance was made for "selective forgetting" of trivial episodes. Fourth, there were among the well-authenticated cases a few "collective experiences" involving several percipients and a few "reciprocal" experiences in which agent and percipient were in interaction. This last problem of the collective and reciprocal cases exposed a difference of opinion between Gurney and Myers. Gurney held that in the collective cases there was one primary percipient who then "relayed" the experience to the other percipients. Myers, on the other hand, insisted that an agent could alter the psychological world of two or more persons as if the agent him- or herself had "invaded" their shared space.

An early problem was to ascertain the number of cases as compared with "chance expectation" for that size population, using actuarial data. The chance that a given person within the British Isles will die on a particular day (that is, within twelve hours one way or the other of an impression relating to his or her death) might appear to give a base line. There are several serious nuisances in dealing with data of this sort. The data relate to all persons, not only to those who are not at the time known to be ill or in danger of death. Death rates are not adjusted for age levels (e. g. among the aged as contrasted with children). The method raises questions as to the "selective forgetting" of earlier as contrasted with more recent cases; a large number of impressions regarding death may well be received and yet not be confirmed, but because they are of a low order of dramatic interest, may fail to be reported, while those that are fulfilled may be reported in much larger proportions.

These difficulties were pondered and dealt with somewhat better when between 1889 and 1892 a large survey of spontaneous hallucinations was made by volunteers. In this "Census of Hallucinations, " some 410 collectors undertook to find out how many individuals had ever had such an experience. From nearly 17, 000 replies, over 2000 were affirmative, and among these cases thirty representing death coincidences fell within the twelve-hour limit. Barely one case would be expected on the basis of the actuarial data for the British Isles. The margin of safety seems to be considerable and is greatly enhanced by the fact the deaths are often represented in astonishing detail. It is not quite enough, to say, for example, in the case of Mrs. Paquet (Sidgwick, 1891-2, pp. 32-35), that her brother had one chance in 19, 000 of dying on a particular day. Nor is it merely a question of his dying. The specific, fully visualized death by being dragged by a hawser and drowned, constitutes the actual "coincidence" that has to be analyzed. It must, of course, be granted immediately that there is no feasible method at present for getting a proper base line for chance expectation. One simply falls back upon a lifetime of assumptions and expectations. The method, however, sufficed as a starter.

Spontaneous cases are something like the novas that intrigue the astronomer. One could say something about the likelihood of a new star appearing at a new place, and having such-and-such a specific character when analyzed. The astronomer hopes to develop a lawful system for the prediction of new stars, and the parapsychologist hopes for the development of a lawful method for predicting specific types of spontaneous cases occurring to particular kinds of people under particular circumstances. Fortunately, the working principles that emerge from the study of spontaneous cases agree in considerable measure with those that appear as a result of laboratory work.

Some Early Observations

A few general observations may be attempted here, without any statistical pretenses, regarding the taxonomy and possible interpretation to be afforded such types of paranormal experience.

They appear in the great majority of cases to be highly relevant to the core of self, such as an accident to a loved one, rather than to some distant acquaintance. Often the impression comes first in the form of depression or unhappiness gradually taking shape, and often being rejected as silly, meaningless, sheer "nerves," until the time when the impression of the accident or death is actually clear--i. e., the percipient has been developing more and more specific impressions regarding what has happened.

There is also a strong tendency of dreamers to discover what is relevant to their own needs, especially in the form of information about what friends and loved ones at a distance are thinking or doing. Here also, a preoccupation with distant persons is sometimes shared by those who are physically together, and we may in such cases encounter "collective cases." Hornell and Ella Hart (1933) gathered a useful compendium of information about such reciprocal and collective cases.

There is often a certain set that permits the impression to occur, in the sense of an emptiness, absentmindedness, brown study, the mind stopping "on dead center" or more often still, being in a light dream state or a state between sleeping and waking, in which material seems capable of "welling up" or intruding through the interstices of thought.

Often the paranormal impression is carried, so to speak, on the wings of the primary perceptual or memoric effect. One percipient looks at a highly polished oak door and sees on its surface the face of a sea captain who has in fact just died at a distant point; the message was organized around and also reorganized the shining surface of the oak. One student of mine reported the case of a man in a restaurant perceived as another man, who at that moment had just died at a distant point.

Dreams, on the other hand, have a notable capacity to be concerned with the future and the past. When systematic analysis is applied to the orientation of the dream to the past, the present or the future, it appears that paranormal contact is striking indeed with events that have not yet occurred, but that do occur within a few hours or days thereafter. Dreams such as these are reflected in the classical studies of the early years, then later in the systematic work of H. F. Saltmarsh (1934) and in several confirmatory studies by Louisa E. Rhine (1954). While the waking telepathic impression deals, for the most part, with contemporary events, the dream often deals with events about to happen, events of the next few hours or days.

Side by side with these precognitive cases we must note a fair number of those that seem to make contact with the past in a way that permits authentication of the reality of the contact with the past event, although neither the dreamer nor those nearby at the time were in any position to know normally about the past event in question. These "retrocognitive" cases are not numerous enough to permit us to say that the preoccupation of the dream with time displacement appears symmetrically in the cases of precognition and retrocognition.

We shall now take up in detail the ideas of a person critically significant to the history of research into the psi process.

C. FREDERIC W. H. MYERS

During this same era Frederic Myers, beginning with an interest in psychical research, was studying psychopathology, too, trying to understand the states of dissociation and ecstasy that appeared in Charcot's clinic, in the pilgrimages to Lourdes, in the trance phenomena of spiritualist mediums, and in the "prophetic" deliverances of people carried beyond the realm of normal human contact. Myers began to develop a conception of "the subliminal self," that portion of human personality that functions without being observed or controlled by consciousness. In an early paper (Myers, 1891-2) on the subliminal self, he undertook to cover both the medical phenomena of Charcot and Janet, and the telepathic and clairvoyant phenomena reported in the psychical research of the period. Becoming more and more absorbed in this conception, he spent a large part of his time, through the eighties and nineties, in organizing a systematic presentation of the theory of the subliminal in relation to human personality. His conclusion, with regard to the subliminal, is as follows:

> I suggest, then, that the stream of consciousness in which we habitually live is not the only consciousness which exists in connection with our organism. Our habitual or empirical consciousness may consist of a mere selection from a multitude of thoughts and sensations, of which some at least are equally conscious with those that we empirically know. I accord no primacy to my ordinary waking self, except that among my potential selves this one has shown itself the fittest to meet the needs of common life. I hold that it has established no further claim, and that it is perfectly possible that other thoughts, feelings, and memories, either isolated or in continuous connection, may now be actively conscious, as we say, "within me," in some kind of coordination with my organism, and forming some part of my total individuality [p. 301].

Myers's theory of the subliminal is not a theory of the morbid, although it deals with a realm in which both the morbid and the highly creative can coexist. The works of genius can come along with pitifully disorganized, non-human material. The Myers conception is broad enough to be ethically significant, while not insisting that all the materials of the subliminal are ethically significant. It is the structure of the mind and its capacity for functioning at many levels and reaching this broader articulation that is most significant for Myers.

The idea of the subliminal is still being hotly debated today. Some challenge it, while others in effect say: "But didn't Freud establish the reality of the unconscious?" Yes, but in some respects it is almost as if we were still back at the period when Myers first presented these ideas. The issues are in fact inordinately complicated because what is involved is the notion that there is a kind of consciousness of which we are not conscious. We are conscious of our immediate present surroundings--the people around us, their voices, the evening sounds out there--and many other things at different levels of awareness. Some things are not in consciousness until we mention them, like the pressure of the clothing on one's body or the breeze coming in from the open window, for example. Until these things were mentioned, perhaps they were not in awareness at all, but they can easily be lifted into awareness. The actual status of that which is both conscious and non-conscious is actually partly a metaphysical question and partly an experimental and scientific question. And if one gets the feeling of Myers as troubled about the nature of all these strange awarenesses and impulses that are often thrown into action without our deliberate intent, one will see why he found it so urgently necessary to dig deeper and to try to get an empirical answer as to what is involved.

Human Personality

Myers great two-volume work was Human Personality and Its Survival of Bodily Death (1903), which he started writing in the early 1880's, along with the time of the founding of the SPR. It was not quite finished at the time of his death at the turn of the century, but through the devoted labors of his SPR colleagues Richard Hodgson and Alice Johnson, it finally saw the light of day in 1903.

Human Personality is laid out in such a way that everything seems rather obvious, interrelated and clear. First we have to distinguish between that which is integrated and that which is automatic. The term "automatism" is defined by Myers "as expressing such images as arise, as well as such movements as are made, without the initiation, and generally without the concurrence, of conscious thought and will." Myers distinguishes between sensory and motor automatisms: the motor automatisms are those that spring from the muscles of the fingers, the hands, the arms; the voluntary musculature is thrown into activity involuntarily in a task such as automatic writing. These motor automatisms are often easier to produce than the sensory automatisms that involve visual or auditory effects, since in the latter case there may be an image or an articulate sound that comes to mind, as it were, in spite of yourself and without your bidding; this may occur as you fall asleep, or as you awake, or as you gaze into a crystal ball or hold a conch shell to your ear.

While both motor and sensory automatisms may sometimes be in conflict, working together they can also lead us

on into activities of a very complex order, as in a great
writer's realization of a denouement, or the solution of a
difficult problem through a sudden integral performance. For
example, Robert Louis Stevenson (1892) before going to sleep,
used to tell his little "brownies," as he called them, to work
on a series of story themes. Upon awakening he would find
that the "brownies" had achieved an intricacy and beauty of
plot that he believed he could not possibly, as Stevenson in
his conscious mind, have achieved. Or take the celebrated
case of H. V. Hilprecht, Professor of Assyriology in the
University of Pennsylvania. For many weeks he had struggled to work out the meaning of two fragments of Babylonian
agate marked with cuneiform characters. Despairing of finding a solution, he fell asleep one night and in the course of
a vivid dream he encountered a priest in his high robes who
explained to him that if he would place the two fragments
together he would find the answer to his problem. The next
morning he examined the fragments again and to his astonishment found that they did indeed belong together; research
carried out several months later in a distant museum proved
that they had originally been a part of "one and the same
votive cylinder" (cited in Myers, 1903, pp. 375-379).

Experiences such as these are subliminal and yet at
the same time they are integrative in the sense that they
bring together the brilliant light of pure consciousness at the
highest creative level of genius. Indeed, this is one of the
many contradictions, partly verbal, partly conceptual, that
still dog us. In the closely similar issues that confront
psychoanalysis with regard to the nature of the preconscious,
there is also the question of dynamics: can one say that the
ego--the highest central, organized, directive force of the
individual--is responsible for the little furtive activities attributed to the preconscious? This question would seem to
raise the same complex conceptual and clinical problems with
which Myers was beginning to struggle in the eighties and
nineties.

To return to Human Personality, there are chapters
on sensory automatisms and motor automatisms; on disinte-
grations of personality, genius, sleep, hypnotism, phantasms
of the dead, trance, possession and ecstasy. All these give
life to a system of the subliminal that Myers believed constitutes the real extent and range and depth of the personality; they all belong to his one general, unified scheme.

We finally come to the adventure par excellence that
makes all the earlier passing references to telepathy and

clairvoyance seem almost incidental; namely, the task of pulling them together into a conception of human communication. Myers, while writing a book on human personality-- on memory, imagination, dreaming and genius--ingeniously allows all the phenomena of psychical research, the phenomena of telepathy, clairvoyance, precognition and all the rest, to slip into the interstices wherever they belong. For example, a telepathic dream comes easily into the midst of a discussion of the dream as a subliminally guided process. In the same way, the precognitive impression, the clairvoyant vision, are regarded as subliminal phenomena that sneak past a sort of psychic censor, a process similar to that of censorship in analytic dream theory. There is a process by means of which the hidden material is allowed easy access to a higher level. We begin to think of the mind, then, as a series of levels, or concentric disks with each smaller one a little higher than the one below it, as if we had a tower made of very large disks at the bottom, and then higher and smaller until we finally get a brilliant, shining little orb at the very top. Thus Myers provides a normal and easy way to slip the telepathic, the clairvoyant and the precognitive into the texture of the same divided, multi-level self.

Now what kind of personality manifestations are we concerned with at the highest levels of this analysis? With meaningful communication from person to person whenever the message is deep and significant: a message regarding values, ideas and aspects of human living that are most precious. That is what we should be able to communicate through these subliminal strata of our personality. For the ordinary tasks of daily living it may be sufficient to work with simple, conscious symbolism, but to communicate something vastly significant and broadly human may require the use of all the levels at once. It may require a telepathic message that is more than a telepathic message.

Subception

Myers, then, is an early originator of the concept of the integral quality of mental function. For him, psi was another aspect of that integral function. It interpenetrates all aspects of the mind. The particular mechanism of psi was less important to him, since he had to live with much ignorance of the mind, ignorance that we have begun to overcome in the nearly a century since he began to write and reflect on this issue.

About twenty-five years ago some experimental work began to be published in the psychological journals under the term "subception." This is a compression of "subconscious perception," perceptual responses made at a subconscious level: organized, systematic interpretations of the environment despite the fact that the symbols being interpreted do not get into consciousness.

Here is a quite dramatic illustration, utilizing the "rebus effect." A rebus is a kind of puzzle in which pictures of objects, by the sound of their names, suggest another word: for example, the picture of an "ax" followed by the picture of a "cent" (penny) is a rebus for the word "accent." If we see these two pictures consecutively, adjacent, we may think of "accent." What would happen if we were shown these two pictures at a subliminal level, with illumination so low or at such a rapid exposure that we simply couldn't see anything at all? If in responding to this we began to think, say, of people talking with a French accent, or a Russian accent, it would indicate that the stimuli had begun to summate or to integrate into a new pattern, though plainly neither the ax nor the cent got above the threshold.

Howard Shevrin with Lester Luborsky (1961) have been working with the rebus technique for a number of years. They used the rebus "tiny," showing the picture of a (neck) tie with the picture of a knee (bent very sharply as if one were kneeling). The tie and the knee were shown at an exposure of only one-fiftieth (in later experiments at one-hundredth) of a second, which is merely a blinking flash. At one-hundredth of a second, no matter what the lighting, one is not conscious of seeing anything meaningful at all. But what happened was that even though the rebus pictures were shown at that exposure, the subjects' images and associations were clearly related to the rebus. In view of experimental results like these, it is hard to see how anyone can still deny the reality of subliminal perception.

Subception has an important implication for psi research today. Material thus absorbed may not initially exist in consciousness, but may ultimately filter its way upward as part of a subconsciously mediated response, at the appropriate time.

D. WILLIAM JAMES AND THE MEDIUMS

William James was active from the first in developing a psychical research effort in the United States. He persuaded the well-known astronomer Simon Newcomb to become president of an American organization that soon became a branch of the London SPR; in the years 1904 to 1906 J. H. Hyslop established an independent American Society for Psychical Research.

But the entry of William James into this theater of operations did much more than extend its geographical scope. He was not simply "interested"; he stumbled upon what he regarded as major facts requiring intensive research. Mediums were easily to be seen in Boston in his early professional years. His wife and her mother had sittings with a Mrs. L. E. Piper. In deep trance, messages were communicated that startled her sitters. Family matters that simply could not be known to strangers were correctly conveyed--not once, but repeatedly. William James had to have his own sittings. He was immediately convinced. Despite much bludgeoning from the incredulous, he proceeded to give more and more reports of the extraordinary character of this woman's powers.

Mrs. Piper

The story of Mrs. Piper's life has been told in part by Dr. Richard Hodgson, an Australian student of philosophy and psychology, who had made a study of Madame Blavatsky, and was in general known as a very tough investigator and critic of the claims of the spiritualists. He offers some biographical material in the reports of her sittings. We find in this record no evidence that Mrs. Piper was "trained" as a medium. She did, however, know about mediumship, and consulted another medium, a Mr. Cocke: during a sitting with him she spontaneously fell into trance. It did not take long to cultivate the capacity to relax, slump over a table or chair and remain in a state of deep unconsciousness for an hour or more.

She was a quiet, inconspicuous person with a very limited education. But she did express herself with clarity and dignity both in speech and in writing. The Jameses made her a personal friend and took her with them to their summer home in Chocorua, New Hampshire. There was no orderly research program for her in the mid-eighties, but Hodgson, becoming convinced of the importance of this new scientific instrument, took over the responsibility for her sittings: making the appointments; preserving the incognitos so that she might have no basis for guessing the attributes of her sitters; arranging for the European trip; keeping the records in order; writing and publishing the reports.

The mediumship went through a series of well-defined stages. At first the purporting communicators were characters from history or odd unidentifiable persons who gave vivid accounts of things going on at a distance, several of which were strikingly correct. The sudden death of Hodgson's friend George Pellew in 1891 was followed immediately by communications purporting to come from him. This episode faded out, and there began a long and vivid series of communications from an august body of ancient prophetic figures with the names "Imperator," "Rector," "Mentor," etc., among whom Rector soon became primary. It was Rector who spoke when the voice was activated, and who wrote when the hand was writing. After the initiation of deep trance, it was he who began to speak, then write, for a while holding his cupped hand to the mouth of the sitter as if this hand were an ear. The script was large and clear, and was rapidly read back to Rector, to allow assent or dissent as to the correctness of what had been recorded. After about an hour and a half there would be signs of "failure of light"; the hand would slump; the pencil would fall; then there was a "waking stage" in which the hand was inactive. Instead of a solemn masculine voice purporting to be Rector, Mrs. Piper would speak in her own voice and report what she saw--a sharp change from the dull, heavy intermediary of a lump-like body to a conscious report by her of the figures who had been communicating and who were then making their departure, and some of the words that they were asking her to convey to the living.

Henry Sidgwick died in December 1900, and Frederic Myers the following month. On any theory whatever, one could have expected communications to be offered shortly thereafter, purporting to come through Mrs. Piper from the two deceased leaders. Actually, only a little was purportedly received from Sidgwick, but a great deal from Myers, and the story of the decade of a Myers or pseudo-Myers communicating through Mrs. Piper and other sensitives is one of the more fascinating historical themes in all psychical research.

The Verralls, Mrs. Holland and Mrs. Willett

Among Myers's friends at Cambridge were Professor A. W. Verrall of Trinity College and his wife Margaret, of Newnham College. At the turn of the century, shortly after Myers's death, Mrs. Verrall undertook to learn to write automatically. She sat in quiet and expectation, and after some weeks words would drop into her mind as from nowhere and she would write them down, until in time coherent messages, in English, Latin and Greek, were recorded. Some of the messages referred to events going on at a distance of which she had no knowledge. Some of them, however, were plainly regarded as messages from Myers.

In India, in the meantime, Mrs. "Holland" (this is a pseudonym; the woman was in fact Rudyard Kipling's sister, who had recently read and been deeply impressed by Myers's Human Personality) began to write automatically in a script that likewise offered itself as material from the deceased Myers. She was instructed by the script to communicate with 5 Selwyn Gardens, Cambridge, the address of the Verralls, not at the time known to Mrs. Holland. When the two women were in touch through correspondence, it began to be evident that each one had been writing automatically about themes that were meaningful to the other, and several of these themes had to do with classical lore, highly characteristic of Myers.

At the same time, the Verralls' daughter Helen (later, Mrs. H. W. Salter), began likewise to write automatically and several of the messages received through her offered striking similarities to the messages written by Mrs. Holland. Indeed, the three women, together with the two others writing in England, began to refer frequently to one another's script, so that the research personnel of SPR, always concerned with problems of extreme secrecy of research materials, could hardly avoid the conclusion that telepathic "leaks" were occurring. Therefore, carefully prepared attemps to prevent leaks were made.

Mrs. Coombe-Tennant was a woman very prominent in British public life and politics, a member of the inner aristocracy with Fabian as well as Conservative Party affiliations, who, through a desire to protect her public image in the world of the elite, never revealed her identity. She was known as Mrs. "Willett" in the SPR investigations. Mrs. Willett was one of the more unusual of the British mediumistic group.

Her mediumship arose under conditions of exposure to the elite Cambridge group, which had no trance mediums, nor for that matter did Mrs. Willett usually succeed in achieving full trance. She did, however, go farther toward "automatism" than did the Verralls, Mrs. Holland or the others. She could throw herself into a receptive state somewhat like that of the waking stage in Mrs. Piper's trance; that is, she was listening both to the living and the deceased, and talking to both. She was like a person standing in the doorway between two rooms in which interesting conversation is going on, but she is the only one capable of hearing and being heard by each group. (For a sample of her work, see pp. 152-153.)

At the very least, then, it appeared to the investigators of automatic writing that subliminal telepathic interchanges were the order of the day. Many of these messages are in fact cross-references to Myers-like messages coming through the others. Often the reference in Mrs. Piper's trance to one of the British automatist's production was very simple and obvious. Others were less so.

Of the direct type of message that might be expected, in which Myers refers to his life on earth and gives "evidential material," there was almost nothing at all. There were, however, many specific references to classical literature, prose and poetry in both Greek and Latin, that were well known to Myers, plus a great deal of material from English literature interwoven with the classics. Since Myers had been a Fellow of Trinity College, Cambridge, and was steeped in this literature, this was not surprising. The references were, however, often very complicated and made a good deal of work for the scholars to unravel, and this was odd, particularly when it came from the very unclassical mind of Mrs. Piper.

The focus of the SPR group was on the question of whether there was in fact direct evidence of the participation of the deceased Myers in these cross-correspondence messages. There are several ways to portray the possibilities here. We can for argument's sake posit telepathic leakage from the SPR researchers to all of the automatists as a group. This would further assume something resembling a "group mind," with each automatist joining the group, establishing rapport with those deeper strata of the interacting minds, to produce these group effects. In continuing the assumptions, we have to see each automatist alternately playing the role of Myers, while in the trance-like state. Then, too, could not the requisite classical information also be drawn from scholarly sources that knew what type of material would have a Myers-like quality to it? Another important question surfaced here: Who leads? Who selects? Which is the initiative point? There had been enough preoccupation with Myers in American experiments involving Mrs. Piper to suggest that she might well be the presumed repository of these group efforts. After a study of the dominant Piper personalities in the "Imperator Band" and the communicators who appeared to speak through these controls, Mrs. Sidgwick early (1900-01) came to the conclusion that in every instance one is dealing with "secondary personalities," and that there is no direct confrontation of George Pellew or Myers or any other deceased individual. To her, telepathy between the medium and other living personalities was rather well established. However, she could not see why telepathic sensitivity should be limited only to contacts with the living. If much of the material of the cross correspondences, she argued, is best conceived to be a mode of interaction between the subliminal levels of various living individuals, and if there are some items that psychologically make much more sense as coming from the deceased than as coming from the living, there is no sound theoretical objection to the hypothesis of telepathy from the deceased. To be sure, the evidence for the continued existence of the deceased is the major point: but it is much better to deal with this directly as a problem of evidence. Moreover, one should not be forced into a position of accepting the Piper trance personalities as in some sense the literal surviving personalities once known in life. As a matter of fact one throws off a great load of sheer burdensome baggage when one deals simply with a version of Mrs. Piper's role-playing, subconscious self, and with survival evidence as a separate problem. A deceased Myers could influence the trance utterances without our needing to conclude that Myers is incarnate and controlling Mrs. Piper's hand and voice.

Intriguingly, the Piper material fits well with both the hypothesis of postmortem communication and the hypothesis of a psychological group structure unconsciously developed, organized and directed by the minds of the living automatists, perhaps under the leadership of one strong individual, such as Mrs. Verrall. (It should be noted that the cross-correspondences tended to become weak after Mrs. Verrall died in 1916.)

Hodgson dropped dead playing handball in 1905, and the Piper sittings were not again subject to such close observation and control. Many of the regular sitters did, however, continue to come, and William James played an important part among them. The communicator now was frequently Richard Hodgson, bringing with him his deceased psychical research friends. It was during this period that James had a chance to evaluate the actual quality of the Hodgson communications, to which he devoted a long and serious "Report on Mrs. Piper's Hodgson-Control" (1909). Sittings of this period also offered an opportunity for G. Stanley Hall, President of Clark University, to trick the purporting Hodgson personality into a series of statements about a nonexistent person, with the conclusion that the suggestible trance personality, rather than a surviving Hodgson, was at work (Tanner, 1910, p. 254).

James's Final Views

James sums up his views on mediumship as follows (cited in Murphy and Ballou, 1969):

> The phenomena are as massive and widespread as is anything in nature, and the study of them is as tedious, repellent, and undignified. To reject it ["psychics"] for its unromantic nature is like rejecting bacteriology because penicillium glaucum grows on horse dung and bacterium termo lives in putrefaction. Scientific men have long ago ceased to think of the dignity of the materials they work in... [p. 316].

> The first difference between the psychical researcher and the inexpert person is that the former realizes the commonness and typicality of the phenomenon here, while the latter, less informed, thinks it so rare as to be unworthy of attention. I wish to go on record for the commonness.

The next thing I wish to go on record for is the presence, in the midst of all the humbug, of really supernormal knowledge. By this I mean knowledge that cannot be traced to the ordinary sources of information--the senses, namely, of the automatist. In really strong mediums this knowledge seems to be abundant, though it is usually spotty, capricious, and unconnected. Really strong mediums are rarities; but when one starts with them and works downwards into less brilliant regions of the automatic life, one tends to interpret many slight but odd coincidences with truth as possible rudimentary forms of this kind of knowledge....

We are thrown, for our conclusions, upon our instinctive sense of the dramatic probabilities of nature. My own dramatic sense tends instinctively to picture the situation as an interaction between slumbering faculties in the automatist's mind and a cosmic environment of other consciousness of some sort which is able to work upon them. If there were in the universe a lot of diffuse soul-stuff, unable of itself to get into consistent personal form, or to take permanent possession of an organism, yet always craving to do so, it might get its head into the air, parasitically, so to speak, by profiting by weak spots in the armor of human minds, and slipping in and stirring up there the sleeping tendency to personate. It would induce habits in the subconscious region of the mind it used thus, and would seek above all things to prolong its social opportunities by making itself agreeable and plausible. It would drag stray scraps of truth with it from the wider environment, but would betray its mental inferiority by knowing little how to weave them into any important or significant story.

This, I say, is the dramatic view which my mind spontaneously takes, and it has the advantage of falling into line with ancient human traditions. The views of others are just as dramatic, for the phenomenon is actuated by will of some sort anyhow, and wills give rise to dramas. The spiritist view, as held by Messrs. Hyslop and Hodgson, sees a "will to communicate," struggling through inconceivable layers of obstruction in the conditions. I have heard Hodgson liken the difficulties to those of two persons who on earth should have only dead-drunk servants to use as their messengers. The scientist, for his part, sees a "will to deceive," watching its chance in all of us, and able (possibly?) to use "telepathy" in its service.

Which kind of will, and how many kinds of will are most inherently probable? Who can say with certainty? The only certainty is that the phenomena are enormously complex, especially if one includes in them such intellectual flights of mediumship as Swedenborg's, and if one tries in any way to work the physical phenomena in. That is why I personally am as yet neither a convinced believer in parasitic demons, nor a spiritist, nor a scientist, but still remain a psychical researcher waiting for more facts before concluding [pp. 322-323].

Thus James concludes, as baffled by the problem as we are perhaps today, but always the alert researcher, willing to pursue the search.

E. EUROPEAN EXPERIMENTALISTS

The essentially amateurish character of most of the telepathy experiments in the late nineteenth and early twentieth centuries is evident through the chaotic and almost random selection of materials to be used as targets, the impromptu selection of methods and controls and, except in the case of conspicuously successful clairvoyants and mediums, the casual selection of subjects. For the most part the hypotheses being tested (beyond the hypothesis of the sheer existence of some kind of paranormal perceptual function) had to do mainly with a "favorable state," such as the hypnotic, semi-sleeping, or high-concentration states. It was at this level, for example, that the experiments of Professor Gilbert Murray were performed. Standing in an outer hall beyond the closed door of a large room in which a number of people were undertaking to test his telepathic powers, he picked up a number of impressions very similar to those which had been agreed upon as targets.

Because of the character and the eminence of Gilbert Murray these studies have evoked wide interest (see Dodds, 1972). The traditional flaws--the hit-or-miss selection of target material and the "let's make do" attitude regarding the absolute exclusion of sensory cues, rather than genuine severity in controls--kept the work at an interesting but scientifically inadequate level by today's criteria.

René Warcollier

One large exception needs, however, to be noted regarding this work of the early twentieth century. The French chemical engineer, René Warcollier, developed definitive hypotheses to be tested, indeed, a systematic psychology of the transmission process, which he subjected to rather thorough testing over a quarter of a century. It must be admitted that he did not succeed in getting his Paris group of "telepaths" to accept a statistical control, and there is obvious failure throughout his work to establish reasonable canons of evidence as to what is a telepathic "success." Yet one example from his Experimental Telepathy (1938) will illustrate the ingenuity of his approach:

> From among our best percipients we chose the person who was to act as agent. She relaxed into the passive state, the usual state for percipients. A characteristic object was then, in darkness, placed in her hand, and her descriptions were recorded. Percipients in a distant room recorded their impressions. The results rewarded our trouble.
>
> In one experiment, the object was presented to the agent, under the conditions described, by D. The object was the lower jawbone of a woman found in the crypts of St. Etienne du Mont. Only D, in this case an active agent, as distinguished from the passive agent (who received the object in her hand), knew the nature of the object, shown in Figure 1. It is obvious that the image itself was not transmitted, but that what the agent thought of the object was. The thoughts of the passive agent are found in her description of her part in the experiment. She felt the object and said, "Horns of a little deer, or rather of a roe; not made of wood. I put it against my forehead--idea

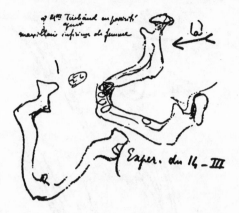

Figure 1: Warcollier Experiment A

of a mountain, wild animal, wild springing, very difficult to catch. In the middle of a little point, the nail by which it is attached, a little movable knob, like a joint. It is a stag's horn." The association of ideas is evident.

And what did the percipients receive? In a room at a distance, R., one of the percipients, drew the Greek letter gamma, R. W., another passive percipient, drew a tined pitchfork, a claw, and antlers. These are shown in Figure 2. The experiment was a complete success. The thought provoked by mistaken interpretation in the passive agent's mind was transmitted, while the actual object, and what the experimenter knew about it, were not transmitted.

In this case the explanation of clairvoyance cannot be applied. The phenomenon is one in which the state of consciousness of the passive agent plays an important role. To employ a term from physical science, a certain "potential" of thought is involved.

To continue with the above experiment. The hour was now 6:00 p.m. At 9:30 that evening, March 14, 1925, I was to send a message to the

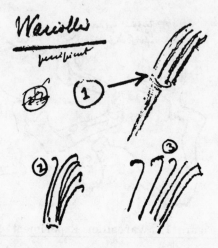

Figure 2: Warcollier Experiment B

American group in New York with whom we had
been experimenting for three years. I had tried
on that evening not to concentrate my thought upon
any object, but to remain passive, and to note
whatever images might pass through my mind, in
order to see whether they would be the ones transmitted to America. I eliminated the image of the
stag's horn of our experiment at six o'clock ...
and the only image which I visualized clearly at
the fixed hour of 9:30 was a glass funnel, a memory image from the morning. At the same hour
a percipient in New York drew a sort of funnel
with handles, which he called a Visigoth helmet,
upside down. Another percipient in New York, at
the same moment, drew a large compote glass
with handles, as she remarked, "like the horns of
a stag." Her drawing is illustrated in Figure 3.
Here the factor of the intentional disregard of an
image, whose importance we had, in fact, suspected, played its part... [pp. 25-28].

During the years in which the level of success was
said to be rising, the group was, of course, becoming con-
solidated, and each member might have some furtive guess
as to what others would be likely to choose for target mate-

Figure 3: Warcollier Experiment C

rials; and we have no assurance that all the data collected were published, or evidence that the published data are representative of the general trend of the material secured. There remains, however, the following psychological contribution: (a) there is evidence that the successful telepathic experiments involved, on the part of the percipient, a state of enriched imagery, or even "mono-ideism" in approximately the sense developed by Janet; (b) there is evidence that the relaxed physical state and general psychomotor relaxation and retardation appear to predispose to the best results; (c) there is much evidence of dream-like processes, such as fragmentation, duplication, symbolization, resynthesis--much that suggests psychoanalytic dream psychology, and also specifically eidetic and other familiar types of image enrichment.

It is likely that these are attributes of a relaxed, attentive seeking state, a state of general readiness for enhanced imagery, or indeed a state in which the subjects expect near conscious, preconscious, unconscious materials to emerge that will lead them to a correct guess as to the target material being used, and while in this state many factors of past conditioning and many modes of sensitization for their own sub-threshold messages may be at work. This would probably tend to produce materials that, have appeared in earlier experiments, especially earlier experiments with the same group of friends. Novelty in experimental conception has therefore the special advantage that it may break the existing set and not only serve as a guard against the intrusion of old material, but actually encourage receptivity.

The Groningen Experiments

From the point of view of an orderly and sophisticated psychology, dramatic indeed is the change of pace as one moves from the earlier twentieth-century studies to a series of experiments conducted in 1921 in the Psychological Laboratory of the University of Groningen by H. J. F. W. Brugmans (1922) and two of his colleagues. This series is usually considered one of the early experimental classics, and we quote it as follows:

> Our subject, a young man of twenty-three, a student of mathematics and physical sciences, became aware of his telepathic talent on the occasion of the public performances of Rubini, a young Austrian, who through his demonstrations revived in Holland an interest in paranormal gifts.

> ... the talent of the student, whose name was Van Dam, has seemed to us very real ... we have been able to give the experiments such form that, in my opinion, no possibility of sensory communication was allowed....

> ... Our idea was to get the subject to choose from among about ten objects as the subject sat before them.... Instead of this group of about ten objects, we ended up at last with a sort of checkerboard (Figure 4) with forty-eight little compartments in which the horizontal direction gave the letters from A to H, and the vertical direction, the numbers 1 to 6.

> The small compartment was chosen each time by lot. We had eight letters and six numbers, and each time before the beginning the experiment we had drawn twice, and among the three of us only he who was to influence the hand of the subject knew the result of the drawing, such as A2 or G3.

> The eyes of the subject were always blindfolded. In addition, he was always seated in a sort of little cubicle closed on three sides. Through a slit the hand alone was visible. All the rest was hidden by a curtain. In addition, the subject was placed in a room other than that containing the experimenters. We were in a room above his room.

6	6	6	6	6	6	6	6
5	5	5	5	5	5	5	5
4	4	4	4	4	4	4	4
3	3	3	3	3	3	3	3
2	2	2	2	2	2	2	2
A	B	C	D	E	F	G	H

Figure 4: Board Used in Telepathic Experiment at University of Groningen, Netherlands

We could follow the movements of his hand through a hole filled by two sheets of glass with an air cushion between. . . .

Thus, as you see, there were three precautions: blindfold, cubicle, and the use of another room. During the experiments the subject's room was well lighted, while ours was pitch dark.

As to the results of the experiments, first I shall give a general view, and later the details. [Of a total of 187 experiments, there were sixty successes]. . . . After each series of six experiments, using the two rooms, we made six experiments in the same room in which our subject sat. We wished to know about the influence of distance. in the two rooms the distance was about three meters; in the same room about half a meter. Among the experiments in two rooms, 32 out of 80, or 40%, were successful. Of the experiments in one room, 23 out of 77, or 30%, were successful. Perhaps this is a chance difference. In any

event, a greater distance did not reduce the phenomenon. Indeed, the two rooms present advantages. If as "conductor" (if the word be permitted)
one finds oneself in another room from the subject, it is unnecessary to inhibit expressive movements. In the same room (though the subject had
his eyes blindfolded and was placed behind a card-
board cubicle) one controls one's expressive movements. All the same, I believe that the better results with the two-room procedure is a consequence
of the absence of this inhibition.

All three of us acted to guide [i.e., influence]
the hand of the subject. All three served as "con-
ductors" and with success. There is no notable
difference from one experimenter to another. However, one of us who is short-sighted had scant results in the two-room experiments, but in the same
room had fine results.

The experiments were made after giving our
subject 30 grams of alcohol [ten minutes before];
... at other times nothing at all.... As to the
alcohol, we may say that it improves the results
considerably. Without it we obtained 22 successes
in 104 cases, or 21%; with alcohol we obtained 22
out of 29, or 75%. Looking back, the result is
not surprising. We know that alcohol overcomes
the normal inhibition of the individual. The reduction of self-control and the presence of more superficial thoughts are symptoms of the lack of inhibition. If we wish to describe the same thing in
Otto Gross' terminology we may say: Secondary
process is reduced and at the same time primary
process is increased....

Thus, if we use our entire psychic energy for
our practical life, our problems and preoccupa-
tions, there is nothing left to receive the messages
which seek a place in our awareness. Our awareness is like a fortress well defended. It is less
completely closed in sleep, and the proof of this
is the fact that spontaneous telepathic cases are
found more often in dreams. I have, moreover,
the impression that the mental state of hystericals
and neurasthenics offers a relatively favorable
situation. We need a state of awareness which

suffers from a handicap.   Alcohol is a crude method of realizing, to some degree, artificially, this state of mind.

   I do not wish to weary you with numbers.   We have seen that the correct squares were chosen more often than would be expected on the basis of chance probability....   Sixty hits in a total of 187. Probability would have given us only four ... each of our seven sessions gave results above chance expectation.   If we have not yet committed some error (and it is to ask your opinion regarding matters which we may have overlooked to which I would especially draw your attention) the existence of telepathy is established... [pp. 396-408; translated from the French by G. M.].

   In this classical experiment from the Netherlands, there are several questions which might be of interest to the careful analyst of the data.

   What did the experimenters do when the subject pointed, not directly to a square, but to the line between two squares or on a corner marking the intersection of four squares?   While one would think that there might be occasional cases of uncertainty, it is clear that the theory of probability would incline us not to expect as many hits as were obtained, even if all the uncertain cases were counted as hits--indeed not by a wide margin, since only four hits would be expected in 187 trials.   This is a significant puzzle.   It would be nice to know whether a record of the slips drawn by lot was made prior to the record of the subject's actual response.   Probably so, but it is unfortunate to be left guessing in this matter.   The old question: could one or indeed two of the experimenters have been in collusion with the subject, or would it have been physically possible for one or two of the experimenters to "fake" the results? These questions do not appear to be answerable today.

   The psychological yield from the experiment--quite aside from the strictness of its methodology, experimental and statistical--lies in its direct evidence for the importance of the relaxation factor.   Small doses of alcohol markedly raised the scoring level.   In the matter of sensory cues it is striking that the results were much better when the experimenter and subject were in two rooms than during those tests in which they directly observed in the same room the moving hand on the target board. They suggested that the effort to maintain strictness of control, for example, through the exclusion of any possible unconscious whispering, probably distracted them from the concentration desired in the telepathic experiment.

The Brugmans experiment was done to "satisfy" the individual experimenters, and was not repeated. Since the one successful subject whom they used had himself faded out, the question might well be raised whether this kind of physical set-up in itself had any special advantages. As a study, however, it offers the beginning of statistical treatment; suggests control of sensory cues; begins to examine the margins of preconscious functioning; selects the preconditioned subject who has seen an apparently successful stage demonstration of the same process; and finally, encourages empathy between subject and experimenter. As criticism, it lacks the essential element of adequate controls.

Whately Carington

Much of the modern experimental work with telepathy and related processes limits the experimental subject to a specific range of objects among which he must choose. There may, for example, be numbers from one to one hundred, letters of the alphabet, fifty-two playing cards, states of the Union, a fixed list of flowers, birds, etc. All experiments conducted with materials of this sort permit some sort of statistical control. There are, however, two rather serious psychological objections. First, they call for a more or less cut-and-dried choice among existing possibilities. The subjects are not free to let their minds roam and think of anything they like, because there is no way of scoring their successes. (Though they may think of something very unusual, we do not know how many of these very unusual things would come up by chance alone in the course of experiments of various kinds.) The other psychological difficulty with the fixed or limited range of materials is that the subjects may become so bored with the limited possibilities that their attitude toward the experiment is no longer positive. Granting the enormous difficulties in setting up a "free" procedure, it is to the very great credit of Whately Carington, a Cambridge University scholar, to have developed a suitable technique for the use of free material in psi experimentation.

Carington's (1944) usual procedure in his early experiments was to open a large dictionary at random, preferably by inserting a pen knife; select the first "drawable" word, that is, a word that could be embodied in a drawing; make the drawing; place the drawing on his desk; and go out, locking the door. By prearrangements with his subjects, who were scattered throughout all of Great Britain, he would ask that impressions received by the subjects be drawn and sent to him within a certain period.

Regarding the statistical treatment of the data, he decided first that it was necessary to have a large pool of empirical material as to what people in such experiments actually think of, and this could easily be derived. Suppose a subject correctly guesses anteater and claims a hugh success on the ground that anteaters are thought of relatively rarely; and claims some credit also for a cat and an albatross. If a thousand people take part, it is not difficult to show that the cat should get very limited "credit," because so many dozens of people reported cats. The albatross should get a great deal more and the anteater more still, because these are rarely submitted. And consequently if the subject's guess actually coincides with a drawing of an anteater placed upon the desk in that particular experiment, we know what the "chances" of a successful hit on such an object are. We proceed now to give credits to all the objects reported by all the persons taking part in all of the series of the experimental trials. If there are many anteaters in the course of an experiment in which anteater was actually drawn by the dictionary method, and very few anteaters in other experiments preceding and following this particular experiment, we may pile up a considerable amount of "credit." Whereas, if the subjects waste their guesses either on very common objects or on rare objects that were not actually shown at the time of the particular experiment, they will have to be penalized. The total credit is going to depend on the number of hits weighted by the rareness value of the item. We have then a crude but forthright way of demonstrating whether items newly drawn by percipients at the time of experiments worked better than material used in previous or subsequent tests.

Carington successfully repeated his experiments on numerous occasions, notably in an experiment involving Scottish and English universities. Each university group scored higher on the materials set up for it to guess than on the material set up for the other groups. It has been clear from subsequent work, however, that it takes a very large amount of material (many subjects and many guesses) to yield a statistically significant result, and a satisfactory repetition of Carington's experiments with large quantities of material has not yet been reported.

Often in science, as in everyday life, it is the thing that is so simple as to be overlooked that constitutes the very core of what needs to be done. For over fifty years psi researchers had carried out experiments in telepathy, and one could still argue very plausibly on either side of the following question: are experimental telepathic phenomena limited to a few special sensitives, or are they the common property of the human race, capable of being realized in some degree by everyday persons of both sexes and of every age, degree of endowment and personality makeup? On the whole, the evidence seemed to support the view that the former alternative was correct; that except for a few special sensitives, the rest of us were completely without a capacity for paranormal responses under experimental conditions. Repeatedly inviting large unselected groups of people to take part, Carington put to test the hypothesis that a telepathic ability, in a form susceptible of test, is a common property of the human race, and through the remaining years of his life he drove home one blow after another in support of this conception.

In the earliest experiments, the procedure consisted simply of placing a line-drawing in his study, leaving it there overnight. Reports were received from scattered percipients who had attempted to duplicate the drawing. He then asked a friend to act as "umpire" to determine the degree of success obtained by these percipients. One control was automatically provided through the fact that the order in which the drawings had been exposed night after night through the course of the experiment was unknown to this umpire. Thus, in stating that a given drawing submitted by a percipient should be counted as a hit in relation to a given target prepared by Carington, the umpire could not know (except perhaps paranormally) whether the agreement was with a true target actually used on the occasion in question or with a wrong target belonging to some other date. Massing all the material, one could ask whether there was a tendency for the percipients' drawings to come in at the right times and to agree with the target drawings that were set up at the time when the percipients' responses were made. After some experimentation with this and with a related method in

which part credit for part success was given, encouragement
came from the clear evidence of a "mass effect" on the part
of the percipients, making them send in the right drawings
on the right occasions.

Now, as to results. Even in the first stages of his
work, Carington found clear evidence that subjects were hitting the intended target, but that they were also to some degree hitting the target that came next; that is, a target that
would be exposed at the time of the next experiment. So,
too, they often hit a target that had been exposed on the occasion just preceding the one officially intended. It was just
as if the percipients were a little confused as to the time
in which they were functioning, or the time in which Carington was functioning, or both. As early as 1941, Carington
had accepted the evidence for precognitive processes that
came from these experiments. Control data showed clearly,
however, that this tendency to hit future targets was not an
artifact and that the more remote in the future was the target, the smaller the number of hits upon it.

It occurred to Carington that the percipients who took
part in his experiments were somehow in touch with his own
mental operations. This was obviously not due to any intimate or emotional relationship; he was often unknown to individual percipients, and in the inter-university experiments
we have the further problem of subjects scoring successfully
on targets prepared by persons in no way in rapport with
them. On the other hand, it appeared that the distribution
of a photograph of his study, showing the location at which
the target drawings were to be placed, enhanced the scoring
ability of his percipients. He began to wonder if classical
association psychology might not be applied to the problem;
so as he prepared for an experiment he associated a certain
drawing with the "idea of the experiment"--with the room in
which the drawings were to be placed, with the date, etc.
There was, then, a network of associations having to do with
the experimental situation, a great many of which were thoroughly known to the distant percipients--for they knew the
general plan of the experiment, had an opportunity to see
the photograph of his study, had in mind the dates for the
various tests, and so on. One item connected in Carington's
mind with all these things--namely, the specific drawing
used--would also become accessible to the percipients if it
happened that the distinction usually made between different
human minds should turn out to be an artifact or philosophical prejudice.

There is a conception that all human minds are one mind, arbitrarily viewed through a sort of prism that artificially separates them. This doctrine was early developed by the sages of ancient India, then by Plotinus and by many Western mystics; and there is a great deal in Myers, Bergson, Croiset, Warcollier and in the writings of many other psi researchers that tends in this direction. If, consequently, experimenter A has in mind a group of inner-related items, and some of these items (or, indeed, only one of them) are supplied to subject B, the latter will, by association of ideas, come into possession of the missing item or items. It is, however, important to note an essential and important difference between Carington and the other advocates of such doctrines. He brought to the problem both the disciplines of long philosophical as well as experimental training, and he saw that the theory was of value only insofar as it could be put to work in rigid experimental tests. He showed, for example, that the "laws" of association as they have been tested under laboratory conditions can in some degree be directly transferred to the psi situation. The law of frequency says that the tendency of one idea to arouse another will depend upon the number of times the connection between them is made. Accordingly, Carington showed that the more frequently repeated and the more firmly established the associations were between the two events in the mind of the agent, the more clearly the first of these events will give rise to the second (i. e., the distant target) in the minds of the percipients. The Carington hypothesis cannot be lightly pushed aside on the ground that one does not like "philosophical theory." The theory has by now become a guide to experimentation; it will be tested and finally accepted or rejected in terms of empirical results.

In his book Telepathy (1945), published first in England two years before his death, and in 1946 in this country under the title of Thought Transference, he began to develop a theory of survival. As he saw it, a cluster of associations belonging to a single mind--a "psychon" system--is only loosely hung together, as we know from such phenomena as absent-mindedness, sleep, trance and multiple personality. It is possible that just as during our lifetime the system may become more strongly or more weakly organized (or may display the accretion of new elements, or the tendency toward fission or collapse), so the process of dying may grossly alter the properties of the psychon system. Some individuals may be able to survive the shock of bodily death, others not. Post-mortem existence will not be fed by new sensory impressions, but psychon systems may well continue--and indeed under certain circumstances may in death make progressive consolidation.

Carington's work offers much for us to reflect on in the subsequent studies of Ian Stevenson (1974a, 1975) on reincarnation, and in the drawing work of the dream participants by the Maimonides group (Ullman and Krippner, with Vaughan, 1973). It further appears in our adaptations of Tart's conceptual frameworks for viewing the interaction between minds.

F. THE AMERICAN SCENE

G. H. Estabrooks

G. H. Estabrooks (1927) conducted an interesting experiment in the Harvard Psychological Laboratories in 1924-5. Approaching individual subjects after classes in Emerson Hall, he invited them to the third-floor laboratory rooms offering to show them, individually, "the three-card trick." Here, in a large double room with the door closed between the two rooms, the subject simply guessed every thirty seconds the card that had been selected by the experimenters in the other room by cutting with a penknife. The results with eighty subjects showed very high levels of success in the first few calls per subject, but the results began to fade off for each individual subject during the course of twenty calls, so that they fell to the chance line; in other words, the positive results were all concentrated at the beginning, and soon fell off. A second series was attempted in another room without success. The Estabrooks experiment is one of many in which it is impossible to tell whether the failure of replication is due to something different about the new working conditions, but it is to be noted through the decline curves that individual scores had already fallen to a chance level before the second series was undertaken--that is, individual performances had not demonstrated a capacity to continue beyond the few initial successes. The Estabrooks experiment must be added to the rather long list of not easily explainable series.

It is worth noting in this connection that the scoring level in almost all the early published experiments is surprisingly high. This is true likewise of J. E. Coover's experiments (1917) at Stanford University, to which Coover himself assigned a negative evaluation. Treated by standard statistical methods the card-guessing studies that he carried out indicated results that exceeded the chance expectation by about four probable errors. In those days it was a rather generally accepted custom to regard results at this level as non-significant, and in view of Coover's own great caution and reluctance to accept anything paranormal, it is not surprising that he rejected these data of his own as contributing to any support for the telepathic hypothesis.

J. B. Rhine

Except, then, for the Groningen experiment, the scientific evaluation of telepathic claims had brought nothing strongly and clearly positive during the first quarter of the century. It is therefore no exaggeration to say that the field altered immediately, dramatically and profoundly when, in 1930, William McDougall offered the hospitality of the Duke University laboratories to Drs. Joseph Banks Rhine (1934) and Louisa Rhine, who were determined to define a clear and orderly research program relating to types of perceptual responses not understood through their prior training in biology. Their aim was to establish simple and clear procedures for the testing of paranormal powers, standard sets of target materials, methods of statistical evaluation of deviations from mean chance expectation. The standard deck made use of the five symbols, represented in Figure 5, five of each symbol appearing in each deck of twenty-five cards. A hit was the correspondence of a call with a target--star for star or waves for waves. Fundamental in the new conception is the clear distinction between telepathy and clairvoyance. Much prior research in this field had attributed successes in hitting a target to a telepathic process, the transmission of an idea, percept, etc., from one mind to another. Clairvoyance, or the direct contact with an object by means other than the senses (e.g. in dowsing), was in general regarded as unlikely, and experiments in which subjects apparently made contact with objects rather than minds were usually assumed to be really based upon contact with the mind of someone who was perceiving or remembering or thinking about that object. For Rhine, however, telepathy and clairvoyance constituted independent research

Figure 5:   ESP Symbols

problems, and from the beginning almost all of the work associated with Rhine has related to object perception (e. g.
clairvoyance).

Another radical innovation was to base the method
upon the phenomenon of recognition rather than recall.   In
psychological experimentation the term "perception" relates
to the response to a present stimulus.   The experimenter
can later ascertain whether the subject can recognize it when
presented.   In most of the early "telepathy" experiments
"free response" was used, as subjects were asked to describe the target material.   With the Rhine procedures, however, the subject's task was to state which of five cards was
presented, using classical "recognition" procedures.   So
great was this innovation that for a long time experimenters

were inclined to assume that the favorable conditions for this type of performance lay in various experimental parameters of motivation and such psychological factors as Gestalt structure of the target material or interference between lists of symbols, whereas the conditions favoring recall are by no means the same as those favoring recognition. For that reason the generalizations emerging from Rhine-type experiments must be related to general psychological principles that derive from recognition rather than to recall as such.

Of major importance, however, was Rhine's conception that both telepathy and clairvoyance--particularly the latter-- are forms of basic organismic (or total) perceptual capacity; together they were labeled "extrasensory perception." Experimental series were compared under conditions favoring or not favoring telepathy and/or clairvoyance. The basic model being conceptualized as a form of perception, it was natural to ask: what facilitates (or inhibits) perceptual response? Not only were control methods concerned with ascertaining the genuine extrasensory character of the perceptual process, but psychological dynamics were invoked to throw light upon rising and falling scores. In general, sensory cues were excluded by three methods: (1) by screens between subjects and target objects, (2) by opaque envelopes concealing cards or whole decks, (3) by distance.

Armed with simple experimental and statistical methods, Rhine proceeded both to attempt group experiments and to seek highly gifted subjects. Between 1930 and 1934, he found eight subjects who over a period of months maintained high scoring levels, typically averaging six or seven hits per twenty-five as against the chance expectation of five. These were scores that had never been reported in control series, and any one of these high-scoring subjects would be expected to fall to chance levels within a short time if there were simply a "run" of luck at work. The hypothesis naturally appeared that extrasensory perception was an attribute in which various persons are lavishly endowed.

The work done was mostly clairvoyance testing, in which subjects called straight "down through" (DT) a shuffled deck, and the call order was immediately compared with the target order. In a few experiments the card was taken off the deck after it was called, the subject always calling the card at the top; this was one of the cruder methods in which several types of sensory contact may well have been responsible for the high results reported. The down-through method, particularly when the cards were at a considerable distance, came gradually to be preferred. Other methods were soon developed to make possible the presence of experimenters and subjects in the same room without giving opportunities for sensory cues to produce spurious positive results. In the "screened touch matching" (STM), a bit reminiscent of Groningen, a screen separates the subject from the experimenter. On the experimenter's side of the screen the five target symbols are fastened. The subject pokes underneath the screen with a stylus at one of the five points corresponding to the five targets on the other side. The subject is in this way instructing the experimenter, who holds the cards face-down, where to place the card that lies at the top of the deck. In this way J. G. Pratt (1937), for example, in the Columbia University Psychology Laboratory, tested the ability of a high-scoring subject to respond appropriately to the top card in a deck as the cards were distributed, one by one, to the appropriate piles corresponding to the five symbols visible on the experimenter's side of the screen.

Rhine's work encountered much hostile criticism, but it also stimulated a large amount of research. The Journal of Parapsychology was launched in 1937 and contained, within a few years, research reports from over a dozen American colleges and universities and a few overseas. Some failures to get any positive results were reported, but a large number, using Rhine's or related methods, got encouraging results. Strict repetition was rarely attempted. Rather, the Duke University investigators and their adherents elsewhere were constantly launching new studies of the effects of various changes in working conditions, such as changed motivation, attitude, incentives, drugs and stimulants.

Enthusiasm and horror were more or less equally matched. The American Psychological Association set up a symposium at its 1938 annual meeting in Columbus, Ohio, to present attacks and rejoinders. For a long time there was a tendency to refight the same battles over and over again. In general it was clear that some of the experiments were indeed weak, but that there was a considerable amount of material involving opaque envelopes, screens and long distance to make a universal negative very hard to establish. The case settled down to the summary made in Columbus by Donald Hebb: "In view of the precautions taken any of us would ordinarily accept such findings, but there is one reason against it and that is that they do not make sense."

Clearly they did not "make sense" in terms of the general matter-energy-time-space conceptions of the physical universe that have been held--by most psychologists, that is--and will be held until someone can find new time-space-energy formulations that will make possible long-distance contact with target materials. When the physicist Leo Szilard visited our Columbia University laboratory in 1938, he said, after looking at the cards, "If anyone can perceive them at a distance, you are not dealing with radiant energy." By an extreme stretching of various "brainwave" theories of telepathy (a practice still encouraged among many Soviet investigators), telepathy can be somehow squeezed into the scientific package, but clairvoyance is excluded by the same process, and precognition of course is beyond the pale. There remains, of course, the possibility of new time-space definitions; new scientific models; mutual adjustment of parapsychological findings and contemporary--and rapidly changing--scientific constructs.

For the parapsychologist of the post-1930 era the problems remaining have to do with observable and measurable differences in the level of extrasensory perception as a result of such factors as motivation, excitement, satiation, relaxation, Gestalt organization of the target material, incline and decline effects, competition, distraction; such various parameters of personality as extroversion, introversion, expansion, compression; and a variety of attributes emphasized in projective testing (as with the Rorschach inkblot test).

G. R. Schmeidler

One of the main tasks of the Duke University Laboratory in the first decade of its existence was to test the various hypotheses, already noted, related to motivation, the effects of rewards and punishments, interpersonal relations between subjects and experimenters, enjoyment of the task and the effects of various drugs. Several studies dealt with the impulse to succeed, the conscious or implicit need of a subject to score high, as shown for example in self-competition or competition with other subjects.

Numerous studies dealt also with widespread occurrence of "psi-missing," the consistent tendency to score below chance expectation. A subject who is forced to work against his will, may not just occasionally, but steadily, maintain a score below chance expectation. Under certain working conditions it is possible to predict that the scores will deviate not in a positive, but negative, direction from chance level. Or, at times the subject may be blocked in the attempt to perceive a particular target and may, to a highly significant degree, make use of some other symbol, for example, tending significantly to call a cross when the target is a square. The subject may be both avoiding a particular symbol and using a personal substitute for what he or she will not see.

This combination of positive results when one desires them, with negative or below-chance results when one does not, came prominently to light in the work of G. R. Schmeidler at Harvard in the years 1942-5, and at the City College of New York in subsequent years. Schmeidler's (1943) first major hypothesis was to the effect that subjects who believe in the reality of extrasensory perception, as a possibility under the conditions of the experiment, will score significantly high while subjects who reject this possibility will score at or below chance. In the initial three cycles of experimentation done at Harvard, in Emerson Hall, the results were in accord with this hypothesis. Indeed, subjects who disbelieved in the possibility of success not only failed to score significantly high; they scored significantly below chance expectation. This trend of the believers to score significantly higher than disbelievers continued in the next three cycles of the experimental work, at the Harvard Psychological Clinic, and they have continued now for many years in the laboratories of the American Society for Psychical Research and the City College of New York. Those who believed in the possibility of success under the conditions described Schmeidler called "sheep"; those who disbelieved in this possibility she called "goats." The sheep-goat difference has been rather consistently maintained in a series of more than twenty of Schmeidler's published experimental studies since 1945, and in about twenty studies by others who have used these methods. These studies appear then to indicate the releasing effect of a positive attitude. The same kind of releasing effect is expected in the sphere of normal sense perception and perceptual defense, one of the many instances in which the psi capacities are released or inhibited or given a special direction by the subject's attitudes and personal attributes.

G.   THE PSI SCENE TODAY

The work of J. B. Rhine has provided the background for many of today's researchers. He alerted a generation to the possibility that psi existed, and as a result many were recruited who might have remained forever out of the field. Rhine's card and dice experiments and his and Louisa Rhine's books are familiar to a great many Americans, whether they believe or not in the possibility of psi.

Long preceding Rhine, another small group of devotees met periodically at the ASPR in New York (and in London at the SPR) who maintained a faith in scientific process, with varying ups and downs, depending on the phenomena and persons being tested at the time. Until the time of Rhine, mediums were seen as the experimental base for demonstrating the possibilities in psi, but once Rhine began his work with cards, the mediums gradually faded into the background, and with the death of Mrs. L. E. Piper, the last of the older great mediums passed.

Gardner Murphy, first as research director and later as president, helped turn the ASPR into more modern psychological research channels. From participants who saw psi as a hobby, he redirected its research work and recruitment down more professional lines, so that psychologists and psychiatrists, profoundly interested in psi as a research challenge, began to devote increasingly larger segments of their professional lives to the field. As a professor of psychology, first at Columbia and then at City College and the New School for Social Research, he inspired numbers of young psychologists to consider the field seriously. Then, when he and Lois Murphy transferred to the Menninger Foundation, he influenced many young psychophysiologists to study the puzzling problems that inhered in biofeedback and body neuromuscular functioning, as well as the relation between psi and creativity.

Since the Second World War research in psi has grown steadily. Immediately after the war there were but two significant points of research in the U. S.: the ASPR and Duke University. Since then more than a dozen focal

points of work and interest have emerged, usually under one
or two key researchers, keeping a small group of graduate
psychology students busy, with little funding but much genuine interest in the problem. Because of personal predilection, those in one setting tend to study a given problem, so
that specialization has begun in psi, as elsewhere. Some of
the primary research concerns may be delineated, as follows:

Under what circumstances does psi emerge? Here,
the growth of knowledge is slow but steady. Belief, as indicated by Schmeidler, may influence performance positively
or negatively, depending upon the attitude of the participants.
The concept of the participants has now been expanded to include the experimenter (White, 1977), so that the attitudes
that pervade the research setting are now seen to be perhaps
one of the more important elements of what may be a rather
complex process. Thus, the experimenter's beliefs about
psi and the experiment may be significant to the process, as
well.

For that matter, depth of the experimenter's emotional involvement may be one part of the "decline effect" that
pervades all psi studies, wherein a pattern of highest scoring
is present at the beginning of the study and the run, and
then a decline appears, with an occasional lift again at the
end of the study and/or the run. Charles Tart also suggests
that the decline effect may be an extinction phenomenon,
wherein one learns the wrong response steadily, in the absence of cues as to the right results, and he has designed
much of his learning work on this positive feedback theme.
Repressed emotion may well be a factor in the appearance
of poltergeist phenomena, as William Roll, of the Psychical
Research Foundation, Durham, North Carolina, has suggested (1974).

The particular brain state during the experiment has
absorbed a tremendous amount of research concern. For
instance, Montague Ullman and Stanley Krippner, working at
the Maimonides Hospital in Brooklyn, developed a Dream
Laboratory that systematically began to pick up on the work
of Aserinsky, Kleitman and Dement, sleep and dream researchers of the fifties. Ullman and his colleagues were
interested in studying REM sleep as a possible staging point
for psi phenomena, since the earlier researchers, especially
in England, had suggested that the hypnagogic and hypnopompic stages of sleepiness, leading both into and out of sleep,
were quite rich in extrasensory processes and experiences.

A part of this payoff has since been published in the book Dream Telepathy (Ullman and Krippner, with Vaughan, 1973). The study was positive, since the results suggested that during the REM stage of sleep, as well as the stages leading up to and out of it, psi phenomena apparently abound, and the organism is seemingly receptive to psi experiences.

Along this line the focus of much experimentation has centered around the low alpha, high theta brain wave dominance stages, with many different techniques employed to induce this: hypnosis, meditation, relaxation, drugs and sensory deprivation. Among the leading experimenters here are Charles Honorton (now in Princeton, New Jersey); William Braud of the Mind Science Foundation, in San Antonio; Charles Tart, of the Psychology Department, University of California, Davis; and Rex G. Stanford, of the Center for Parapsychological Research, in Austin, Texas.

They now seem to be reaching agreement on the need for an internal alert state, coupled with a willingness to permit psi to occur, however it occurs. There is some similarity to the paradoxical dream state, with a striking mix of activity and passivity, wild dream action plus very relaxed muscle tone. How to recreate this in a waking state is, of course, a real challenge.

Who make the best subjects for experimentation? There have always been a few superstars in the field of parapsychology at any give time. Formerly, they were mediums, but with the shift to the laboratory good subjects become experimenters in time, with interest, systematic training and graduate study. Rex Stanford and Robert Van de Castle are good examples of this. Ingo Swann remains a strong subject, over the years, as does Blue Harary. However, there is a conviction growing that apparently psi exists everywhere, and everyone has some of the ability (the difference or spread in scoring between those with sheep versus those with goat attitudes helps explain negative scoring, previously seen as the absence of psi). The job of the experimenter, then, is to bring this skill or ability to the fore, in the given experimental setting. Also, with some of the mass screening techniques that Tart and Helmut Schmidt have developed, it is now possible to sort potential participants into better and poorer performers fairly early in the study protocol.

Can the mind influence physical events? This is the
area so persistently studied by Rhine with his dice at Duke
over the years. But now, a new generation of researchers
has begun to shrink the arena of the action down to microprocesses, including the atom and random physical decay
events, rather than bulky (by comparison) dice. The mind
may be subtle, but then, too, so are the atom and its nucle-
us. Here, a physicist such as Helmut Schmidt, of the Mind
Science Foundation in San Antonio, Texas, has shown extraordinary inventiveness in developing random number generators (RNG's), random event generators (REG's) and electronic
equipment that speeds up test items by hundred and thousands
of events, thereby rapidly increasing the mathematical odds
against chance expectancy, when psi seems to be operating.
Schmidt employs techniques like the feedback researchers,
leaving only the final event for the subject to try to influence. This may be a dial, a needle, a clicking in the ears,
a light on a TV screen, without the puzzling circuitry to
ponder over (and possibly get lost in).

Is there a psi body paralleling the physical body?
As we learn more about brain chemistry, we begin to appre-
ciate the extraordinary computer mechanism that operates
on our behalf inside our skull. But psi would complicate
this mechanism far more. For many researchers there is
a parallel self, perhaps non-material, by our current definitions. This is being studied at a number of locations. For
instance, Harold Puthoff and Russell Targ of the Stanford
Research Institute in Palo Alto, California, have conducted
a series of studies of remote viewing (a form of clairvoyance) that suggest that an alternate self may be "going" to a
distant location, to report what a party of experimenters
are looking at concurrently. Karlis Osis of the ASPR has
specialized in studying such out-of-body experiences, conducting a series of ingenious experiments to determine whether the subjects "viewed externally" or "stepped into" an experimental box that appeared quite different, in each case,
depending on the viewpoint. Osis (1961) has also surveyed
out-of-body deathbed phenomena, studying the experiences of
dying persons in the United States and India. A followup
study was printed recently and was very widely read, making the best-seller lists (Osis and Haraldsson, 1977).

Carrying this theme to the next logical step, Ian
Stevenson, a Charlottesville, Virginia, psychiatrist who
teaches at the University of Virginia Medical School, has
assiduously tracked a number of times around the world in

search of apparently valid reincarnation cases. He has combed cultures friendly to the concept of being reborn, such as among Eskimos, Lebanese and Indian groups, seeking cases that have a strong measure of validity by his very rigorous standards. His books, including Twenty Cases Suggestive of Reincarnation (1974a), Xenoglossy: A Review and Report of a Case (1974b) and a new series, Cases of the Reincarnation Type, have become in a very short time the standard reference points for study of this phenomenon.

Can psi be made to fit into normal psychological processes? In a sense all the researchers are concurrently trying to answer this question, at least from the vantage point of their own special knowledge and insight. Charles Tart has provided one of the more important concepts in recent years, with his examination of the nature of consciousness and his suggestion that we examine the marginal experiences on the borders of what he calls the "basic state of consciousness." These altered states help to provide insight into many of the personation aspects of multiple personality, drug states, dream states and the states that emerge between waking and sleeping.

One who has devoted much attention to theory building in this regard is Rex Stanford (1974). He postulates one form of psi as a scanning mechanism employed instrumentally in the service of the organism, modified by motivations, emotions, attention, extent of needs, relevance and adjacency in time. It interties with the rest of the psyche, including thoughts, memories and feelings. Guilt and negative feelings can produce blockages and negative actions, as with any neurotic patterns. It can operate at unconscious levels, probably more effectively than when the conscious self gets in the way.

A second form of psi for Stanford is psychokinetic, producing changes in persons and objects outside the person. This person/PK he calls MOBIA (mental or behavioral influence of an agent); it follows all the above modifications for psi, while in the service of the organism. An optional feature of MOBIA is its mobilization when the person has done all apparently possible, and then "surrenders" to other "forces" in the universe.

Stanford's ideas have continued to evolve rapidly. He now postulates what he calls a "conformance model," which subsumes telepathy, clairvoyance and psychokinesis. Three

elements are required: a disposed system, in this case an
organism with a need or other disposition; a random event
generator (the brain serves as this for the human); a contingency wherein the REG produces the events that control
the probability of occurrence of unequally attractive alternative futures with relation to the disposed system. In that
case the REG will tend to influence the alternative future
most favorable to the organism's disposition. This goal orientation he calls "conformance behavior." Stanford does not
pretend to explain how these events occur, only that they do
occur, based on his studies in the laboratory.

The Recognition of Psi as a Legitimate Research Field

R. A. McConnell of Pittsburgh, Parimal Das of New
York and Rhea A. White and Laura A. Dale of the ASPR
have lent strong support to education for psi, with information and curriculum structures that have proven very useful
to the hundreds of courses now emerging on campuses
throughout the United States in psychology departments trying
to cope with a rapidly growing awareness of psi and humanistic psychology.

The growth of humanistic psychology, the broadened
American experience with psychedelic drugs, continuously
widening study and practice of meditation and altered states
of consciousness--all these combined to permit a broader
acceptance of psi in America. In December 1969, after a
dramatic appeal by Margaret Mead, the professional organization of parapsychologists, the Parapsychological Association, was accepted into affiliate status with the American
Association for the Advancement of Science. In the decade
since, the few hundred serious research students of psi have
thereby achieved a new status, although that has yet to pay
off in research grants or the opening to respectability in the
university on a broad scale. If anything, the serious researchers have had to be even more assiduous in the task
of defending responsibility and professional study, and in at-
tacking irresponsible and careless work in the field.

The current status of psi research may be symbolized
by a brief excerpt from a report by Braud (1978) as follows:

> ...positioned two feet directly ahead of the volun-
> teer's eyes (for Ganzfeld stimulation), a Sony TC-
> 440 reel-to-reel tape deck, a Schmidt binary ran-

dom event generator (REG), and a Sony TC-110A
cassette tape recorder. Another room, 70 feet and
two closed doors away, housed a six-channel poly-
graph (Stoelting Multigraphic Recorder, Model
22656), a Realistic stereo cassette tape recorder,
and an armchair.

When W. G. B. was satisfied that the volunteer
clearly understood the experimental protocol, he
attached two electrodes (silver/silver chloride, each
embedded in a plastic insulator disc, Autogenic
systems) to the volunteer's right palm, using adhe-
sive electrode collars (Beckman Instruments) and
Spectra 360 electrode gel (Parker Laboratories).
He then placed translucent acetate hemispheres
(halved ping pong balls) over the volunteer's eyes,
moved the chair to a semi-reclining position,
turned on the red Ganzfeld light, placed headphones
over the volunteer's ears, then left the room....

During the initial three-minute music section of
the tape, W. G. B. recorded the volunteer's basal
skin resistance (BSR) and adjusted the sensitivity
of the GSR amplifier (Stoelting Model SA 1473) so
that the internal calibrating signal of 1 K ohm resulted in a 10-mm deflection of the recording pen
[p. 125].

Psi is also under study abroad, as always thinly sup-
ported and funded. The Eastern Europeans, working from
a base that considers psi a possible variant of biological
energy, do not have quite as many of the emotional hangups
that block many American scientists from even weighing the
problem in a dispassionate framework. The Czechs and the
Russians conduct study in some ways similar to our work,
but psi research is still dealt with gingerly in government
circles. Also, the possible military uses of psi hang in the
background, an ever-present possibility in a world of rapidly-
shifting scientific assumptions (see Wilhelm, 1976, Ch. 14).

Conclusion

Psi research today is seen differently by two groups.
The first is puzzled as to what all the struggle is about:
obviously psi exists, since most of them have either had one
or more experiences that are inexplicable except through

psi or know someone who has had such an experience. For
this group the struggle for scientific recognition is a waste
of time, since psi will be recognized in good time, when
science moves into this area on a broad scale.

The second group is composed of the professional scientists who are upset at the idea that such nonsense is being
studied seriously by adults who should be doing better things
with their time. For them there is no problem, either,
since psi does not and cannot exist--because it simply doesn't
make sense.

Despite these attitudes the research-oriented parapsychologist is now being joined, albeit slowly, by the physicist,
who does not find the ideas of psi so disturbing, nor out of
conformity with the current ideas of space and time. Furthermore, the younger physicians, biologists, psychiatrists,
philosophers and others who encounter the field are beginning
to listen with fewer preconceptions and a greater openness.
And now we propose an assault on the walls that separate the
paranormal from the normal. On the debris we hope to build
a new paradigm that could encompass the world of psi. Perhaps if the new paradigm can be developed to reshape the
framework for our inner experiences, we could begin to see
a different approach to the problem. Our efforts in the discussion that follows will be devoted to that task.

Part II

Philosophy

INTRODUCTION: THE MIND-BODY RELATION

While the intimate interdependence of body and mind is attested by every study of the normal or of the abnormal--with continuous manifestation of the mental consequences of bodily functioning and the bodily consequences of mental functioning--it can hardly be said that great progress has yet been made in the search for the actual relation between the two. We still encounter in medical and in experimental psychology the same working conceptions that were developed in the seventeenth century-- some of them, in fact, defined by the Greeks and the Indians of two millennia ago. With all the exquisite subtlety of the modern methods of studying the living brain through electrical excitation and through observation of its electrical and chemical activity, and with all the knowledge gleaned by postmortem studies of brain pathology brought into relation with the mental pathology of the living, one might expect better. Is it not, indeed, somewhat of a paradox that in an era of huge progress in neurology, psychiatry and psychology, almost nothing new and clarifying has taken shape regarding the mind-body problem?

Of course, the problem may prove to be insoluble. Or perhaps its solution requires more and more facts of the same general sort we have already begun to accumulate and to use. Perhaps, however, we have been looking at the problem in the light of too limited a kind of evidence; it may be that we have not brought all of our present knowledge to bear on the issue.

Indeed, the most striking thing about the present philosophical situation, as it relates to this and similar issues, is the inability or unwillingness to use some of the data that seem to bear most directly upon the problem. These are sober, factual data, not known in any systematic way to the Greeks or to the seventeenth-century European; but they stand before us today and wait to be used. These are the data of psychical research, which is concerned every day of its existence with the empirical relationship of body and mind. Our purpose here, then, is to ask how the great classical conceptions of philosophy regarding the mind-body problem are affected--strengthened, weakened or ruled out-- by the evidence from research into psi, and what new philosophical conceptions the data seem to suggest. The whole undertaking is, of course, tentative; it is speculative and asks only to be studied, not to be accepted as a demonstration.

In referring to the data or facts deriving from our research, we should include nothing that is still controversial among research investigators, but only those general classes of data that have been repeatedly published, analyzed, evaluated and subjected to the criticisms of alert readers.

A survey of all the mind-body theories is out of the question; those interested in a systematic condensation of the various possibilities might do well to begin with C. D. Broad's (1925) The Mind and Its Place in Nature, in which the various contending doctrines are expounded and discussed. We will limit ourselves here to a few of the doctrines best known to the history of philosophy and to a few concepts of distinctly modern flavor. Of the six concepts to be outlined here, four are monistic; i. e., they state that mind and body are one. They assert the ultimate identity of mind and body, arguing that mind and body are appearances of, or ways of apprehending, the same ultimate reality. Two of the concepts are dualistic, arguing that mind and body are two distinct things.

A. MONISM

The four doctrines to be discussed under monism are: idealism, mechanism, emergence and panpsychism.

Idealism

Both Indians and Greeks were familiar with the view that the world of physical things, including the body, is an illusion; the one reality is mind. At times the term "illusion" is used loosely or even playfully. But with Bishop Berkeley we have the reasoned insistence that real things are in fact simply the things as we perceive them, and that there is no real thing except insofar as it is perceived. There is no "objective world" beyond the world as we experience it. There is no reference here to "degrees" of reality; there is just one reality, that of our personal and conscious experience.

While Berkeleian idealism is in poor repute today with professional philosophers, it is intriguing to note the resurgence among scientists, including physicists and astronomers, of ways of thinking that are almost as explicitly monistic as those of Berkeley. The late Sir Arthur Eddington was among the most eloquent of those to whom the findings of physics lead more and more explicitly into the abstract, the mathematical, the purely ideal. In The Philosophy of Physical Science (1939) he became explicit as to the reality, the knowability, of the things of the spirit. In contrast to this world of the spirit he held that we have very little knowledge of the physical world since it is permeated by the intervening properties of our subjective makeup.

How does such a philosophy adapt itself to research into psi? Whatever the intellectual satisfactions of an idealism in which mind is the one, or the primary, reality, the gravest difficulties appear when a simple case of telepathy or psychokinesis knocks at our door and demands an explanation. Take Mrs. Sidgwick's (1924) study of "hindrances" in telepathic communication. If there is no knowable body, but only a mind, the telepathic process can hardly be either "hindered" or "assisted" except by purely mental processes. There are in fact such mental processes: states of physical weariness, or drowsiness, or sleep; states induced by relaxing or stimulating drugs; states of deep trance involving circulatory changes. All these physical states seem clearly relevant to paranormal experience. Yet they must be denied to exist as genuine aspects of physical reality, or they must be translated into purely ideal terms, by anyone who seriously holds to such a monism. Psychokinetic effects must, in the same way, be treated by Berkeleian monists as occurring in an ideal non-physical world,

for there is, for them, no other. There is therefore no
very clear and practical way of dealing with the partial--and
complete--failures of PK; having no physical object whose
motion has to be altered, they have no place for the struggle
--successful in small degree or large--to cope with a world
alien to that of the mind. They of course have the privilege
of asserting that paranormal physical effects belong in the
same category with normal physical effects; namely, the
category of perceptual responses in the observers. But
whereas they have agreed to reduce the perception of normal
physical events to orderly lawful principles (which fortunately
coincide in practice with the principles that we all agree
govern the movement of objects), they must invent another
set of laws for the paranormal, and so might as well become
a dualist. It is not an accident that Eddington avoids the
paranormal; his orderly system has no place for it. What
is ordinarily called physical becomes with him (he actually
uses the word) spiritual; and the consequence is that there
is no place for the invasion of a physical world by a non-
physical force.

The conception that research into psi imposes upon
the investigator is that of a physical order into which there
sometimes breaks, and from which there sometimes emerges,
a non-physical order. The word "physical" is a great nuisance here. Everyday words are indeed poor things when
one wishes to convey all that is foreign to the "common
sense" from which they arise, and the word "physical" is
certainly insufficient, both because it leads (as with Eddington) into the metaphysical and because physics as a science
is gradually reaching out to embrace more and more of the
intelligible world, so that no boundaries can today be safely
imposed upon it. But, as things now stand, we can distinguish between physical energies on the one hand, which obey
certain definite laws as to distribution in time and space
(such as reduction of energy with the square of the distance),
and on the other hand the energies known to psi research,
which behave in no such way--which, through the fact of precognition alone, slip through the mesh of the whole system
of physics. The nature of such events is trans-spatial and
trans-temporal; the individual personality does at times know
without making physical contact with the thing known in the
ordinary way through the senses; and at times it makes contact with things that have not yet (physically) happened. The
idealist's "one world" is beautiful in its simplicity, but its
simplicity is misleading, for the world order that it lays
down must either be a space-time world (as it is with Ed-

dington) or a world of the trans-spatial and trans-temporal,
which would dissociate it from scientific laws as we now
know them.   If there are, as we have argued, two systems
of processes, two worlds of reality, the idealist can embrace
one, but not both of them.

Mechanism

A second variety of mind-body monism, generally
known today as mechanism, regards "mind" as the name for
a group of functions carried out by the body, especially the
brain. It is true that the term mechanism, like the term
idealism, is in some disrepute today, owing largely to the
common tendency of the older mechanists to make too close
a parallel between the behavior of living things and the behavior of machines.   But for all that, most of the "naturalistic" scientists and philosophers do believe in an essential
continuity between the simplest physical events and the most
complex brain activity, the latter serving as the basis for
mental activity in about the same way in which the movements of a gaseous particle in a closed box serve as the
basis of the pressure that the gas exerts on its sides.

From the point of view of one concerned with research
into psi, mechanism and related philosophies are neither
more nor less adequate than idealism.   They are simply
helpless when confronted by such phenomena as clairvoyance
and precognition.   Indeed, the mechanists, of all the philosophers, are the most afraid to study the phenomena of psi,
the most insistent that the phenomena cannot exist because,
considered philosophically, they have no "right" to exist.

Since both idealism and mechanism are self-contained
systems that can easily be integrated with physical science
but not with psi, serious confusion can arise from espousing
the idealistic position and eschewing the mechanistic on the
basis of some vague feeling that higher realities are saved
by the former and neglected by the latter.   This bias arises
from the notion that ideas are nobler things than physical
particles.   But the problem is not one of nobility; it is a
problem of serviceability in making phenomena intelligible,
and most idealists make no more serious attempt to come to
grips with them than do the mechanists.

Emergence

Yet, it would be a mistake to suggest that all the twentieth-century descendants of an earlier mechanism are equally naive, or that the monistic, "naturalistic" science of today is incapable of moving in the direction of a philosophy that might ultimately do justice to psi. Of the greatest importance in this connection is the modern concept of "emergence," which defines the properties of a compound in terms transcending the properties of its constituent ingredients. Just as sodium chloride has properties that belong neither to sodium nor to chlorine, so the living cell has properties that belong to none of the atoms, none of the molecules within its structure, but that do belong to the structure itself. Indeed, following this line of thought, there may well be emergent qualities of the living cell that are not properties of the non-living. A whole philosophy may be based upon this distinction; Broad calls this "emergent vitalism." So too, there are properties of the many-celled structure that could not be predicted from a knowledge of individual cells. Slime mold is a good example of this. There may be properties of the human brain that are not predictable from the physics, the chemistry and the biology of individual nerve-cells. Human brain-functioning may be a true "emergent," a kind of thing that never happened at all before in the evolution of living things. Indeed, consciousness may be an emergent, something really new under the sun. It may have properties incommensurable with any of the properties of other, simpler, things in nature. This line of thinking could give us, we are sometimes told, a true and consistent naturalism, and at the same time carry us along into the open air of great human potentialities freed from the manacles of the older mechanism, which made complicated things behave, as do the simpler things, according to a "push me/pull you" system of mechanical thrusts and counter-thrusts.

This whole doctrine of emergence is surely music to the present-day philosophical ear. But we seem to be moving rather too fast. What the properties of an emergent whole can be will depend on the ingredients. It is true that when a new integration is found, we may not be wise enough to predict what the emergent properties will be; but when we examine them, we find them depending upon an interrelation of specific components, and without the specific components the emergent cannot come into being. The new phenomena do not conflict with the old. The basic laws that hold through nature at a simpler level hold also at the higher level. The laws that a biochemist uses in predicting an individual's endocrine or nutritional needs are at a "higher level" than the laws of inorganic chemistry, but they do not violate the general laws that hold for all chemistry.

If the doctrine of emergence is to be helpful for research into psi, it must show how paranormal phenomena can be reconciled with the general scientific laws that hold in the physical and biological sciences. Does the doctrine of emergence really help us with phenomena that decline to participate in the space-time order; does it help us with telepathy, clairvoyance, precognition, psychokinesis? It makes no difference at what level one puts these things; they simply do not belong in the monist's scheme. Emergent vitalism, with its derivatives just described, is useful for general biological problems, but it is still too safe, too conservative, too limited, to meet us in our new terrain. It is certainly a good theory, but a theory that stays too "close to home" to do the pioneer job that is waiting to be done.

Panpsychism

But the monists may take an utterly different direction. The boldest of all the mind-body theorists begin, as do the idealists, with the raw stuff of which experience, or personal consciousness, is made; but they work in the general manner of the mechanists. They postulate a primitive or elementary kind of consciousness, a sort of "mind-stuff," as William James called it, and undertake to put it together into myriad combinations, to make the whole universe. They are generally called today "panpsychists." I shall attempt here to present only one kind of panpsychism, taught me many years ago at Harvard by L. T. Troland. Here is Troland's theory insofar as I can do justice to it:

As you read, you are a conscious self; your experience is not just an event in a material brain, but an act of consciousness or awareness. Someone watching you read observes your body, but does not observe your consciousness. Even with electrodes attached to your head to show your brain-waves, the observer would not see your thoughts, but only a manifestation of them. Our first premise, then, is absurdly simple; namely, that consciousness, or personal experience, is the one reality. But whenever there is consciousness there is an external manifestation of it, such as the brain-waves or the brain-cell changes, and this manifestation is a physical activity.

Now imagine the brain becoming simpler as we trace it back to infancy or to embryonic life. All the time the reality, which is consciousness, grows simpler; and the external manifestations likewise grow simpler. Even the single cell has its rudimentary consciousness. From physical and chemical studies of living and of non-living things we may conclude that the differences are relative rather than absolute. It is therefore not fantastic to suggest that an oil drop may have a consciousness not altogether different from that of a simple living cell. Indeed, the simpler the thing, the simpler its consciousness. But there is no reason to make a sharp break at any point; in the pansychist theory, everything that exists has a consciousness of some sort. Thus all the events of the physical world--considered from the inside--are psychical events. Every chemical attraction or repulsion, for example, is in its inner reality a psychical pull toward or away from something else.

But when we say that there are external physical "manifestations" of each psychic event, what do we really mean? By "manifestations" we mean conscious events in the observer, such as a visual perception of brain-cell activity as evidenced in an electrical process such as brain waves. What we call the "external" manifestation of one consciousness is actually the conscious experience of another, the observer. Thus, if someone watches you as you think, the observer's experience of you, even the experience watching your brain-waves, is still consciousness, not a non-conscious physical event. If the observer could open your skull and watch the surface of your brain, or even peer into its chemical reactions, he or she would still be dealing with consciousness--his or her own consciousness of brain surfaces and chemical reactions. With Bishop Berkeley, the panpsychist agrees on one essential point: it is meaningless to speak of things as they would be if they were not observable; it is what is observed, experienced, by the thinker, or by the one who observes the thinker, that science can deal with.

On the other hand it is the physical scientist with whom the panpsychist agrees when it comes to the way in which conscious elements are put together. In conceiving the universe, the panpsychist postulates a very large number of small, simple particles, each of which is a droplet of raw, primitive consciousness, such as a little ache, or a shrill simple tone, or a patch of pure color. If you analyze the furniture of your mind, you will find it composed of such mental contents, sense-impressions and feelings, which when compounded, make aggregates like musical chords or sunset colors. Now these elementary particles of consciousness move about in what we call space; they obey all the laws of physics. But if they are to become the subject-matter of science, they have to be perceived and then clarified and grouped in an orderly, logical way.

Of course, the qualities of the observer's experience are not necessarily the qualities as they exist in and for themselves in the particles observed. For the qualities in the observer's mind are determined by those conscious particles that we know as the brain. To pursue the example given above, suppose you examined the observer's brain, and saw a pink, furrowed surface. This would not mean that the observer's thought is pink or furrowed. The thing that you observe as the brain is the guise in which the observer's consciousness is manifested to you; these are the obverse and reverse of the same coin. And, in turn, the pink and furrowed qualities are qualities that are primary elements of your experience, corresponding to those activities that a student of electrical brain-waves would report going on in your brain. The essence of anything is its conscious quality, but the qualities of color, size, extent, etc., present in anyone's experience are "projected" into an outer space, a world where they are taken to be real. Actually they are real, and occur in time and space just as they are observed to occur. But we, the observers, never perceive their inner quality, but only their location and motion; and as we perceive them we impose upon them the qualities of our own inner experience. Thus, to the panpsychist the whole world of physical objects is regarded as real, and science goes on exactly as it does for the mechanist.

The panpsychist theory has indeed great subtlety and great esthetic and religious appeal--it may, for example, lead into pantheism. It is probably the most consistent, the most free of paradoxes, of all the aspects of current monism. But, as it is usually taught, it has the weaknesses as well as the strengths of monism. And, having bound the psychic realities to the space-and-time laws of physics, just as idealism and mechanism have, it appears to have given up all its opportunities to reach into the new trans-spatial, trans-temporal world to which research into psi has afforded a clue.

Nevertheless, panpsychism has much to offer. It does combine two fundamentally healthy and absolutely necessary ingredients in any viable philosophy: first, a respect for immediate experience, which it tries to explain rather than to explain away; and second, a respect for the methods and the laws of physical science. It makes the impression of going in the right direction. It might be turned into something more adequate if it would forego the negative note by which it insists that psi events can obey only those laws that are known to us in the form of the laws of present-day physics. This gratuitous assumption might well be stripped away, and we might find ourselves recognizing two forms of psychical reality, one form operating in space-time terms, and known to existing science, and the other operating across --or rather outside of--the spatial and temporal categories. The first form includes the ordinary data of physical and biological science, and of psychology, insofar as it is an expression of biological existence. The second form includes ESP and PK, and every other process that research into psi may discover in which people make contact with something that is not a part of the space and time in which they are placed. There is a similarity here in some regards between gravity on a large scale and gravity at the sub-atomic level, where it apparently follows different laws.

But where will this lead us? Two kinds of psychical laws, the one bound by space and time, the other free from them? And still this asks to be called monism? No, this surely will not do. It becomes clear that a real dualistic cleavage in nature is suggested to us--not between "mind" and "matter," for in following the arguments of the idealist and the panpsychist we have found that we no longer know what matter is--but between those types of natural events that conform to physical laws and those that have a different kind of lawfulness of their own. The panpsychists had not intended us to go so far; but facts have priority over theories, and the panpsychists, who were willing for us to go up to the gates of dualism so long as we did not enter, will now have to allow us to go into new territory, armed with the ideas that they have lent us. We therefore turn to a study of dualism. But we start with a predilection for a dualism not of "material" and "immaterial" things, but of two kinds of conscious operations; the space-time kind and the trans-temporal kind.

B.   DUALISM

Parallelism

There are many ways of differentiating between bodily function and mental function that still deny genuine dualism; for they regard "bodily" and "mental" as simply aspects or expressions of a single basic process ("double-aspect" theory).   Thus, Stanley Cobb (1944) writes in his <u>Foundations of Neuropsychiatry</u>:   "Indeed, up to the present there is no hint of any fundamental difference between the 'mental' and the 'nonmental' functions of the central nervous system, whether they be studied by chemical, physical, or microscopical methods" (p. 92).   By dualism we indicate a much more profound cleavage of mind and body than is implied by such reference to two aspects; we mean a belief that mind and body are different in kind, differing as stars differ from virtues, or as words differ from pyramids.

The two great modern forms of dualism took shape in the seventeenth century, in the hands of Descartes and of Leibniz, respectively.   Descartes differentiated between the body as an "extended" thing and the soul as an "unextended" thing, but asserted that the influence of soul upon body must be exerted at a specific point in space.   Indeed, he went on to argue that this point is the pineal gland, which "by inclining this way or that" in response to the soul's influence, caused this or that bodily response to occur.   All body-mind views that postulate in one way or another that there are two distinct entities that act upon one another are bracketed together under the term "interactionism. "

Leibniz, on the other hand, could conceive no way in which a physical event could properly be caused except by another physical event, or a mental event except by another mental event.   While the attempt to put the essence of Leibniz's thinking into a phrase is even more misleading than in the case of other philosophers, we may best refer to his extraordinary analogy of the two clocks: if two perfect clocks are set going and continue to function independently, the time as given by one is always the same as given by the

other, although neither ever "causes" the movement of the
other's hands. In similar fashion, there is always perfect
agreement between mind and body. A light flashes into your
eye, and you see, but the light does not cause your seeing,
which in the economy of nature, was predestined to occur at
precisely that moment; and as you decide to reach out your
hand to sign an agreement, your hand is concomitantly, but
independently, extended by virtue of physiological processes
in your body. This is the best known of the many forms of
"psychophysical parallelism."

Parallelism seems clearly disqualified as a system
of thought appropriate to research into psi, since the processes are inevitably straightjacketed within the same system
of laws that govern the bodily movements, for the two systems can never get out of step. If normal perception is explainable through the parallel activity of brain and mind,
then extrasensory perception involves the sheer omission of
an essential link--it is a mental process without a parallel
physical process--while PK involves the thing that parallelism can least of all admit, the action of mental upon physical.

Interactionism

We noted that parallelism is as inadequate as a base
for psychical research as are any of the monisms treated
earlier. Our phenomena require the establishment of a
definite functional cleavage between orders or classes of
events based upon the applicability or non-applicability of the
familiar laws of spatial and temporal organization. To perceive that which is occurring at a point from which no appropriate physical energies have reached us, or to perceive
that which has not yet physically happened, or by our thought
to influence that which is not physically controlled by our
bodies--all these are prima-facie cases of dualism, and of
that particular kind of dualism called interactionism.

There are, however, two huge enigmas here. First,
how can things that are fundamentally different interact?
We may smile at the quaintness of Descartes's dutiful pineal
gland, which took the whole onus of the interaction problem;
but our own view is likely to appear just as quaint, unless,
simply to avoid quaintness, we conveniently forget to indicate
any specific organ or method for the facilitation of interac-
tion--escaping the appearance of absurdity only by being

evasive. We shall have to admit that interaction is possible only if the interacting things have some similarity and are governed somehow by similar laws; at the very moment of stressing the cleavage between the two, we shall have to acknowledge their sharing in a dynamic unity. There must be laws that transcend the limitations of mind as such, and of body as such.

Of all the monists, the panpsychists appear to be the readiest with assistance here, for they have already suggested that mental laws and physical laws are two aspects of the same thing. Confronted with the data of our research, their task is to find a way to postulate two kinds of interacting conscious activity, one of which presents a physical appearance, the other of which does not. Admittedly this is a large order. But all fundamental progress in science and in philosophy is a large order, and it is doubtful whether the assignment is any more difficult than the successfully assumed assignment of reconciling corpuscular and wave theories of light. When the panpsychists determine, on the basis of evidence from research into psi, that they must become interactionists, the beginnings of a workable philosophy of mind and body will be at hand.

This will provide the beginnings, but not the completion of the task. Much labor, both empirical and theoretical, will be needed. But with a view to the developmental unity of the living organism, and the general nature of the evolutionary process, the working assumption would be that behind a genuine dualism there is some form of superseding unity expressed with two realities. For all the conscious processes--normal and paranormal--of each living thing are in some measure integrated to make use of whatever realities there are in the environment that may be useful in meeting its needs. The paranormal processes that transcend the space-time order--whenever the individual is gifted with the capacity for their use--have indeed been found to be utilized in close integration with the normal processes. As Rex Stanford (1974) has conceived the problem, we may utilize the paranormal in the service of our life purposes in close conjunction with our everyday utilization of the normal, and without even realizing that our manner of knowing the world is twofold.

The other enigma presented by interactionism is one that has caused much uneasiness among psychical researchers in the last few years. The question is this: granting a world of mental or conscious events, are these events self-sufficient, to be taken at their face value as an irreducible kind of reality, or are they simply aspects of a deeper, unobserved psychical reality--a soul or mind? Are mental events things in themselves, or are they reflections or shadows that betray a unitary reality beyond? (The issue reminds one of Berkeley and Hume, and even of Socrates and the Sophists.) Carington (1945) insists flatly that the psychons (conscious elements or clusters) are to be taken as non-physical entities in their own right; H. H. Price (1939) among others, holds out for a deeper psychical reality, of which ideas are but expressions. It is not the aim of this discussion to debate this huge problem, but simply to observe (a) that the term "interaction" might mean interaction of the body either with the soul or with the psychon system, and (b) that while the introduction of an unobserved soul, lying beyond the actual mental processes known to us, may indeed ultimately prove to be philosophically necessary, nevertheless at present it simply complicates the picture. The evidence from psychical research seems to relate the interaction of knowable mental states (ideas, feelings, etc.) with knowable bodily states.

It is equally clear, however, that this interaction leaves residues; it does not, so to speak, cut through the empty air, leaving no aftereffects, but definitely alters the world. Memory involves the re-presentation, within us, of earlier interactions; personality is an accumulation, a progressively integrated network of new and old impressions. Part, but not all, of memory consists in impressions left within the brain; there are rote memories depending on brain mechanisms, and there are also meaningful memories that appear to survive brain injuries, and to live on indefinitely as holistic processes, being subject to no simplistic principle of biological disintegration. Some of our meaningful memories may not die with us. If, then, we argue that part of the psychic existence of the individual is not governed by the familiar space-time laws, it is likely in turn that this accumulated nexus of personal associations may be unaffected by the physical disintegration of the body. Most of the survival evidence in hand cannot differentiate between continuity of a "soul" or persona and continuity of subsidiary elements of personality, such as personal associations or psychon systems.

We have hinted at one among many possible solutions of the mind-body problem; at least a direction has been sug-

gested in which an answer might in time be defined. Many
other possible solutions exist, and research alone can tell
which is the most promising path to follow. It is possible,
for example, that the most rigid of the dualisms, even the
interactionism of Descartes, may be revitalized by new dis-
coveries; and it is quite likely that newer theories of emergence may find a way to obliterate the difficulties here
pointed out. The advances of physics may find a clue to
cosmic structure in which the paranormal appears as another
aspect of reality intimately expressive of laws that lie at the
very heart of all physical processes; we may find that the
spatial and temporal are simply two "special cases" of universal kinds of structural relations. We see in a glass
darkly, and dogmatism is the only unpardonable sin.

Yet something is gained by emphasizing, for explora-
tory purposes, one immediately promising direction. The
mind-body problem has not been solved by the preceding discussion, but it has perhaps changed its locus to a position
from which it can be better observed. A point of attack has
been suggested. The problems of psychical research appear
today to call for a dualistic answer. But perhaps these
problems need no longer be stated in terms of two irrecon-
cilable, incompatible elements, physical and mental. Rather,
it may be a problem of two types of psychical functioning,
one defined by and expressed in the spatial and temporal orders, the other lying beyond them.

We now turn our attention to the construction of a new
framework, a paradigm or model that can permit us to insert psi appropriately into place as a meaningful part of our
mental world.

Part III

A Theory of Psi

A.   INTRODUCTION

There is an elevator in which I ride up to my work, and it has a defect that intrigues me.   I step from a seemingly solid floor into a seemingly solid room that floats in a shaft on a cable.   I ignore the small line that divides the room from the floor, and I do not normally look into the shaft when I step into the elevator.   But once within the car, there at eye level, the plastic sheets that make up the walls of that floating room do not join perfectly: there is a space that permits, no, compels, me to look out into the shaft. This crack in my microscopic egg makes me aware of one illusion under which I labor, that the world in which I struggle is so solid and real.   It is not.   Try as we may to complete the incompleted figure of our world, there is far more to the nature of ultimate reality than our Gestalt-ridden brains can ever hope to complete and cover over.   And it is not a plastic-covered empty metal cube, either.   It surrounds us like a rich, complex, ever-changing jungle, defying our best efforts to explore its multitudinous paths.

We probe deeper and deeper into the mysteries of nature.   She forever eludes us, and surprises us by her complexity.   Each layer of understanding we finally uncover reveals another mystery beneath.   We pulverize grains of matter down to molecules, smash them into atoms, bombard them into protons, neutrons and electrons, and then the mystery really begins.   Sub-sub atomics reveals still more complex particles, glues and processes, and the whole structure dissolves into a shimmering field of radiative forces. Each theory, like the field, is found to be full of holes.

There is much about psi functioning that fits in well with everything else that we know about the person and human functioning. Ours is an attempt to normalize psi, to set it in a framework essentially human, social psychological, and--within the current limits of knowledge--biophysical. This approach postulates categories of psi that relate closely to the rest of human mental and physical functioning; biophysical causes and effects of psi, in a matrix that tries to link together a great variety of mental and psychic phenomena hitherto unexplained and unexplainable. It builds on much that has gone before, the work of the major experimenters of the past and the present. What emerges here is an interim resultant of many fine minds, each of whom provided parts of a giant mosaic still slowly being assembled. Our hope is that this tentative construction is along lines suggestive of what can emerge as a durable theory of psi.

We group many assumptions about psi and human nature, some of which are unproven, others of which are merely suggestive, at present. The virtue of this position is that each assumption is testable and researchable, and can be either proven or disproven, or new lines of study can be set out.

In the discussion that follows in Parts III and IV, all of the psi phenomena are examined in detail, some more than others, to include comments, induction and some typical cases, spontaneous and laboratory, to provide a feeling of the experience, without insisting that these examples are in any way proof of the phenomena. Finally, each section has research suggestions for follow-up, since all the postulates ultimately demand the most rigorous study and proof.

B. THE INDUCTION OF PSI

The Sympathetic and Parasympathetic Nervous Systems

Roland Fischer (1971) has provided us an important conceptual clue in his discussion of ergotropic (aroused by the sympathetic nervous system) and trophotropic (tranquilized as a result of an activated parasympathetic nervous system) processes and their relation to inner states of being and awareness. The basic personality, certainly in the West, is usually centered upon the outer world, functioning with Hertz brain-wave levels in the alpha and beta ranges and EEG amplitudes between 15 and 35. Moving toward either extreme of excitation or tranquilization results in turning the self inward and away from the outer world. At the extremes of system function, whether these are states of extreme hyperarousal, with a collapse that follows (as in dervish

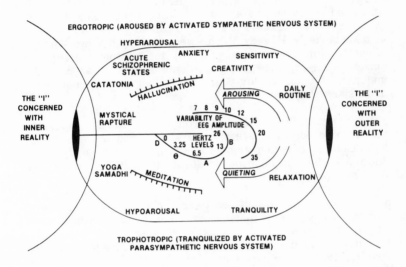

Figure 6: The Outer and Inner "I's" (adapted from Fischer's Cartography of the Ecstatic and Meditative States, 1971)

dancing and similar heightened activity states) or of extreme quietude (as a result of meditation or drugs), the result is essentially the same: a deep inner self-concern and self-absorption. Figure 6 illustrates Fischer's concepts, but adapted to the current context and modified somewhat.

Functional Modes

The studies of Myers, James and Stanford summarized earlier have suggested that psi has many lawful features. Most of all, it should be seen as embedded in typical mental functioning, rather than as operating on its own. It is not literal, nor are simpler expressions of it, such as clairvoyance, photographic. Rather, it takes place in the total matrix of mental functioning. This is an important concept for us to grasp, since we so often tend to think simplistically about new concepts, and then are so surprised to find, rather, that they continually flow from everything else we know about ourselves.

First of all let us try to define the mental matrix in which psi operates. For one, we apparently can relate to others who have experiences important to them and to us, at a distance. Already, then, we have implied two aspects of mental functioning: empathy, or feeling into the experiences of others, and perception, albeit at a distance, and under circumstances for which we do not even pretend to understand the mechanism.

For another, there are some very strange experiences that involve body and spatial awareness, and more particularly muscle functioning: automatic writing, psychometry and dowsing, wherein psi process seems to utilize some aspects of motor process.

Thus, we have at least three aspects of mental functioning (and probably many, many more) that can be listed as involved with psi: perceptual or sensory processes; empathy or feeling; and motor, or more narrowly, muscle functioning.

Altered States of Consciousness

The process by which a person induces an altered state of consciousness (ASC) is as varied as the cultures of humanity. Long ago, ancient peoples discovered that dozens of factors can upset the delicate balance that holds the "normal" consciousness in operation. Stress, starvation, intense rhythms, staring at the sky, immolating the flesh, extreme pain, imbibing certain liquids, eating certain plants, rocking back and forth, turning till one is dizzy, rapid sensory variation--the list is endless. Arnold Ludwig (1968) has suggested that extremes of modality function seem to induce an altered state, which apparently becomes a "final common pathway" for any of the dozens of forms of altered response and function. A listing of these extremes is shown in Table 1, broken up into our three categories.

Table 1

EXAMPLES OF FUNCTIONAL EXTREMES LEADING TO ASC'S

Ergotropic (arousing)	Trophotropic (quieting)

Perception

Sensory overload:
  7/sec. flicker frequency
  Rapid alternation of colors
    or light and dark
  Certain drugs
  Fever
	Sensory deprivation:
	  Ganzfeld screen
	  White sound
	  Immersion in water at
	    certain temperatures
	  Prolonged vigilance (sentry duty, crow's-nest watch)
	  Fog, sky, sea, arctic, highway hypnosis

Empathy

Threats to significant others, including death, injury or illness	Sudden removal of threat to significant others Suggestion process, including hypnosis Mass religious ceremonies Being in love

Motor/Spatial

Motor excitation with much adrenaline Sudden emergence into larger space Music and rhythmic patterns Panic, rage, running berserk Battle fatigue Hyperventilation Turning in place rapidly Witches cradle Orgasm	Motor stillness or acute sense of confinement Body immobilization Motor paralysis Curare

Charles Tart, in States of Consciousness (1975), has offered yet another very useful model for us to study (see Figure 7). He postulates a baseline state of consciousness (b-SoC), which we would recognize as our normal state, sub-

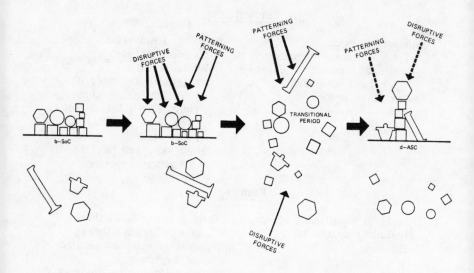

Figure 7: Steps in the Induction of a Discrete Altered State of Consciousness (from Tart, 1975)

jected to disruptive forces, as well as patterning forces. Under the impact of these two a new discrete altered state of consciousness (d-ASC) is established, with a new stability pattern. For our purposes this is a highly creative paradigm of the process, that offers much for follow-up. For instance, extremes of modal function, such as sensory deprivation, could serve disruptive purposes, while social pressures, social norms, family or tribal practices, prior experiences with trance or medicine men would serve as patterning forces. Latent abilities that are unused or underused in one state may serve important functions in other states. Conversely, important elements of the baseline state of consciousness may well be missing in any of several altered states.

Tart's concept suggests the concept of "reassembly" of latent elements of personality into new configurations that would be unfamiliar to and different from the baseline personality.

How Psi Comes About

If we assume that there are certain consistencies among all psi processes, then a paradigm can possibly be designed for the induction of psi. For this purpose let us further assume the following:

Input into a given mental mode is modality specific.

> Perception: sensory processes.
> Empathy: relations with and feelings about others.
> Motor/spatial: motor and muscle activity, plus
> awareness of body in space.

Input into a mental mode normally falls in a middle range of performance, based on the evolution of the mode. Modulations of the input tend to keep absorption of the input close to the middle range for optimum functioning. Actual input, however, can fall well below or rise well above the middle range of optimum functioning. This can result in demands upon the modality function beyond its ability to cope at optimum levels.

Since consciousness is multiply stabilized, attempts are made by the system to maintain stability, drawing upon these varied resources. However, when input passes a certain point above or below the range of optimum functioning, a shift then occurs in the total system (see Figure 8). This shift occurs first in consciousness, with preconscious functioning taking over for a brief period. The shift to preconscious functioning is characterized first by dissociation, and then a new stability is achieved in the induction of an altered state of consciousness. At the same time, a modality-specific psi system may come into play, in one form of rebound against the alteration that has occurred in modal functioning (see Table 2). The altered state of consciousness is thus a necessary but alone not a sufficient condition for psi to occur.

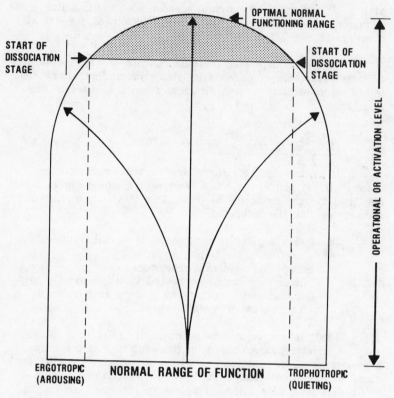

Figure 8: Modality Process Leading to Dissociation

This threefold process can be portrayed in another way, to illustrate some of the dynamic features. Crudely pictured, the three input systems may in some ways resemble different train tracks, coming into a railroad roundhouse, because an emergency has compelled them to come to a switching point (see Figure 9). Restated in psychological terms, if a system is forced into extreme functioning, dissociation may begin and preconscious functioning may take over for a few moments while a new stability is being sought. This is the entry point into the roundhouse, which is an altered state of consciousness, or final common pathway. At this point many choices lie open to the organism. The normal rule would be to see the input continue on its former trip, and this is the usual pattern: input into a modality tends to continue, after the crisis, in the same modality, as

Table 2

THE INDUCTION OF PSI (THREE PRIMARY MODES ONLY)

Typical Modality--Specific Extreme

Mode or Function	Ergotropic (arousing)	Trophotropic (quieting)	Form of Psi Induced	Shorthand Term
Perception	Sensory overload	Sensory deprivation	Clairvoy-ance	ψr
Empathy	Threats to signifi-cant oth-ers	Suggestion process	Telepathy	ψe
Motor/ spatial	Motor ex-citation; sudden emergence into larger space	Motor still-ness or acute sense of confine-ment	Psycho-kinesis	ψk

a rule. Thus, a motor crisis would tend to be motor-expressed, just as a perceptual crisis would tend to be perceptually expressed, since that is the system active at the particular moment.

However, this is a complex, dynamic system. The roundhouse permits many choices, and each organism has its own unique history of patterning forces for the resolution of intra-psychic tension. Thus, a mother whose daughter has just been injured at a distance may feel the bump of the bicycle against her leg and hear her daughter cry out at the same moment--motor and sensory processes. The suggestion here, therefore, is that many possibilities lie open. A single modality may experience and respond; a single modality may experience, another may respond; several modalities may experience, one may respond; a single modality may experience, and several may respond; finally, and we should

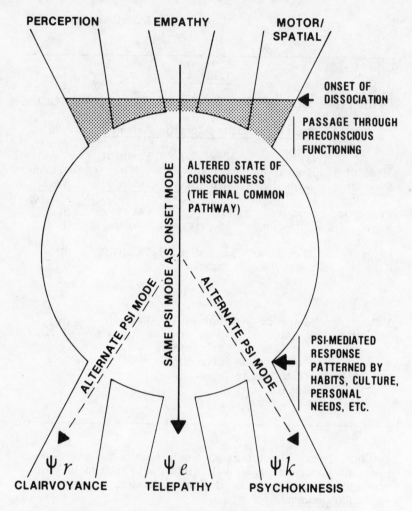

Figure 9: Basic Modality Exceeding Optimum
Function (Empathy as an Example)

assume most commonly, several modalities may experience, and several, in turn, may respond.

This should help us understand why the process has not been well understood. We have assumed too simply that process A leads to A^1 result. Experience, on the other hand, suggests that the range of possibilities is almost endless, owing to the extraordinary complexity of human personality. Experience A may lead to A^1, A^5 or A^{27}.

Part IV

The Psi Matrix

A.   THE MAIN THREE SINGLE MODE PSI PROCESSES

We shall first sketch the list of the three psi processes that essentially derive from and relate to a single mental mode.   These are the same three as listed in Table 2:   Perception--Clairvoyance; Empathy--Telepathy; Motor/Spatial--Psychokinesis.   These are now portrayed (see Figure 10) on a matrix that arrays both the modes and the extremes of their function on a three-by-three array.

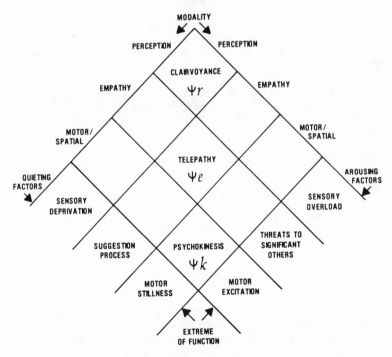

Figure 10:   The Main Three Single Mode Psi Processes

Clairvoyance

This is a complex process that does not conform to current physical theory, bound as it is by the inverse-square law. Pure clairvoyance is assumed to take place when the mind perceives an object extrasensorily, without the intervention of another person's mind.

Induction: Assume profoundly reduced familiar sensory patterning input, which can be as extreme as sensory deprivation. The eyes may be involved (Ganzfeld screen-- with ping-pong ball halves over the eyes); ears (white sound --a shshshing sound, repetitively played on a tape); skin (floating in water at body temperature or a little lower, or wearing special gloves).

There may be variations on this: furry, blurry perceptions that are confusing, shapeless, meaningless, that compel the sensorium to organize an input (e. g. --crystal ball; neutral rug or wallpaper with meandering pattern).

For certain sound experiences, which are linear rather than global, it may require highly repetitive materials, such as a tape loop saying the same phrase over and over again.

An alternate mode can involve sensory bombardment: rhythms, flickering light, repetitive sounds, vibrations, frequently at rates identical to low alpha and high theta rhythms in the brain.

As the familiar patterning of input is broken up, there is the gradual emergence of dissociation and the induction of an altered state of consciousness.

Spontaneous Case: Milan Ryzl (1970) cites the case of a Dutch clairvoyant who had a striking success with some lost jewelry:

> Mrs. S., from the Hague, lost a pearl necklace in 1942. She suspected that it had fallen into a sink. Her insurance company made a search, and, on the basis of the plumber's expert evidence, concluded that the necklace could not have stuck fast in the discharge pipe, but that it had floated into the central drain and must be regarded as lost. However, the insurance company suspected that

Mrs. S. might have lost the necklace elsewhere, and called in a paragnost. He confirmed the statement that the necklace had fallen into the sink, but assured them that it got stuck in the discharge pipe. After visiting the house he indicated the exact place. Although the plumbers denied the possibility that the necklace could get stuck in the discharge pipe, the insurance company nevertheless had it opened at the indicated place. The necklace was found there [p. 197].

Experimental Case with Spontaneous Elements: Additionally, external shapes may be sought to "justify" an inner experience, a shape that seems to "conform" to what is occurring inside at some level. Taves, Dale and Murphy (1943) reported on a particularly revealing case in this regard:

One subject, Miss L. L., calling her first deck ... obtained a score of 17, the first 15 cards of the deck being correctly guessed. An unbroken sequence of 15 hits at the beginning of a deck would be expected to occur by chance once in about 30,000,000,000 runs. It will be recalled that all decks used were arranged in accordance with random numbers....

In the "17" run she had started out by looking around the room and certain objects there, which she associated with the five symbols, had successively caught her eye. For instance, when the coils of the radiator seemed to "attract" her she chose the wave; dry cell batteries on a nearby shelf indicated the circle; the corner of the table indicated the star; the square was symbolized by a chair-bottom, and "something she saw in the design of the rug" meant the cross. (Actually there is nothing in the design of the rug, which is of Oriental type, that even remotely resembles the form of a cross.) Then, as the run progressed, this procedure began to seem too stereotyped, too "automatic," and another approach to the task took its place. She felt that she should call, say, a circle, and then she looked around the room until she found an object the outline of which would "justify" her impression. She further stated that after a while (whether towards the end of the "17" run or at the beginning of the next run could not be exactly ascertained) she "got bored with looking around the room and just tried to imagine what symbol Mrs. Dale was looking at, but thought it silly." She was not told at the end of this sitting, as were all the other subjects, what her exact scores were, nor was she paid the reward for her score of 17 until after the last sitting [pp. 116-117].

Experimental Case: Honorton and Harper (1974) offer the summary of a study that attempted to combine various sensory deprivation techniques in the laboratory, as follows:

Abstract: Converging evidence from the laboratory, spontaneous case trends, and introspective accounts of "gifted" subjects suggests an association between psi-receptivity and states or conditions of sensory isolation. This is consistent with the hypothesis that ordinarily weak psi inputs are masked by sensory "noise," and that reduction of such "noise" may result in amplification of psi input and facilitation of ideation, imagery and other forms of mentation which may serve to mediate psi information into consciousness. Thirty subjects each participated in a single thirty-five minute session in which their auditory and visual perceptual inputs were regulated via a homogeneous visual field (Ganzfeld) and a repetitious auditory tape. Ss gave continuous reports of images, thoughts and feelings throughout the session. In prior research this procedure was found to facilitate the flow of ideation and imagery. At a randomly selected time period, an agent in another room viewed a series of thematically related, stereoscopic images, attempting to influence Ss mentation. Blind assessment of correspondence between targets and mentation revealed Ss were successful in identifying the correct targets to a statistically significant degree ($p = .017$). Inspection of the correspondences supports prior theoretical and empirical work suggesting that psi information may be encoded in memories.

[The foregoing abstract covers an experiment that successively included clairvoyant and telepathic work. What follows includes a few instances of the pre-sending, or clairvoyant hits. --M. L.]

Example 3. Mike. Target: "The American Indian." Pre-sending: "A long highway in Mexico....
Lots of thoughts of Mexico, but maybe because I
just read Journey to Ixtlan...."

Example 5. Jacklynn. Target: "U. S. Air Force
Academy." Pre-sending: "...An airplane floating
over the clouds.... Planes passing overhead....
Thunder now, angry clouds.... Airplanes....
Ultrasound.... A blaze of fire, red flames. A
five-pointed star.... An airplane pointing down...."

Example 7: Lance. Target: "Project Apollo."
Pre-sending: "Almost like I was flying, flying
higher into the sky.... The sky changed to dark
blue with stars. Now, something that doesn't belong there, spinning, crescent-shaped and rounded.
Going faster, looks like stars in the background..."
[pp. 163-164].

Research Suggestions: The difficulty in the design of
clairvoyance research is the complication of telepathy, plus
other elements, such as time displacement. Most instances
of laboratory work around the theme of clairvoyance can be
explained alternatively in terms of telepathy plus precognition. Occam's Razor, with its emphasis upon the simpler
solution comes to our rescue here. The concepts of psi are
complicated and difficult enough, so that simplicity is always
called for. For this reason clairvoyance has its own domain
for study.

The problem, then, boils down to a question: can we
design an experiment in which the experimenter can never
know the individual target, nor anyone else for that matter?
Then the questioning outside scientist can rightly ask: but if
the experimenter doesn't know the exact target, how can you
get a valid score that can be counted as a part of the growing body of evidence for analysis?

The answer, as some researchers have now discovered, lies roughly as follows: set up a target-creating and
scoring mechanism that is random, accurate, mechanical and
repetitive, but with varied targets so as to maintain interest. Once a score is laid down, the machine records the
total score, destroying the individual hit records, as it goes
along. This eliminates the possibility that any future experimenter can ultimately come to know an actual run of targets.

The important element, of course, is a high degree of accuracy, since so much of psi research hangs on small and subtle scoring differences.

Helmut Schmidt (see, e. g. , 1975) has provided one answer with his electronic equivalent to a "coin-flipper, " which works so quickly (i. e. , 300 or more decisions per second) that the individual can only know the total results. In this case it comes down to clicks in the right or left ear, for the equivalent of "heads" or "tails. " The psi element comes in trying to influence the random events so that more clicks arise in one or the other ear.

For the biophysicist other problems arise. For too long we have assumed that the five senses were the full range of perception of the outer world. The reality, as always, is infinitely more complex, and as time goes on we become suspicious that the range may be much greater than we are willing to acknowledge at present. In this kind of examination we must assume the similarities of life forms and the essential continuity of the life process. Thus, once a mode has been developed we should assume that it can and will be developed again and again, in many different forms (like flight in birds and bats or swimming by fishes and mammals). In addition, there are probably scores of forces in the universe and dozens of ways of perceiving them. We should assume that if a force is relevant to the survival of the organism, some means of perceiving the exertion of that force will evolve or be developed, often to a high degree of sensitivity.

A good example of the full development of a perceptual mode is the evolution of the eye. In humans, it plays a primary function, and the eye-hand coordination is one of the keys to the mastery that humans show in coping with the outer world. The area of the brain that is devoted to the work and functioning of the eye is significantly large. By comparison the world of the dolphin and porpoise is dominated by sound perception. The area of the dolphin brain devoted to sound perception is correspondingly enlarged, while the area devoted to the eye, not surprisingly, is significantly smaller. In the dog the nose plays much the same dominant role, so that it has been estimated that a smell-sensitive dog, such as a bloodhound, using the nearly one-third of its brain devoted to its nose, can perceive with one million times the nasal sensitivity of a human.

The exploration of animal senses is now proceeding apace, so that for the first time we are beginning to examine polarized light perception in the bee and in certain birds; magnetic senses in a number of animals (e. g. , snails); time sense in cockroaches; heat perception in snakes; electrical perceptions in fish and eels; vibration senses in bats; geographic orientation in moles; the list goes on and on.

What does all this mean for the current discussion? Basically, this: that the margins of the currently known senses are significantly wider than we can ever suspect. Many persons can see into the infrared or the ultraviolet. The limits of skin perception of light and color are not known at this time. Certainly light can be perceived right through the skull by the pineal gland of some birds that have been blinded.

People who are blind or deaf demonstrate in their very being the astonishing widening of sensory ranges that takes place when one sense is eliminated. This, too, should make us very cautious about ruling out any ranges of sensory perception. We may be reactive to cosmic rays, as we are to gravity, for all we know (the astronauts seem to have perceived them as tiny orange-red flashes that also damaged the corneas of mice sent into space).

For the experimenter in sensory and extrasensory perception, however, this problem lays on a special burden. Conceivably some aspects of what is regarded as psi may involve a poorly understood sensory process, similar to the recently discovered heat sense in snakes. Conversely, however, there may be forces outside of our experience (similar, perhaps to cosmic rays) that another generation will accept casually, while we would be astonished to know the ultimate truth. Certainly, successful long-distance testing suggests this possibility. Either way, we should tread cautiously and be a bit less dogmatic about our "knowledge. "

Model of Psi Process--Clairvoyance: This model (see Figure 11) posits activity on the part of the person, but the activity on the part of the object is unknown. We should assume that some form of information is encoded thereon. Psi is assumed to be occurring during preconscious levels of functioning. An encoder-decoder is shown to function between different modalities. If there are biological (and hence mechanical) aspects to this process, the encoder-decoder becomes an important part of the process, since it involves

(Ψγ - CLAIRVOYANCE)

PERSONALITY

STATE OF AFFAIRS

ENCODING PROCESS

NOISE

CHANNEL (TRANS-MISSION MEDIUM)

NOISE

ENCODER/DECODER

PRECONSCIOUS ENTRY

MIND

CONDITIONINGS, LANGUAGE STRUCTURE, A PRIORI CATEGORIES

WORLD VIEWS

(IMPLICIT) INTERACTIONS

PHILOSOPHIES

(IMPLICIT) BELIEFS

PERCEPTUAL LEARNING

COGNITIVE EXPERIENCE

EMOTIONAL EXPERIENCE

LIKES AND DISLIKES

DEFENSE MECHANISMS

UNCONSCIOUS COMPLEXES

INSTINCTS

EMOTION

PLEASURE-PAIN CONDITIONING

(IMPLICIT) INTERACTIONS

Ψ STIMULI FROM OTHERS

BODY EXPERIENCE

COMPLEX SKILLS

STYLE OF MOVEMENT

POSTURE

CHRONIC MUSCLE SETS

SIMPLE MOTOR PATTERNS

REFLEXES INSTINCTS

BODY

taking material in message form and translating it into psychologically meaningful terms. It can also, using Stanford's (1974) approach (see pp. 50-51 above), translate these into action, muscle, or other non-conceptual processes, as well.

A channel is assumed, if some form of message process is also assumed. Noise that gets in the way of the message is present as in any complex system. Entry point is unknown, with inner interactions not shown, since they are too numerous to represent.

Telepathy

This process demonstrates interrelations, the going outside of the self. Though it is often a product of withdrawal, as so frequently occurs, the rebound resulting from the withdrawal shoots the self outward dramatically to those important to the self. As with much of psi process, which is so intimately related to primal or basic thinking, the closer to the self in psychodynamic terms, the more likely is the outside person to be involved in the psi experience. Conversely, the farther from the integral self, the less likely is the outside person to be involved in the experience.

Induction: An intensive relation with another person is assumed. The relation can be genetic, as between mother and child or between siblings, or social, between husbands and wives, or close friends. Most instances of spontaneous telepathy demonstrate this kind of basic relation between the two (or more) participants.

We must further assume that suggestion process is involved, that the "rheostat" of belief is fairly strongly turned up, thus reinforcing the relationship assumed above. Suggestion process may take many forms. It may have developed over many years, as between a mother and her daughter, reinforced by common experience. It may be further developed by a cultural milieu that sanctions such

opposite--Figure 11: Model of Psi Process--Clairvoyance (adapted from Tart, 1966, 1975) joint experiences, if only at the verbal and folklore level within the family or larger social setting (e. g. , "Mother had second sight"; "She had a touch of the witch in her"; or similar traditional descriptions that help to set the scene).

Spontaneous Case: Ronald Rose (1956) reports instances of apparent telepathy among Australian aborigines, as follows:

> First to tell us of his experiences was Walter Page. He had no clear-cut, unequivocal psychic knowledge of Combo's death, he said, but he had an unusual, disturbing feeling that subsequently he felt sure was associated with it.
>
> Walter, an unusually intelligent native, one indeed who had represented his people as the aboriginal member of the Aborigines' Welfare Board, put it this way:
>
> "I'm sure something happened to me when Billie Combo died, and I'm sure it was caused by his death. I was on the station here at Woodenbong that day. Suddenly I felt dopey--it was as if a cloud came over my mind. I couldn't think; I was depressed and upset.
>
> "When I went to lie down, my wife asked me what was wrong. I said, 'I don't know, but it's serious. ' She said, 'Is it one of our people, Walter?' I said, 'No, ' because if it had been one of our people, that is, someone related closely to us your way or by the totem, I would have seen my totem rooster I always see when one of us dies. The rooster is the one that tells me of such things.
>
> "But I had this strange feeling just the same. I tried to find out. I asked myself who it could be, but I didn't know. Later that day my wife went into the township and they told her they'd just heard that Billie Combo died. "
>
> "Was Billie related to you at all?"
>
> "He was a cousin, but he was not a totem relative. "

Later in the day we heard a similar story from Rene Robinson. Lyn and I were carrying out some routine investigating following our questionnaire.

Rene was asked: "Would you know if a relative some distance away had died, had an accident, or was seriously ill?" Then we went on to explain, "We don't mean knowing because of a letter or telegram or someone telling you, but by something else, like a feeling."

She watched Lyn and me carefully as we noted down the conversation. She was a half-caste aged something over seventy. But her eyes were keen and her faculties sharp. Normally, she was a cheerful woman, but as we mentioned this subject her wrinkles deepened, her eyes became thoughtful, and she became downcast.

"Has this sort of thing happened to you, Rene?" Lyn asked.

"Oh yes. Great sorrows come on me. I can't do no work. I lie down and I think and think, and this feeling lays heavy on me.

"I got like that when Billie Combo died last week."

Tears came into her eyes. She pushed a wisp of gray hair back on her head, and sat down.

"It comes awful heavy, that feeling. When I had it last week, I knew one of my people was gone. It was a feeling full of death. All our people know it."

"Did you know at the time that it was Billie Combo who had died?"

"No. I didn't know till I was told--but when I had the feeling, the great sorrow, I knew it was one of my people, for sure."

We told Rene that earlier Walter Page had told us of a similar experience. We asked her if she knew of anyone else who had been affected.

"That Danny Sambo," she replied. "He came over to my house that morning, and when he saw me lying down he said, "You got that feeling, too?" And I said, "Yes." He said, "I know, it's that Billie Combo died." I said, "You bin told?" He said, "I bin told by my black crow that tells me these things'."

Danny Sambo confirmed her story. "These things often happen to my people. More in the old time, of course, but with Billie Combo, both him and me was crow totem, so I must know, see?" [pp. 144-146].

<u>Experimental Case</u>: During the fall and winter of 1937-8 Sir Hubert Wilkins and Harold Sherman (1942) arranged for long-distance ESP experiments three nights a week ranging distances from 2,000 to 3,000 miles. For much of the time there was no radio communication between Wilkins's camp and New York. Material was recorded and cross-mailed, with Gardner Murphy as the recipient of a copy of Sherman's notes, mailed just after they were written. A few sample excerpts, of the more dramatic instances of psi hits, follow:

December 7

Sherman

Don't know why, but I seem to see crackling fire shining out in darkness of Aklavik--get a definite fire impression as though housing burning--you can see it from your location on ice. I first thought fire on ice near your tent, but impression persists it is a white house burning, and quite a crowd gathered around it--people running or hurrying toward flames-- bitter cold--stiff breeze blowing.

Wilkins

While I was in Radio Office at Point Barrow the fire alarm rang. A long ring on the telephone (there are only four telephones at Barrow). It was an Eskimo's shack on fire. The chimney blazed up, and the roof took fire, but it was soon put out. Some damage resulted, mostly from the efforts of the zealous firemen. Was pretty cold that night, with a light wind [pp. 225-226].

December 21

Sherman

Sudden severe pain comes
to me--right side of head--
I record this because it happened at this time and not,
at the moment, because I
attach any significance or
relation to it--other than
passing physical disturbance
in me--sometimes, however,
I seem to see or feel physical ailment affecting another....

Wilkins

Am not sure that it happened
this day, but each one of us
could not seem to avoid
bumping our heads on a
sharp-edged stove pipe in
the kitchen of our quarters.
I bumped mine only twice
but Dyne and Cheeseman
bumped often. Cheeseman
was "laid out" by the blow
twice in one day. The pipe
was at an awkward height
[p. 237].

January 6

Sherman

You much in company young-
ish looking man, a trifle
shorter than you--appear to
have much in common--he
seems to have been vicinity
of Point Barrow about two
years--believe he has en-
gineering background--in-
terested in natural resources
--particularly oil. You discuss matters with him.

Someone has entertained
you with quite a collection
of phonograph records--
some of which recall old
tunes.

Wilkins

Mr. Morgan, radio operator.
We often talk oil. There
are oil seepages near here.
He has invented a "distiller,"
which he wants the government to develop and furnish
the Eskimos who may, by
that means, recover oil.
Now they buy oil, but can
burn the black pitch from
pitch houses nearby.

Correct. A toy Christ-
mas present machine with
thin paper records--old time
tunes [p. 245].

March 10

Sherman

"Diamond mine"--why I
should think of this is mys-
tery--almost as though you
had discussed existence of

Wilkins

That night was telling people
at table, at about the time
you were sitting, of visit to
African diamond mines--

diamond deposit in Alaskan mountain area or north region--to my conscious mind this seems absurdity, but I record impression nevertheless....

discussing Cullinan and Jonker diamonds, and so forth [p. 323].

Research Suggestions: Any researchers working on telepathy quickly discover that what they had thought to be a simple process, operating from mind to mind, is in reality far more complicated. Assume for a moment, for instance, that no direct telepathy could exist, but that clairvoyance could, from mind to object (and back). A great deal of apparent telepathy could be explained alternatively by such clairvoyance, since much of what passes through our minds also has physical concomitants with the external world. The researcher has often gotten around this by using the concept of General Extrasensory Perception (GESP), which embodies both telepathy and clairvoyance in an inextricable mix. Thus, the five ESP symbol cards can be tested in settings wherein either the experimenter or the cards may have been the originating point for the ultimate psi perception by the subject.

A technique developed more than a dozen years ago by Tart (1969) has been seriously neglected, and rarely duplicated since then, yet it offers precisely the tools that we are seeking in the resonance of two minds postulated by current theory. This is the approach of mutual hypnosis, or, in this framework, suggestion process.

Two subjects, Bill and Anne, were hypnotized, as follows: the experimenter hypnotized Bill, who then hypnotized Ann; she, in turn, hypnotized Bill. This mutual hypnosis produced the profoundest type of hypnosis, especially for Bill, but more important, produced an even more profound type of empathy between the two subjects. In one of the sessions they were walking down a tunnel; in a later one, they were climbing up a rope ladder (Bill) or a golden rope (Anne). Most remarkable was the following:

Changes in self-concept and body image were usually together. The Ss at times perceived themselves as bodiless, or possessing just parts of a body. They also felt there were changes in psychological functioning over and above the alterations in body image. An example of this would be the use of modes of communication between themselves that they did not know they possessed. The alteration that most impressed (and later frightened) the Ss, however, was the feeling of merging with each other at times, especially in the final mutual hypnosis session. This seemed like a partial fusion of identities, a partial loss of the distinction between I and Thou. This was felt to be good at the time, but later the Ss perceived this as a threat to their individual autonomy.

Several times during the sessions the Ss said nothing for a time, but when I questioned them replied that they were communicating, so there was a feeling at the time of the experience that paranormal communication of some sort was going on. Even more striking material regarding the Ss' feelings about this heightened empathy and communication was obtained a couple of months after the final session when the tapes of the sessions had been transcribed. Anne and Bill read the transcripts over and were both shocked. They had been talking about their experiences to each other for some time, and found they had been discussing details of the experiences they had shared for which there were no verbal stimuli on the tapes, i. e., they felt they must have been communicating telepathically or that they had actually been "in" the non-worldly locales they had experienced. This was frightening to both Ss, for what had seemed a lovely shared fantasy now threatened to be something real. This feeling of the Ss does not constitute any sort of proof for genuine telepathic interaction, of course, for there were no independent records of the details of the Ss' experiences made before they had an opportunity to talk with each other, but the feeling of the Ss that there was telepathic interaction and their reaction to it was one of the most impressive aspects of the experience [pp. 305-306].

Deriving from the above, a suggested research protocol is as follows: Locate a mature, stable married couple, interested in and accepting the possibility of psi phenomena. By biofeedback train them separately and at different times, to get into preconscious functioning at will. Discourage them from doing this outside the experimental setting at the same time. Induce mutual hypnosis in them, with the experimenter as controller for all activities. A second experimenter, also under hypnosis, may serve as a safety factor and an additional control. Place them in separate rooms, out of sensory range. Monitor both subjects on the EEG. Induce sensory dissociation by using the Ganzfeld screen and white sound. Induce disorientation by placing them in two witches cradles. Have them switch down to preconscious functioning simultaneously. Keep the protocol loose the first few experiments. See what they say (keep recording equipment available for sound), do, experience, keeping time records in parallel for all actions, from the mutual hypnosis, on. Once "resonance" is established, psi tests for telepathy can begin. We may be quite surprised at the results.

One leading West Coast researcher has suggested verbally, based on a laboratory experience several years ago, that the two subjects can "home" in on a resonance, perhaps both watching on a feedback screen until they both hit alpha-wave levels simultaneously. He describes it somewhat like merging with another personality, possibly the eeriest experience he had ever lived through.

This experimentation should not be indulged in lightly. Personality disturbances should be anticipated, and psychiatric assistance should be available. Personal growth counseling may even be necessary. Our culture does not know how to cope with such intensities of interpersonal experience, and subjects involved in this kind of experimentation should be chosen on the basis of great personal stability and the ability to understand and cope with at a mature level what the experimentation is doing to them and their relations with each other. One experience will demonstrate what is being suggested, but by then the damage may have been done, and further work might be seriously interrupted while repair of altered egos takes place.

There is an additional aspect of such research that requires special study by physicists and mathematicians, following up on work by Osis (Osis and Turner, 1968) and the ASPR, a few years ago. With "resonance," long-distance testing can be undertaken, to determine any fall-off effects based on distance. These become important for helping to determine the nature of the physical laws involved, if any, and thereby help to pin down the nature of the forces. Measurements can take place to varied cities, to space satellites, or to locations deeper in space, as well.

Modeling the Telepathic Process: Figure 12 provides a model that could be useful to the experimenter, based on

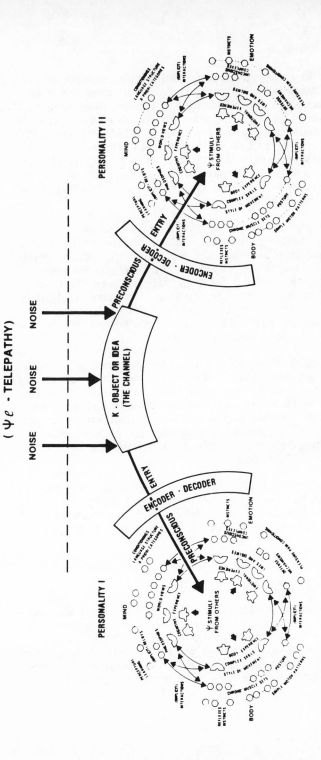

Figure 12: Model of Psi Process--Telepathy (adapted from Tart, 1975)

Carington's ideas about telepathy and Tart's concepts of personality. Essentially, it posits two personalities linked at a particular time, in synchronization. Whether they have to be synchronized at the same time should be studied, since it is also possible that "messages" can be filed (like telegrams) at one time, to be picked up by a second personality, when it is ready to "receive" at a later time. As a part of each personality, and certainly part of the perceptual system, is an "encoder-decoder," which is essential if a "message" (of whatever sort) is being relayed.

Carington (1945) posits that "communication" occurs when two (or more) personalities share a common field, the so-called "psychon" system (see p. 38 above). Then, within the field, the carrier or channel is the K-object or idea. The stronger the common features, the stronger the field; also, the clearer the K-object or idea, the more likely is a message of some sort to be shared. "Noise" (interfering with the channel), it should be noted, can be internal or external, and lots of it should be shown.

The diagram shows a linking arrow entering the inner system of each personality. Psi experiences may conceivably enter at any one of several levels and modalities. The possibilities of inner interaction are therefore boundless, and for that reason the number of mutually concatenating arrows cannot be drawn, since they would blur the picture completely. Nevertheless, they should be envisioned as if they were included in the sketch.

Models of this kind have their limitations, but they are useful in the sorting out of elements of a process. Those inclined toward such model-building are especially welcome to a field that is notoriously lacking in satisfactory models.

Psychokinesis and Poltergeists

Here is the magnificent puzzle of how, if at all, mind can move, predominate or prevail over physical events. It is the problem of "mind over matter," with which J. B. Rhine and others have wrestled for so long, in their millions of laboratory-measured dice throws over the years. Whatever forces are involved must be micro forces, as they are manifested in the studies.

The typical subject in spontaneous PK cases is usually passing through a period of profound psychophysical change, such as adolescence or menarche, when the phenomena first appear. These changes may be creating tension with unsatisfactory physical outlets. When PK appears, there is an intense experience of relief, even some satisfaction. There may also be a strong sense that the individual is not responsible, that the motivating forces are external. The PK expression is highly need-oriented, and helps solve certain personal problems, while creating others, by the mere manifestation.

Induction: For purposes of the hypothesis, assume motor blockage, which may take several forms:

Keeping the body still. Or, concurrent with body stillness, a buildup of physical tension within the body system, with muscles still but with no usual form of physical release utilized. The buildup may also take the form of repressed rage. Adrenaline may also build up concurrently. Some cultures may employ a form of external vibration that pulses through the entire body (e. g. music, drumming, humming that resonates through the head). In some belief systems, there may be an aspect of "surrender" to "other" forces, apparently "external" to the self.

Spontaneous Cases: W. G. Roll (1972), who specializes in the poltergeist phenomenon, reports on a spontaneous instance that occurred in his presence:

> At five minutes past midnight, on Monday, December 16, 1968, I was walking behind 12-year-old Roger Callihan as he entered the kitchen of his home. When he came to the sink, he turned toward me and at that moment the kitchen table, which was on his right, jumped into the air, rotated about 45 degrees, and came to rest on the backs of the chairs that stood around it, with all four legs off the floor (Roger had been in bed and had gotten up when a glass bowl fell from a bedroom dresser.) [p. 148].

A bit later on Roll discusses a similar event in the same house that was witnessed by a fellow researcher and assistant, John P. Stump:

> In some cases, John was in a position to satisfy himself that there was no contrivance by any of

those present and that known physical forces were
not involved. On one occasion, while Roger was
standing with his grandparents next to the kitchen
stove, and John was in the kitchen looking toward
the three people and the sink area which was next
to the stove, John saw two bottles and a glass jar
containing canned berries, which were standing on
the sink unit, move into the sink at the same time,
a distance of about two feet. There was no normal
way in which the three bottles could have moved on
their own. At the same time that he saw this, he
had a view of the three people. They were standing quietly making no movement during this incident. There was no one else in the area and John
could find no ordinary explanation, such as string
arrangements or other means, whereby the bottles
could have been made to fall into the sink normally [p. 151].

Another very dramatic case, studied in great detail,
is briefly summarized by Roll and Pratt (1971):

The Miami Disturbances

Early in 1967 a case of typical poltergeist activity took place in Miami. The disturbances, located
in a wholesale firm dealing in souvenir objects, involved the falling of objects from shelves or their
moving greater distances with loud impact and frequent breakage. The events were connected with a
nineteen year old Cuban youth employed by the
firm as a shipping clerk.

The case was still active when it was brought
to the attention of the writers of this report, and
between them they spent a number of days on the
scene during which they observed many disturbances and also interviewed witnesses to events that
took place during their absence. A total of 224
distinct events were recorded, and approximately
a third of these occurred while one or both of the
parapsychological investigators were present.
Fairly early in the case it was observed that objects were most often disturbed in particular locations, and the investigators were therefore able to
focus their attention upon these areas. In several
instances objects were disturbed that the investi-

gators had placed in selected target areas and had kept under careful surveillance.

In no instance was evidence found indicating that any of the events were caused fraudulently or in any recognized nonpersonal way... [p. 409].

In a follow-up discussion nearly two years later, Roll, Burdick and Joines (1973) observed the following about the foregoing Miami case:

... there was a significant attenuation pattern and this followed the exponential decay function more closely than the inverse function [see Figure 13].

... The tendency for the objects to move in one direction rather than another, whether this be

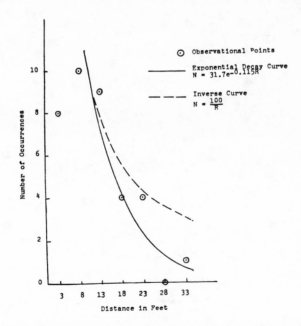

Figure 13: Number of Occurrences in Relation to Julio's Distance from the Occurrences (from Roll, 1973)

clockwise or counterclockwise, is, however, consistent with the hypothesis of a rotating field. But a uniformly rotating field presumably would result in a preponderance of tangential movements which was not observed in the Miami case.

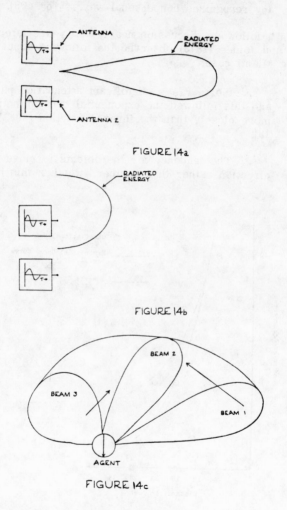

FIGURE 14a

FIGURE 14b

FIGURE 14c

Figure 14: A Theoretical Model for the Occurrences
(from Roll, 1973)

... two antennaes on a plane surface and fed by
identical signals ... will combine their radiated
energies within a cigar-shaped beam perpendicular
to the plane surface as shown in Figure [14]a.
However, if one signal is delayed by a specific
time ... the pattern of radiated energy is rotated
about the origin, diminished in radial extent, and
increased in angular extent; that is, the beam becomes shorter and fatter as shown in Figure [14]b.
Furthermore, by proper adjustment of the time
delay the beam can be swept smoothly from the
long skinny position to the short, fat position and
back again. This is how a phased-array radar
antenna works.

... If energy waves are radiated from different
positions on the agent's body, we could obtain the
radiation pattern shown in Figure [14]c, where three
beams occurring at different times are shown.
Again, depending upon the time delay of the interacting waves ... Beam 1 may occur first, then
Beam 2, and then Beam 3, or the time sequence
may be from 3 to 2 to 1. Now, if objects under
the influence of Beam 3 are carried with the beam
as it becomes Beam 2 ... a typical object movement might be shown by the clockwise arrow in
Figure [14]c. Conversely, Beam 1, having a
greater radial extent, would influence objects further from the agent, and as Beam 1 becomes Beam
2, a typical object movement might be shown as
the counterclockwise arrow in Figure [14]c [pp.
278-280].

Experimental Case: Stanford and his associates (1975)
studied the concept of combined perceptual and motor psi
factors in the following case:

This study tested the assumption of Stanford's
PMIR model that persons can use a combination
of ESP and PK in the service of their own needs,
even when they are not consciously intending to do
so. Forty male college-student volunteers tested
individually first took an intentional ("conscious")
test of PK on an electronic random event generator. Then the subject was introduced to a boring,
tiresome task which potentially could last for 45
minutes. Unknown to the subject the random event

generator was started in the other experimental
room and generated one trial (p = 1/6 for a hit)
per second. Whenever, or if ever, seven hits
occurred in one of the successive blocks of 10
trials, the experimenter released the subject from
the unpleasant task and introduced him to a presumably pleasant task. Subjects knew nothing of
this contingency. Thus, this constituted their non-
intentional PK-ESP task. Eight subjects escaped
from the unpleasant task as contrasted with mean
chance expectation of 2.9 (P = .0069). Overall
results were also significant when mean percentage
of hits per subject was considered in the noninten-
tional PK-ESP task (t = 2.19; df = 39; P < .05).
Subjects showed no overall significance on the intentional (conscious) PK task. Subject scores on
the conscious and unconscious PK tasks were cor-
related positively but not significantly (r = ± .199).
Subjects were tested by two female experimenters
and those tested by the experimenter judged by
R. G. S. and R. Z. as the more extraverted of the
two produced results superior to those tested by
the other (P < .01) [p. 127].

Research Suggestions: For more than forty years
laboratory experimenters have been struggling to affect the
course of the fall of dice, following the traditional aspirations of the American gambler. Possibly the research situations can be still more related to the everyday world, always recognizing the need for the experimental situation to
be controlled. A gambling house, of course, is hardly the
place for such study, although subjects could be monitored
with the assistance and cooperation of the management.
Feedback and the possibility of learning should also be built
in.

The reality situation of challenge and excitement certainly must be interwoven. There is good reason to believe
that many of the U-shaped curves of performance that appeared, whether of the subject or the experimenter, probably
hung on interest in the experiment. Thus, performance was
best at the beginning of a run, or of an experiment, sagging
in the middle and then rising a bit at the end in a final mus-
ter of energy and interest before the experiment ended. The
approach then, should continue to involve instant feedback,
visibility, and a sense of accomplishment, so that the subjects can be reinforced as they work to exert an effect.

Some of the newer work at the Stanford Research Institute may point the way toward utilizing microforces that can very well be controllable by PK. In one suggestive study Puthoff and Targ (1974) utilized a slow electron beam in a divided collector, with inner and outer electrodes. A galvanometer measured any differential voltage between them. The subject was asked alternately to cause the beam to be deflected and then to remain still. The results indicated that the subject did exert some force over the electron beam.

The deflection of such microforces, whether they involve atoms or electrons, altering magnetic fields or rate of radiation decay, may well be easier and more measurable than all the studies of dice heretofore.

Model of Psi Process--Psychokinesis: In this instance one deals with a mind in interaction with a physical object (we are here acting as if the mind of another did not also involve a physical object, the brain). The model (see Figure 15) posits activity on the part of the person, but of course there can also be activity on the part of the object, assuming forms of information are encoded thereon. Again, there is the assumption that psi activity is occurring during preconscious levels of functioning. For psychokinesis, as compared with telepathy and clairvoyance, the place of the decoder is taken by a converter, since if different energies are involved, they have to be transmuted between two different formats: the mind and the physical world. The converter must be assumed to exist within the body, if mechanical correlates to the process exist, and, most likely, within the brain. Again, a channel must be assumed, if action process is to take place. As always, noise exists, to interrupt, confuse, and otherwise hinder the action process. Finally, as with telepathy and clairvoyance models, the entry point and level is unknown, and the possible inner interactions are not shown, since they may well be countless.

B. THE THREE PAIRED PSI PHENOMENA

So far, we have presented psi processes wherein a modality is under pressure and the ultimate form of psi-mediated response takes place essentially utilizing the same

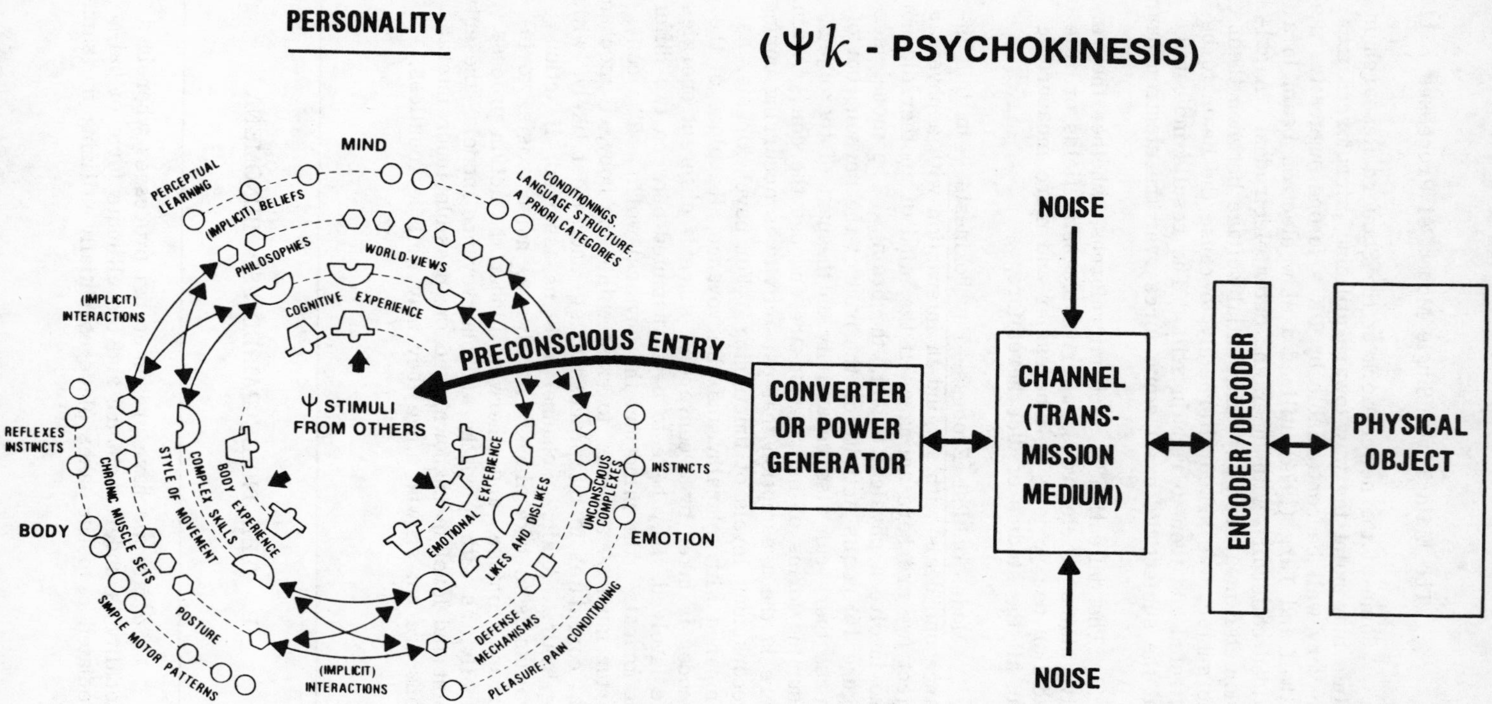
PERSONALITY
(Ψk - PSYCHOKINESIS)
MIND
PERCEPTUAL LEARNING
(IMPLICIT) BELIEFS
CONDITIONINGS. LANGUAGE STRUCTURE. A PRIORI CATEGORIES
PHILOSOPHIES
WORLD-VIEWS
COGNITIVE EXPERIENCE
(IMPLICIT) INTERACTIONS
PRECONSCIOUS ENTRY
Ψ STIMULI FROM OTHERS
REFLEXES INSTINCTS
BODY
CHRONIC MUSCLE SETS
STYLE OF MOVEMENT
COMPLEX SKILLS
BODY EXPERIENCE
EMOTIONAL EXPERIENCE
LIKES AND DISLIKES
UNCONSCIOUS COMPLEXES
INSTINCTS
EMOTION
SIMPLE MOTOR PATTERNS
POSTURE
(IMPLICIT) INTERACTIONS
DEFENSE MECHANISMS
PLEASURE-PAIN CONDITIONING
CONVERTER OR POWER GENERATOR
NOISE
CHANNEL (TRANS- MISSION MEDIUM)
NOISE
ENCODER/DECODER
PHYSICAL OBJECT

modality (e. g. empathy--telepathy, etc.). But, as was suggested earlier (see p. 83 above), two systems can come under pressure simultaneously, thereby resulting in a psi-mediated response that involves a combination of modalities. The matrix lends itself to portraying this process easily. And, since each modality interacts with another twice, this should result in modality response pairs that have essentially similar qualities, yet with some subtle difference in each case. The remainder of the matrix results in three pairs of responses, and these can be grouped and labeled as follows: the hallucinatory pair: crisis apparitions and ghosts; the sensorimotor pair: dowsing and psychometry; and the emotor pair: healing others and motor automatisms.

Each of these pairs will be discussed systematically, its place in the matrix indicated and characteristics, dynamics and examples of each will follow. Each discussion will conclude with suggestions for additional research.

THE HALLUCINATORY PAIR

Crisis apparitions and ghosts are strongly similar: they are both visual illusions that emerge under empathic and sensory stress. They usually appear real to the viewer, are bearers of some kind of message. Crisis apparitions are person-bound; ghosts are place-bound. As a rule crisis apparitions occur once; ghosts tend to be repetitive.

Table 3

THE HALLUCINATORY PAIR

Event	Arousing Factors	Quieting Factors
Crisis apparitions	Threats to significant other	Sensory deprivation
Ghosts	Sensory overload	Suggestion process

---

opposite--Figure 15: Model of Psi Process--Psychokinesis (adapted from Tart, 1966, 1975)

Crisis apparitions can also concern the living, going through an emergency (that may well be critical). The message of the crisis apparition seems to be: I'm in trouble; help me; I am threatened; I need you. The message of the ghost is more blurred, but it generally tends to convey a negative attitude: I hate you; I hate myself; I hate life; I am angry; I am unhappy. The crisis apparition is partly triggered by ergotropic functioning, arising from a threat to a significant other, that can be relayed at a moment of sensory deprivation or perceptual disturbance. The ghost frequently arises in locations of fear and expectation, where the sensory system is keyed up, waiting. Suggestion serves as a resonating chord, an echo within the empathic system of the viewer-participant.

Crisis Apparitions

These are person-bound hallucinations, relatively common in the field of psi, usually occurring in the nearby

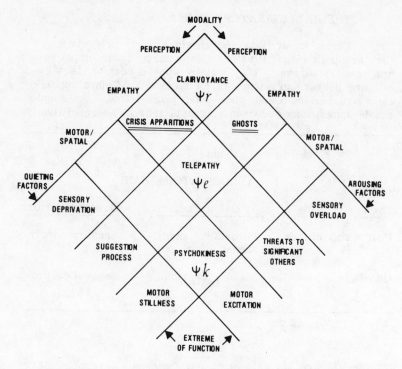

Figure 16: The Hallucinatory Pair in the Psi Matrix

presence of death. The message, in the form of an appearance, is the usual drive for the event.

Those involved may have a strong relation, genetic or social; the two may well be a significant dyad, such as a married couple, or a mother with a favored child. In those for whom the experience occurs only once, the relationship may be the most significant of the pair's existence. The experience, then, would serve important personality needs.

Induction: We should assume an intensive relationship with another person; then add as a reinforcer, belief that psi is possible (under whatever name); a crisis threatening someone close to the self, most usually death or the imminent possibility of death, plus the need to transmit some fact or information. Reduced sensory input helps, as does a furry, blurred perceptual field. Dissociation is a common prerequisite, often as the person emerges from sleep, through an altered state of consciousness, which includes the apparition.

Spontaneous Case: Louisa Rhine (1967) reports the case of a woman whose husband was in the Marines eight hundred miles away from home:

> In December, 1951, my husband was drafted into the Marine Corps. We had only been married three months and of course were very close.
>
> He had been down in Parris Island about a month; it was a very cold spell and according to weather broadcasts even the South was having bad weather.
>
> I stayed at my mother's house several nights a week as I was lonely. On this Friday night I fell asleep and about 1:30 a. m. I woke up and Richard (my husband) was standing in the room next to me. It was as clear as this paper. He didn't speak but just stood there as if sort of pleading.
>
> When I got up the next morning I told my mother I was very worried that something might be wrong. I didn't hear from him that day--but the next day, Sunday, I received a long-distance phone call from Charleston, S. C. , Navy Hospital. He had pneumonia.

At the time he appeared to me on the Friday
night he was standing 12-4 fire watch. As you
know, Marine Corps boot training is pretty rigid,
and when he complained of being sick, they thought
he was trying to plead out of fire watch and he
was forced to stand it anyway.

He had a fever of over 104 and was very sick,
and at those moments when he appeared to me, he
told me that he was walking the watch, just praying
so hard that he could be home with me.

He was wrapped in a blanket and even so the
damp coldness of the night was still making him
shiver and brought him almost to tears. Somehow
--I don't know how--he spanned those eight hundred
miles and came to me [pp. 149-150].

Experimental Case: Milton Erickson (1969), in his
hypnotic work with Aldous Huxley, has an example that is
possibly useful to the researcher into the processes under-
lying apparitions:

Further experimentation in the deep trance investigated visual, auditory and other types of ideo-
sensory hallucinations. One of the measures employed was to pantomime hearing a door open and
then to appear to see someone entering the room,
to arise in courtesy and to indicate a chair, then
to turn to Huxley to express the hope that he was
comfortable. He replied that he was and he expressed surprise at his wife's unexpected return
since he had expected her to be absent the entire
day. (The chair I had indicated was one I knew
his wife liked to occupy.) He conversed with her
and apparently hallucinated replies. He was interrupted with the question of how he knew that it
was his wife and not an hypnotic hallucination. He
examined the question thoughtfully, then explained
that I had not given him any suggestion to hallucinate his wife, that I had been as much surprised
by her arrival as he had been, and that she was
dressed as she had been just before her departure
and not as I had seen her earlier. Hence it was
reasonable to assume that she was a reality. After a brief thoughtful pause, he returned to his
"conversation" with her apparently continuing to

hallucinate replies. Finally I attracted his attention and made a hand gesture suggestive of a disappearance toward the chair in which he "saw" his wife. To his complete astonishment he saw her slowly fade away [pp. 60-61].

Research Suggestions: If one has at one's command good, clear, full, well-corroborated protocols of spontaneous cases, one may look at them phenomenologically, psychologically and dynamically, as G. N. M. Tyrrell (1970) has done, looking for the attributes of various classes of apparitions as conditioned by physical, physiological, psychological conditions, noting what typically goes with what in the more careful reports. One can make a natural history of the spontaneous cases, their phenomenology, their ecology, their taxonomy. Utilizing in this way only sixty-one cases, but cases very carefully chosen from the best authenticated records of the Society for Psychical Research, it was possible for Tyrrell to construct a set of working principles as to the attributes of the various classes of spontaneous cases and the conditions under which they typically appear. He describes the "ideal apparition," in the sense that one may find in sociology an "ideal type" according to Karl Mannheim, or in the world of physics or botany one may find an ideal examplification of some simple physical principle or botanical principle. Tyrrell writes:

Let us suppose ... that the "Perfect Apparition" is standing beside a normal human being. We should find the following points of resemblance:

(1) Both figures would stand out in space and would appear equally real and solid. The apparition would be just as clear and vivid in matters of detail, such as the colour and texture of skin and clothing, as the material person.

(2) We should be able to walk round the apparition, viewing it from any distance and from any standpoint, and as regards distance and perspective we should detect no difference between it and the living person.

(3) If the light happened to be poor, both figures would be badly seen, and if more light were turned on, both figures would appear brighter. If the lights went out, both figures would disappear in darkness.

(4)   Both figures would obscure the background.

(5)   If the apparition happened to be wearing a rose in its buttonhole, we should probably smell the scent of it.

(6)   On approaching the apparition, we should hear it breathing, and we should hear the rustle of its clothes as it moved and its shoes would shuffle on the floor.

(7)   The apparition would probably behave as if aware of our presence, looking at us in a natural way and possibly smiling and turning its head to follow our movements.   It might even place its hand on our shoulder, in which case we should feel an ordinary touch.

(8)   The apparition might speak to us, and possibly it might go so far as to answer a question; but we should not be able to engage it in any long conversation.

(9)   If a mirror were fixed to the wall we should see the apparition reflected in it at the appropriate angle, just as we should see the reflection of the real man.

(10) Both figures would probably cast shadows, but the evidence on this point is uncertain.

(11) If we were to shut our eyes or turn away our head, the apparition would disappear just as the figure by its side would do.   And, on reopening them, we should see it again.

(12) In addition to its clothes, the figure might have other accessories, such as a stick or any other object.   And it might be accompanied by a dog or even another human being.   These would appear normal and behave in a normal manner. With regard to a human companion, I do not think it would make any difference whether he had ever existed or not.   Mr. Pickwick or Sherlock Holmes would probably do as well as Charles Dickens or Sir Arthur Conan Doyle, and would appear just as alive and natural.

(13) The apparition might pick up any object in the room or open and close the door. We should both see and hear these objects moved: yet physically they would never have moved at all.

In all these points the apparition's imitation of a material figure would be perfect. But we should find points of difference no less striking.

(14) For one thing, as soon as we came near the apparition, or if the apparition touched us, we might feel a sensation of cold.

(15) If we tried to take hold of the apparition, our hand would go through it without encountering any resistance. In the most perfect case I am not quite sure about this, for the sensation of touch is undoubtedly hallucinated in such cases, and it might be that we should <u>feel</u> our hand stopped at the surface of the apparition's body, as by something impenetrable; but at the same time should <u>see</u> our hand go right through it without let or hindrance. Apparitions when cornered avoid this interesting situation by disappearing.

(16) If we were to sprinkle French chalk on the floor and could induce the apparition and the human being to walk on it together, we should find that only the real man left any footprints, although we should hear the footsteps of both.

(17) If we were to take a photograph of the two figures, only the real man would come out. And if we had sound-recording apparatus, only the sounds made by the real man would be recorded. It is true that these are inferences and do not rest on direct evidence. But the non-physical character of apparitions is so clear that the inference seems inescapable.

(18) After a time, which might be anything up to half an hour or so, the apparition would disappear. It might suddenly vanish; or it might become transparent and fade away; it might vanish into the wall or go down through the floor, or it might, more conventionally, open the door and walk out.

(19)   Sometimes we should probably find that the apparition did not imitate the behavior of the material man quite so closely.   It might, for instance, become slightly luminous; it might show small details of itself when we were so far away from it that normally we could not possibly have seen them; it might even so far forget itself as to make us see it through the back of our head.

This is a picture of what an apparition would be like at its best, according to our collected evidence; and this is what, throughout the ages, has been called a "spirit. "   But clearly it is in reality a psychological phenomenon, the explanation of which must be sought in the processes of sense-perception [pp. 77-80].

Although Tyrrell sees ghosts and crisis apparitions as variations on the same process, perhaps there are significant differences for research purposes.   The "Perfect Apparition" characteristics apply to both, but the crisis apparition has one or two critical elements different from the ghost.   For one, the crisis apparition is person-, not place-bound.   At the moment of personal crisis, usually that of threatened or actual death, it is as if all the energies of the person involved seem to focus toward a single end: to communicate with someone profoundly relevant to his or her existence, usually to notify that person of the crisis, or of the death. There is a quality of the Zeigarnik phenomenon here: an attempt to complete one's life by finishing with a simple announcement of the end, the word "finis" written at the end of the play.   For another, the act occurs almost always once, and is not repeated, except to one or two other relevant persons on rare occasions.   Here may be noted a significant difference from the ghost, for the ghost tends to have a mechanical, repetitive quality, while the crisis apparition has the profoundest purpose: notification of one of life's most important events, the arrival of death (although some ghosts have participated in this, too).   Once the notice has occurred, the event is finished.   On the other hand, a haunting seems to go on and on, in some cases for centuries, if the area is undisturbed.

And crisis apparitions do communicate: time, manner, place and the varying circumstances of the event, sometimes with the most startling details included, so that chance factors can be ruled out fairly easily by any manner of evaluation or analysis.

For the researcher there are dozens of questions that bear examination, based on these differences. The key fact, of course, may relate to the mental state of the person who is dying. What is happening to the person's brain waves? Is he or she in transition from one brain state to another? Is one of the wave patterns dominant at the moment of death? Is there a difference, if a message is being transmitted? For that matter, what about the state of the potential percipient? Is there a "rapport" between the two brains? If so, what are the common elements, at the moment of "transmission" of the message?

It is possible to envision the formation of an "Omega League," organized to study the moment of death, from every conceivable psychobiological angle, in order to determine what the characteristics of that moment are. Survival research, too, would benefit, since a great deal of information could be derived that might be useful here.

Ghosts

These are place-bound hallucinations that may have derived from a single traumatic, usually fatal, event, or repeated similar events over a long period. They may consist of four key elements, to be examined in detail later (see pp. 127-129 below): the setting; the "charging" agent; the energy; and the perceiving agent or percipient.

Induction: An area or specific location in which a highly emotionally charged event has occurred, such as a murder or violent death. Parts of the area must have remained essentially unchanged physically since the "charging event" occurred. Frequently, there may have been a need, at the moment of the "charging event," to transmit some fact or information.

As a strengthening element, a belief on the part of the percipient that psi is possible, plus strong supportive suggestion process. Reduced sensory input, especially in darkened and quiet areas. Dissociation, leading to an altered state of consciousness, in which the hallucination is included.

Spontaneous Cases: The following case was reported by Gardner Murphy and Herbert Klemme (1966):

On October 3, 1963, Mrs. Coleen Buterbaugh, secretary to Dean Sam Dahl, of Nebraska Wesleyan University, Lincoln, Nebraska, was asked by Dean Dahl to take a message to a colleague, Professor Martin (pseudonym), in his office suite in the C. C. White Building nearby. At about 8:50 a. m. Mrs. Buterbaugh entered this building and walked briskly along its extensive hall, hearing the sounds of students in a group of rooms set aside for music practice, and notably a marimba playing. Entering the first room of the suite [see Figure 17],

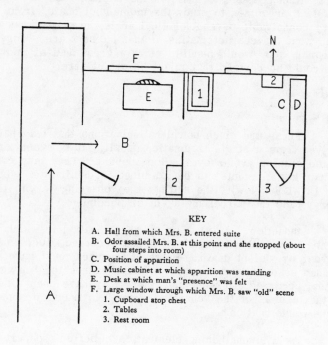

KEY

A. Hall from which Mrs. B. entered suite
B. Odor assailed Mrs. B. at this point and she stopped (about four steps into room)
C. Position of apparition
D. Music cabinet at which apparition was standing
E. Desk at which man's "presence" was felt
F. Large window through which Mrs. B. saw "old" scene
   1. Cupboard atop chest
   2. Tables
   3. Rest room

Figure 17: Floor Plan of Two-room Suite in C. C. White Building Temporarily Occupied by Dr. Martin and in Which Mrs. B's Experience Occurred

she took about four steps and was stopped short
[at point "B"] by a very intense odor--a musty,
disagreeable odor. Raising her eyes, she saw [at
point "C"] the figure of a very tall, black-haired
woman (more fully described below) in a shirtwaist
and ankle-length skirt who was extending her right
arm to the upper right-hand shelves in an old music cabinet. We now continue the account in Mrs.
Buterbaugh's own words:

"As I first walked into the room everything was
quite normal. About four steps into the room was
when the strong odor hit me. When I say strong
odor, I mean the kind that simply stops you in
your tracks and almost chokes you. I was looking
down at the floor, as one often does when walking,
and as soon as that odor stopped me I felt that
there was someone in the room with me. It was
then that I was aware that there were no noises
out in the hall. Everything was deathly quiet. I
looked up and something drew my eyes to the cabinet [point "D"] along the wall in the next room.
I looked up and there she was. She had her back
to me, reaching up into one of the shelves of the
cabinet with her right hand, and standing perfectly
still. She wasn't at all aware of my presence.
While I was watching her she never moved. She
was not transparent and yet I knew she wasn't
real. While I was looking at her she just faded
away--not parts of her body one at a time, but
her whole body all at once.

"Up until the time she faded away I was not
aware of anyone else being in the suite of rooms,
but just about the time of her fading out I felt as
though I still was not alone. To my left was a
desk [point "E"] and I had a feeling there was a
man sitting at that desk. I turned around and saw
no one, but I still felt his presence. When that
feeling of his presence left I have no idea, because
it was then, when I looked out the window behind
that desk, that I got frightened and left the room.
I am not sure whether I ran or walked out of the
room. Dr. Murphy, when I looked out that window
there wasn't even one modern thing out there.
The street (Madison Street), which is less than
half a block away from the building, was not even

there and neither was the new Willard House. That was when I realized that these people were not in my time, but that I was back in their time.

"It was not until I was back out in the hall that I again heard the familiar noises. This must have all taken place in a few seconds because the girls that were going into the orientation class as I entered the rooms were still going in and someone was still playing the marimba. . . . "

Mrs. Buterbaugh made no further attempt to find Professor Martin, but went back to her office in the Old Main Building and tried to work at her typewriter. She found she could not do so, and went to describe her experience to Dean Dahl, who listened with full attention and sympathy. Neither Dean Dahl nor Mrs. Buterbaugh had at this time any idea at all as to the identity of the figure seen or indeed whether it had any "identity." In the course of the day, however, it was suggested by a member of the staff that there might be some resemblance between the figure and the appearance of a Miss Clarissa U. Mills, an instructor in theory and piano, who had many years before used the office in which the figure appeared and who had died suddenly, in 1936, in a room just across the hall. Identifiable features were the extreme tallness, estimated at six feet, the black hair, and the appropriateness of place and action. Evidence of identity, however, has not been offered by anyone as conclusive.

In reply to further questions from G. M., Mrs. Buterbaugh described somewhat more fully what she saw when she looked out the window behind the desk where she had sensed the "presence" of the man:

". . . The window was open. Even though it was fairly early in the morning, it appeared as though it were a very warm, summer afternoon. It was very still. There were a few scattered trees-- about two on my right [east] and about three on my left [west]. It seems to me there were more, but these are the only ones I can be definite about. The rest was open field; the new Willard sorority

house and also Madison Street were not there.   I
remember seeing a very vague outline of some
sort of building to my right and that is about all.
Nothing else but open field" [pp. 306-308].

The following case was reported by H. W. Pierce
(1973):

> Recurrent spontaneous PK effects were reported
> independently by members of two families [named
> Cramer and Henry] living in a three-year-old house
> in suburban Pittsburgh during a seven-month period
> in 1971-1972.   Members of both families also re-
> ported seeing a child-sized, mist- or wave-like
> form on several occasions.   Sounds described as
> "childlike laughter" were reported by both families.
> The phenomena did not occur in association with
> any single living agent.   The traditional literature
> suggested that the violent death of a child might
> have occurred in association with the house.   In-
> vestigation disclosed such a death, although it was
> associated with a former resident of the house,
> rather than with the building itself.   Psychological
> records on the dead child revealed personality
> characteristics consistent with those suggested for
> RSPK agents in general and for the phenomena in
> this case in particular [p. 86].

> ... In November, 1971, about 6 p.m., Peter
> [Henry] saw what he said appeared to be a shadow
> on the stair landing inside the front entrance to
> the house as he was entering the building.   "I
> looked again, " he recalled, "and saw it was not a
> shadow.   It had depth.   It was three dimensional.
> It moved horizontally across the landing, went
> back into the lamp shadow, and disappeared.   I
> went up to the landing and looked around the corner
> and there was no one there. "   Peter said he ob-
> served the form from a distance of about ten feet,
> and looked directly at it.   He is the first member
> of the two families reported to have seen such a
> form, but he did not mention it to the others until
> February 7....

> ... Sometime in January [1972], about 5 p.m.,
> while sitting on the living room sofa, she [Clair
> Henry] saw what she describes as a form made up

of vertical "waves" about three feet high and a foot in diameter. She was able to observe it, she said, only while looking to one side of it, out of the corner of her eye....

...In late January, about midnight or later, Ellsworth [Cramer] woke abruptly in a sitting position. "At the foot of the bed," he said, "there was a grayish mist or cloud. It jumped up and coasted toward the door. It went right through the door." He described the form as three or four feet high. Naomi [Cramer] remained asleep....

...In early February, "for about five or six nights in a row," Naomi observed what she said looked like an oblong white cloud approximately four feet high in a chair at the dining room table. Naomi said she observed this late at night as she passed by the living room door from the bedroom to the bathroom, from a distance of about twenty feet. Initially, she said, she was not disturbed by its presence, although she was unable to explain it. "But after the third or fourth night it began to bother me," she declared....

...On April 22, Naomi was at home alone about 11:30 p.m. in the bedroom but not yet in bed, when the dog jumped from under the bed and ran barking to the living room. Naomi followed and in full light for perhaps two minutes saw a dancing cloud in the middle of the room. The dog continued barking and there was a laugh, more eerie than childlike. Afterwards the dog trembled and panted as though frightened by a thunderstorm [pp. 90-95].

Experimental Case: Maher and Schmeidler (1975) report on an interesting experiment aimed at detecting a ghost under controlled conditions, summarized as follows:

A young woman reported seeing a person in the hallway of the apartment where she lived with her mother, but subsequent search showed no one there. On the following evening, her mother reported a somewhat similar experience.

To investigate the hypothesis that the apartment was "haunted," a floor plan of the apartment was sectioned into comparable units, and a checklist was constructed of items both consistent and inconsistent with the witnesses' reports. Four sensitives and eight skeptics toured the apartment individually. Sensitives recorded impressions of where a ghost was, and skeptics similarly marked the checklist. Two sensitives' records showed a significant correspondence to witnesses' reports ($P <$ .03; $P <$ .04) but no skeptic's record showed even a marginally significant correspondence. Further reports from the sensitives showed some qualitative resemblance to the witnesses' reports.

Research Suggestions: Is there an artificial process that resembles that of the ghost? The latest developments in the field of laser photography offer clues that may be highly suggestive for productive research here. A hologram is produced on a highly stable base, utilizing two beams of laser or coherent light, one of which is slightly out of phase, and reflected from a different angle off the object. The resultant picture is surprisingly three dimensional in its final product and as your vantage point shifts, so does the appearance of the object, with a strong true-to-life characteristic. The most ghost-like representation is produced by a circular film or track, with the object in the center. When the lights are turned off, the object appears, yet you can put your hand through it, despite its apparent solidity.

There is one significant aspect of a hologram that could offer an additional cue for the psi researcher. Every part of a hologram contains a complete view of the entire scene holographed. This suggests that partial disassembly of a haunted area would not eliminate the ghost, but merely thin it: only the total destruction or disassembly would do it, and even then, the ghost could return if part of the elements were still available.

Let us study the elements of a haunting, using the above analogy. There would appear to be several elements necessary to produce a ghost, as follows:

(1) The setting. This is the area in which the ghost appears. It may involve natural elements: trees, stones, earth, bushes, flowers, wood, marble, and other such materials. However, artificial or human-modified materials appear as well: paint, cloth and clothing, carpets, fur, furniture, books, doors, balconies, beds, steps, all figure

in prominent case histories. The area must remain essentially unchanged, although the later addition of stairs and other physical modification sometimes results in ghosts that seem to walk on the former surfaces, not the new ones.

A puzzle exists in reflection on the fact that the leaves of a tree in a haunted area are new each year. The stones and pathway, however, may remain the same for a long period of time. Old houses, therefore, can see the ghosts remain, so long as the essential characteristics of the original area are maintained intact. This could possibly help explain apparitions seen in such areas as the Petit Trianon, which have been maintained essentially unchanged since the days of Marie Antoinette.

(2) The charging agent. This should be a living person, experiencing psychic dissonance of the most intense sort. It could involve the threat of death; profound hatred; blocked love; or any of the human emotions that could conceivably "charge" an area. A variety could exist in long-repeated activities in a single area that went on year after year, in the same small rounds, with essentially identical activities taking place: a group of monks, walking and chanting, through the decades; a woman tending her garden; a lighthouse keeper serving his station; a guard walking the battlements. In such cases, the "charging" that occurs is incremental, rather than taking place during a single event.

(3) The energy. Here we have to assume an analogy to a bioelectrical force, or something like it, that can pervade matter, if only to the extent that a trace is engrammed upon the material, that can eventually be picked up by the fourth element, the percipient. The critical fact about this energy is that it is mediated by a living being, through all the layers of its psychological makeup. There is very little that is mechanical or simplistic about the process. Rather, it is highly complex, varying according to the beliefs, attitudes, fears, aspirations, age, education, inhibitions and life experiences of the percipient. It may vary according to the willingness of the person to believe in the phenomena. However, there may be battery-like characteristics, as well, so that build-ups, discharges, and other peaks and lows may apply, whether based on body-energy, or whatever.

Milan Ryzl (1968), in analyzing the calls of Pavel Stepanek, noticed that Stepanek tended to call a given card a certain way repeatedly (he was working with white and green cards), even if the card was in different wrappers and envelopes. The more often the card was called a certain way, the more likely it was to be called the same way again. He calls this the "impregnation effect," as if the subject has begun to have an effect upon the card by his successive dealings with it in the same way. This clue certainly bears follow-up.

(4) The perceiving agent, or percipient. As indicated above, this element is possibly the most complex of the four. Thus, when critical elements are in alignment: belief, mood, fears, anticipations, wishes, energy levels--then the perception can occur. Talent, too, should not be ignored, since all talents in given sectors are not equal among humankind. For instance, a good medium can perceive ghosts in the daytime, while others may do so with difficulty at night. Training should not be omitted, either. Need should probably be included as well, since some ghosts meet very specific needs of their percipients.

If this alignment concept sounds far-fetched, another analogy from holograms should be remarked on: if the base on which the original picture is being taken is not absolutely stable (it requires tons of stone basing, for this stability) then the picture will not be successful.

The concept of the psychic hologram offers dozens of ideas for research. For instance, it should be possible to dismantle an area systematically over a long period of time, to determine at what point the ghost weakens seriously, or finally vanishes. Or, elements of a setting could be partially disarrayed, split apart, or separated by newly introduced physical or psychical elements, to determine the influence of the change, if any.

Percipients should be tested systematically, not only for belief, but also for the remainder of psychological make-up, to determine which, if any, are the most significant elements that make up a successful percipient.

The phenomenon of exorcism should also be studied in the same way: when performed by an ordained minister; by a lay person; when partially performed; when performed by a person of a faith different from the locality; when performed by a medium.

Haunted areas should be studied for every conceivable type of electrical energy variation; magnetic qualities; polarities; areas of static electricity; areas strongly insulated.

Groups should be tested in such settings, to determine the effect of groups, as well as individuals, upon the phenomenon. Makeup of groups should be varied considerably, specially centering around belief, and psi abilities.

The whole problem of lighting should be examined more than it has, in the past, since an inordinate number of experiences appear to occur in semidarkness or at night.

The phenomenon of cold should deserve special study, since there is an implication of two energy systems intersecting here, one feeling "colder" since it may be vibrating or operating at a different level than the other. This aspect alone could provide entree for other aspects of psi experience, if it could be solved. Thermometers, like cameras, may not work, but other bioelectrical equipment might be able to detect the change in the percipient's temperature system, when it intersects a ghost.

Transparency should be examined with an awareness that double exposure of a photograph also produces transparent images. The question that should be weighed is: at what point did the percipient get "tired" of seeing the ghost, so that what was figure starts to become ground, and the background resumes its role as figure again. With such inner psychological changes, ghosts would naturally tend to fade, as the eye now reacts to two basic perceptual images at the same time.

The Sensorimotor Pair

Dowsing and psychometry are both psi perceptual processes utilizing the motor system (see Figure 18). Dowsing covers items that lie below the ground, essentially geographic and spatial processes. Usually, an object is utilized as a concentration point or focus for the dowser. This can be a stick, metal wand, wire loop or any of a dozen techniques, culturally or personally determined. Tension builds up steadily inside the dowser, until there are explosive jumps, movements or sudden swings, by the wand or indicator, usually on the basis of motor automatism. Dowsers ordinarily do not like to be distracted, and though not, strictly speaking, in a sensory-deprivation environment, they apparently do a good job of shutting out the world of the senses.

Psychometry, on the contrary, seems to be a search for temporal, not spatial, factors. Information is being

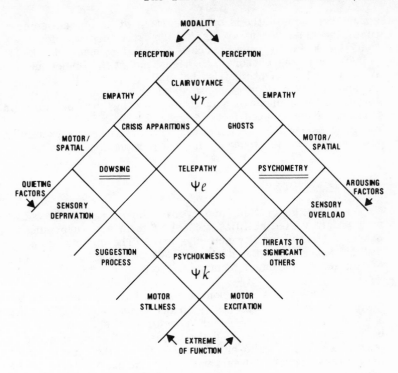

Figure 18: The Sensorimotor Pair in the Psi Matrix

Table 4

THE SENSORIMOTOR PAIR

Process	Arousing Factors	Quieting Factors
Dowsing	Motor Excitation	Sensory Deprivation
Psychometry	Sensory Overload	Motor Stillness

---

sought that apparently is on the surface of an object, sometimes the most recent events (outermost layers of information?). Generally, one searches for what happened to the
object, or to the persons who have handled the object most
recently. The psychometrist holds the object still, or touches
it, and allows a flood of sensory information to "flow" in.
Often, with the mass of data that comes in, the specific item
that one seeks may be lost or ignored. This is typical of
psi process, which is interwoven with preconscious creativity,
imagination and the tendency toward personation.

Dowsing

Every generation, and every culture, has its dowsers
with widely varied abilities. Most of them are surprisingly
proper citizens, usually anti-mystical. The objects of the
search depend upon the item most scarce in the area. Water,
of course, is the favorite target by far.

Induction: A situation requiring location of materials
under the ground. Walking, with the arms extended, holding
a wand, metal, wood or other detector extended from the
body. Concentration around the single focal point provided
by the detector. Build-up of tension within the muscle system. Dissociation and surrender to "external" forces, which
"move" the wand, as aspects of an altered state of consciousness.

Spontaneous Case: M. B. Dykshoorn (1974) reports
from a notary public's record a dowsing experience he had
early in his career, that helped set him on a lifetime of
clairvoyance and psi assistance to others:

> Today, the eleventh of October nineteen hundred
> and forty nine, at half past one p. m. , I, Robert
> Batten, Notary Public, station Middelburg, was in
> the house Seisstraat 28 at Middelburg, in the pres-
> ence of the witnesses to be mentioned hereafter,
> where appeared before me:

> Mr. Marinus Bernardus Dijkshoorn, dowser, re-
> siding at Breda, Wilhelminasingel 7a, born at 's-
> Gravenhage, the tenth of July nineteen hundred and
> twenty and known to me, Notary Public, according
> to his declaration acting in this matter as oral
> mandatary of Mr. Anton Gerard Touburg, pension-
> er, residing at Maassluis, Fenakolinslaan 31.

The appearer declared:

that in said house lived Mr. Jan Hendrik Meijboom, who from there evacuated to Lisse, where he died on the seventh of December nineteen hundred and forty eight; he did not leave behind wife or relations in the direct line and by his last will, passed before the Notary Public H. R. Struve at Middelburg, of the nineteenth of November nineteen hundred and twenty eight, he indicated his sister, Mrs. Johanna Pieternella Meijboom, as his sole heiress, the latter being married to said Mr. Touburg, in entire community of property;

that, according to the communication of his principal, said Mr. Meijboom, before being evacuated from Middelburg, should have buried an amount in silver coins in the garden of said house, which coins, as far as his principal knows, were never found;

that said Mr. Touburg therefore instructed the appearer, to look for this buried sum of money with the dowsing-rod, at the time and at the place as aforesaid.

The appearer therefore requested me to draw up an official report of the looking for these coins.

Complying with said request I was in the kitchen of the aforesaid house, with the appearer and the witnesses, where the appearer, before beginning with the dowsing, gave a description of the appearance of the person of Mr. Meijboom, which came up to the reality. Thereupon the appearer went with the dowsing-rod into the garden of aforesaid house and indicated a place under the back-kitchen where the money should be buried. After digging there, they found there, unpacked in the loose earth, total three hundred silver rixdollars, so total an amount of seven hundred and fifty guilders.

Of which this official report has been drawn up in minute, ah [sic] the time and at the place as said above, all this in the presence of Willem Pieter van Aartsen, lemonade-manufacturer and Janis Marinus Lakerveld, clerk, both residing at Middelburg, as witnesses.

Immediately after reading this deed, signed by the appearer, the witnesses, and by Me, Notary Public

M. B. Dijkshoorn, W. P. van Aartsen, J. M. Lakerveld, R. Batten, Notary Public.

Issued as a copy

[For true translation: Ph. Fickinger--in M. B. Dykshoorn (1974), pp. 172-173.]

Process Observation: Joseph C. Pearce (1974) demonstrates the startling effects of suggestion in this context, as he attempted to use a dowser's forked stick:

I recall watching in semidisbelief as my New England dowser walked along, his forked stick leaping about in his hands, pointing direction and going straight down at the water-spot. The dowser suggested I cut a stick and try, which I did with absolutely no results. So he took my forked stick and I took his. For some forty-five seconds or so his stick twisted in my hand like a thing alive, utterly astonishing me. When its life faded, the dowser handed me the stick I had cut, to no avail, but with which he had been dowsing in the meanwhile. And it, too, was a live thing in my hand for some time. I could not hold it and prevent it from dipping down at some spot. The dowser had given it his power [p. 133].

Research Suggestions: G. M. and his associates at the ASPR (Dale, et al., 1951) conducted an experiment in 1949 that was negative, in that the dowsers were no more able to predict the precise location of underground water than hydrologists, with the latter, if anything, having a slight edge.

A large diamond-shaped area was blocked out (see Figure 19), and dowsers and hydrologists were given the opportunity to indicate where they felt water was most likely to be immediately underfoot, at what depth and with what flow. Drilling then took place, and the holes were determined to be dry or productive, up to certain depths.

Essentially, the same kind of study needs to be done, but not just for water. The rarer the element, the more

O 1A Dowsers' location and number
O 1B Dowsers, blindfold
□ 1 Observation hole number
− − −Boundary of test area

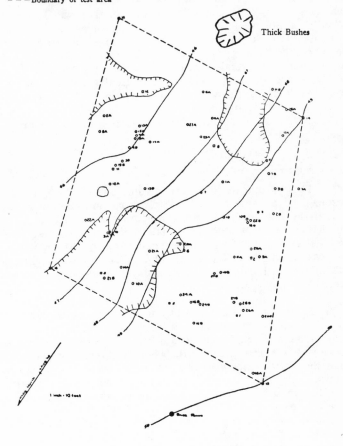

Thick Bushes

Figure 19: Site of Dowsing Experiment Near Liberty,
Maine (from Dale, et al., 1951)

valid will success prove.   Any natural element may be sought.
The principles of randomization need to be applied carefully,
so that the endless tendency to give the subject an interpret-
ive break are adequately countered.   Strict controls must be
applied.   Attitudes may be friendly and cooperative, but the
experimenter must at all times keep in mind that this is experimental, not validation, study.

Some EEG work may be undertaken at the same time. It would be useful to know whether there are any significant changes in brain-wave patterns at the moment that "perception" of the underground material takes place. Other questions remain to be studied, as well. Is there a "force" involved? If so, what is its relation to psychokinesis and poltergeists? To psychometry? How does the organism "receive" the "energy"? What is the role of the "wand"? Why do some materials work for one person and not for others? Or are the materials psychologically determined? How does locating the water, gold, silver, oil and the like, meet the needs of the dowser? More important conceptually, what is the role of psychological need in this entire process?

Psychometry

This is one of the more mysterious of the psi processes, but the answer may simply turn on a better knowledge of the nature of matter. It may well be that a form of information is imprinted upon matter that does not significantly alter it, but that can be read back by the right person, perceiving it in the right way. The same encoding process might well help to explain ghosts, dowsing and clairvoyance at the same time.

There is a useful analogy to keep in mind here. Despite the incredible advances in microbiology, it is still an awesome task to envision the amount of information that is encoded in a single germ cell, whether sperm or egg. Between the fixed processes and the latencies that will permit variation, depending on the accidents of nutrition, radiation and other modifying forces, variability can be expressed, but within a fairly confining range. Thus, for instance, most human babies tend to be born with similar human characteristics, despite very wide variations in physical surroundings and nutritional input differences. And, in the case of the sperm, all the information for the person is initially encoded in a space smaller than the point of a pin.

We should also recognize that the tiniest change at a significant level (in, for example, the nucleotides making up the information-relaying chain) can be highly significant, or even deadly, in future information terms. Also significant for analogy purposes is the fact that until very, very recently, we were ignorant of the very existence of this information system (although we suspected that such a system had to exist!).

<u>Induction</u>: Holding object in left hand, thereby using right side of brain. Concentration on the object, of which key facts may be unknown. Motor stillness, while letting a broad flow of perceptual images enter the system. Dissociation, and an altered state of consciousness, in which a part of the history of the object is hallucinated.

<u>Spontaneous Case</u>: Police Chief Robert B. White, of Palm Springs, California, speaks about the work of Hurkos (Browning, 1970):

> I had heard a lot about Peter Hurkos.... While he was in my office he asked whether we had any complicated cases we were trying to solve. I told him yes, as a matter of fact we had several. I asked Captain Richard Harries to bring in some of the folders of unsolved cases. He brought in several.
>
> Peter Hurkos laid his hand on the top folder, which happened to be the Gallagher case, and began verbally telling us almost verbatim what was in the report. Both my captain and I were amazed. We had never seen Peter Hurkos before. He had no way of knowing what was in that folder. The case was a year old, and it hadn't been in the news recently. Yet Peter began telling us about it exactly as though he were seeing through that folder.
>
> He said it was the case of a missing boy. He named the correct number of persons involved-- three. He identified the vehicle they were driving. He told us there had been a little "party" and there were lots of narcotics involved. This also was correct. The three boys had been off on a little "trip" on LSD.
>
> Peter Hurkos also pretty well described the general area where the missing boy was last seen. He said it was a remote area with lots of rocks and boulders and brush. If you know the Tahquitz Canyon area (I do), you know that's what it's like.
>
> He also saw the boy nude, and it is true that he was last seen in the nude, but Peter also said that he had been in uniform, that he had been recently released from the military, although he did

not see him in the Navy or Marine Corps. The folder contained a picture of the boy in his Army Air Force uniform.

Peter said he saw some blood, and then he stopped. He couldn't do any more. My captain and myself and others were all amazed. We all knew there was no way for him to know the contents of that folder.

They then asked Peter whether he would go with them to the area, and he of course agreed to go. Peter had never been in Palm Springs before, much less in Tahquitz Canyon, but he led them up the mountain to the top of the first falls and to the exact location of the boys' camping area.

What amazed police most was that Peter identified a flat stone as the one on which the missing boy's clothing had been found. "If you know that area, you know it's full of rocks and boulders," the Police Chief repeated. But Peter went over to a certain flat stone and said he visualized some of the boy's clothing on top of that rock. It wasn't just any rock, it was the rock where we had found the missing boy's clothing nearly a year before.

Peter indicated another area, farther on near the upper falls, where he said the body would be found. He said it would be wedged under a rock and partly in water.

My captain's first instinct was to try to reach that area, but it would have been too dangerous to attempt it, especially in the winter months. Tahquitz Creek was extremely high, and there was snow in the mountains. It's hard to get into that area even in good weather, so we decided against it.

But that's exactly where the skeletal remains were found, scattered over an area of about fifteen feet just off a place called Lost Trail, north of Tahquitz Creek in the mountains that border Palm Springs. They were found by two young hikers, who told the police, and subsequently a helicopter was flown into the area to collect the remains [pp. 110-112].

<u>Experimental Case:</u> Lawrence LeShan (1974) tells of his unexpected experience with Eileen Garrett and an ancient Babylonian clay tablet, as follows:

> The materials I assembled for the experiment were all small and very different. They included an old Greek coin, a tiny fossil fish, a woman's comb, a bit of stone from inside Mt. Vesuvius, a used scrap of bandage from a hospital emergency room, and so forth. Each was wrapped in tissue, sealed in a small box, put into an envelope, and given a code number. These envelopes were then given to someone who did not know what was in them and who--working by himself--put each envelope into a large manila envelope with a new code number. Only he had both code numbers, so the end result was that there was no one, not even I, who knew which object was in which large manila envelope. This is typical research procedure in this field. It prevents, for example, the experimenter from unconsciously giving clues to the clairvoyant as to what is in the envelope.
>
> As I was finishing wrapping and boxing the objects in my office (where Mrs. Garrett had never been), I found that I was one box short. The last object I planned to use was an ancient Babylonian clay tablet written in the old cuneiform method. It was somewhere between 3000 and 3500 years old and I have never had it translated. It could be anything from a laundry list to a peace treaty! Certainly a dramatic and interesting object.
>
> Not having a box, I went to a neighboring office and asked the secretary there (a woman I knew only slightly) if she had one. She asked what size and came into my room to see the ones I had been using. There she noticed the clay tablet, picked it up and asked what it was. We chatted about it for three minutes and she departed to look for a box. While she was gone, I found one of my own, identical with the others I had used and put the tablet in that. This seemed a very minor incident in the history of the tablet, and one that quickly slipped out of my consciousness.
>
> Two weeks later and 1500 miles away, Mrs. Garrett sat before a tape recorder. I sat in an-

other corner of the room, facing away from her.
A third person, Jean Andoire (who had no knowledge of the objects either), ran the recorder and
took notes. Mrs. Garrett picked up one of the
large manila envelopes, which I later learned contained the tablet, read the double coded number on
the outside and started to talk about "a woman associated with this. " She then proceeded to describe
the secretary from the office next to mine (whom
she had never met nor heard of) in such detail that
it would have been possible just from the description to pick the secretary out of a line-up of ten
thousand women. She described the two scars she
bore on her body (which later checking showed to
be precisely where Mrs. Garrett had indicated),
her distinctive hair style, her job history, and the
special relationship she had with her daughter.
However, Mrs. Garrett did not say one word that
could possibly be interpreted as having anything to
do with an ancient Babylonian clay tablet, or with
the area of the little shops next to the British
Museum where I had bought it, or even with my
desk in whose top drawer it had rested for the
past year [pp. 29-31].

    Research Suggestions: First of all, experiments need
to be designed so that the telepathic possibility is eliminated.
For instance, in the previously quoted Hurkos case, a simpler
solution is available in a telepathy hypothesis. Still, there
are instances in the literature where a psychometrist first
asserted certain information unknown to living persons, which
was then later verified from additional written or other
sources.

    Then we must raise the same problem that arose with
ghosts: how can information be engraved on matter, possibly
in some manner resembling the coding inherent in DNA,
which can fix complex events in microspace, so that persons
later on, in the right frame of mind, and with the right talents, can read this matter for the information encoded thereon?

    Many questions derive from this statement of the
problem. Are there techniques in which information can be
encoded, without changing the basic nature or structure of
matter? Some physicists have suggested that this is possible, based on current knowledge.

How does emotion "charge" matter, so that the information is more readily available? What is the relation of the "charging event" to the "readout" process? What is the difference between a single, emotionally-laden event, and a long series of similar or repetitious events, which can apparently also produce an information-laden object? In the latter case is there a steady buildup of information, similar in some regards to metal-plating of an object?

Why is the left hand preferred for readout by some psychometrists? Is there a relation between the left hand and right-brain perception?

How long does information thereby encoded last? Does it become a permanent part of the matter? Or does it fade with time?

We need an alliance between parapsychologists and physicists who are willing to try to learn each other's language, exchange problems and thereby enlarge our knowledge in a very shadowy area of understanding.

While approaching the physicists, we may presume to step into their territory and postulate a process that we may call psychokinetic information embedding (or PKIE, for short). It should take at least two and possibly more forms: instantaneous, in cases of sharp emotional events, such as a major crisis or death; and slow-building, in the case of long-term repetitive buildups of similar or essentially the same events. It should be operative on both organic and inorganic matter; long-lasting; resistive to superficial changes in the nature of the material; cumulative, in that the more information provided, the better the resultant picture, hallucination or parasensory impression. It should be non-verbal, reactive directly on the person in symbolic terms.

While considering the concept of PKIE we should also recognize the parallel to the concept of the crisis apparition vs. the ghost. The crisis apparition is an example of the explosive, sharp, emotional event, while the ghost is more frequently an instance of a slow-building, steadily incremental development of information and attitudes over a long period of time. Thus, the two informational processes may parallel the two perceptual processes, two forms of information recording and two types of information readout.

The problem of information readout raises another question, and another hypothesis. Suppose for a moment that the psychometric object served quite another purpose: that of the addressing mechanism, in computer terms? The addressing could well be in any one of several program lines: past or future time sequence; person sequence; most recent contact; most emotional contact; formative contact; most relevant to the most recent handler; and on and on. Again, we run into the problem outlined by Tart, Honorton and many others: the complexity of human personality, in which sensory, motor and intellectual factors confuse even simple processes in the jungle of human body-mind functioning. Nevertheless, this is one of the richer frameworks for studying the problem posed by psychometric process. A host of cases can be examined in precisely this context, with some real promise for significant payoff.

The Emotor Pair

This is a pair that use motor process in the tension between highly positive and negative relations with others (see Figure 20). The key to healing others is the relation

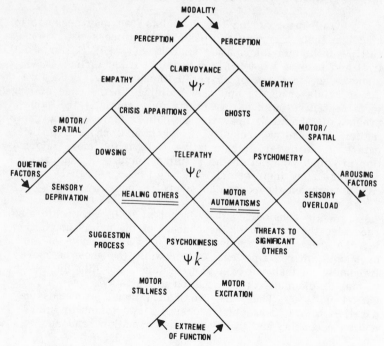

Figure 20: The Emotor Pair in the Psi Matrix

between healer and healed. Hysterical processes, non-psi in nature, can be treated fairly easily in this way. Belief apparently can move personal physical mountains out of the way of cures. Frozen functions that had resisted change melt under the impact of the belief in the healer.

Table 5

THE EMOTOR PAIR

Process	Arousing Factors	Quieting Factors
Healing others	Motor excitation	Suggestion process
Motor automatisms	Trauma or threats to significant others	Motor stillness

---

Motor automatisms, in a sense, are the inverse of this. The person is often concerned about another person who died or is generally concerned about the process of death. Concentration on that concern, extreme body stillness, yet a quiet buildup of tension in the system, and at a certain point the body part, whether hand or lips, begins to perform on its own, presenting aspects of another personality that may demonstrate some significant elements of the prior person, as well. What is expressed, then, may turn out to be a blend of the speaker and the person feared for.

The Healing of Others

The psychological component of healing was well known in the traditional medical world, but it has been underestimated by the modern physician. The old-fashioned family general practitioners understood this process well and capitalized on it every day in their practice. Relationship, of course, was the key to their success.

Healing may conceivably be assisted by the presence of a group of "believing others," who help to strengthen the sense of empathy by all participants in the healing process.

Induction: Belief in the healer on the part of the person being healed. A build-up of tension within the two personal systems--healer and healed. Strong suggestion process buildup in the person being healed, usually by the healer, but it may include other cultural factors, and the presence of other persons as well. A "surrender" to "other" forces, external to the self, thereby building up unconscious forces and effects. Dissociation (especially in extreme illness or fever) may lead to more dramatic forms of healing and cures.

Spontaneous Case: We should count on the essential conservatism of the Roman Catholic Church, since it is very deliberate and careful in verifying the facts that ultimately lead to sainthood. In any event here is a Washington Post (September 15, 1975) report on a healing case in which prayer and her relics played a significant part in the canonization of Mother Seton:

> Carl Kalin, a Swedish-born Lutheran who at the time of his illness worked in the engineering department of New York's Consolidated Edison Co., was Mother Seton's second miracle.

> In 1963 Kalin was admitted to St. Joseph's Hospital in Yonkers, N.Y. suffering from a rare and usually fatal complication of red measles known as primary fulminating rubeola meningoencephalitis. The measles virus had invaded his brain.

> "He was moribund. Death appeared imminent, a matter of hours away," recalled Dr. Frank B. Flood, Kalin's physician at St. Joseph's, who came with him to the canonization.

> "His temperature was out of control. His breathing was labored. He was unable to get sufficient oxygen into his bloodstream. He was blue. He was sustaining one convulsion after another," Flood said. "We did everything we could, but we had no cure for this disease and he appeared to be at death's door."

> Kalin's wife, Anne, is a Catholic and when a nun at the hospital asked if she wanted a novena, an extended period of prayers for him, she agreed.

A so-called primary relic of Mother Seton, a sliver of bone from her body, was brought to Kalin's bedside.

"The change occurred dramatically after the relic was applied," Flood said. His temperature had been close to 106 degrees. The relic at this point was applied and his temperature came down rapidly. His breathing became more normal. His color pinked up. His convulsions stopped and he was peaceful."

Kalin, a vigorous-looking blue-eyed man of 73 with thinning white hair and full mustache, now lives with his wife in Florida.

"It's really difficult for me to say anything about my recovery because I don't remember anything about my sickness or the recovery until the fifth day," he said. "But I was told there were literally thousands of people praying for me."

Last Dec. 20, a week after he had learned that Pope Paul VI had agreed to make Mother Seton a saint, Kalin became a Roman Catholic.

"The miracle had a great deal to do with it," he said. "But I had been associated with Catholics most of my life, and, of course, my wife is a Catholic and has been all her life. I have been in and out of Catholic churches more than any other church."

Kalin said he found it hard to express his feeling about Mother Seton. "I don't know whether it's proper to say she's wonderful," he said. "It's certainly a wonderful thing that happened to me through her."

A complication in interpretation of this case is the fact that so many persons unrelated to him were praying for the patient, who was apparently unconscious during the critical turning point in his recovery.

Experimental Case: Bernard Grad (1965), of Montreal, more than a decade ago conducted an unusual study of a well-known Hungarian healer, Mr. E.:

A series of experiments on animals and plants was conducted in which the effect of the "laying on of hands" as practiced by a man, Mr. E. , was studied.

The experiments on animals involved the measurement of the rate of healing of skin wounds of mice receiving different treatments. In preliminary experiments, the groups that received the laying on of hands healed at a significantly faster rate than either of two other groups, one of which was a control group that received no treatment at all, while the other received as its treatment a warming up by a heating tape to the same degree and at the same rate as that which was produced in Mr. E. 's group by the warmth of his hands. However, there was no significant difference in wound healing rate between the artificially warmed-up mice and the untreated controls (see Table 6 and Figures 21 and 22).

Following this, a more elaborate, double-blind experiment involving 300 mice was conducted with Drs. R. J. Cadoret and G. I. Paul of the University of Manitoba. In this experiment there was an untreated control group of mice called the O group, a group treated by Mr. E. called the E group, and a group treated by medical students called the M group. During the treatment periods, the cages in which the mice were transferred and treated were placed inside opaque paper bags. In half the mice of each group the bag was left open and in the remainder it was stapled closed. In the open bag series receiving the E or M treatment, the hands were inserted inside the bag and the treatment cage held directly between the hands without looking at the mice or cage. In the closed bag series, the hands were placed on top of the paper bag which prevented direct contact with the treatment cage.

On the fifteenth and sixteenth day after wounding the mean surface areas of the wounds in the E group were significantly smaller than those of the other two groups in the open bag series. No significant differences were found in the closed bag series, but here also the mean wound area was smaller in the E group than in the O and M groups [p. 125].

Table 6

THE EFFECT OF MR. E.'S FIELD AND OF HEAT ON THE RATE OF WOUND HEALING IN CF1 FEMALE MICE: WEIGHT (MG.) OF PAPER PROJECTIONS OF WOUNDS

Treatment	On day of wounding	One day after wounding	Eleven days after wounding	Fourteen days after wounding
MTR (Control)	$7.547^*\pm.211^{**}$	$7.705\pm.493$	$3.194\pm.363$	$2.043\pm.379$
STTR (Mr. E.)	$8.051\pm.234$	$7.394\pm.398$	$1.322\pm.326$	$.562\pm.146$
HTR (Heated)	$7.711\pm.284$	$7.299\pm.437$	$3.575\pm.396$	$2.323\pm.442$

*Mean
**Standard error

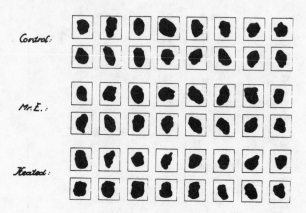

Figure 21: After Wounding, Before Treatment (from Grad, 1966). Surface area of the wound of each of the mice immediately after the wounds were made and before treatment was started. It is obvious that there are no real differences in wound surface area between the three groups despite some variation from mouse to mouse.

Research Suggestions: The most significant element here is the delicate interpersonal role that involves the healer and the healed. We need to explore most explicitly the triggering effects, if any, of positive personal relations. The visceral brain, thalamic functioning, blood factors and the release of significant and relevant hormones, enzymes, trace minerals and other body microelements are all involved in the healing process. Intensity of individual set toward healing especially needs study, since this may well prove a vital factor in many of the more dramatic cures.

The critical physiological mechanism that needs to be studied may well be the limbic system, the seat of emotional functioning, and how and in what way it influences body set toward healing. Suggestion process becomes an important instrument here, and hypnotic studies need to be launched to examine attitudes toward and readiness for healing. Prayer and meditation need to be better understood in terms of influencing the enzyme and hormone processes of the body, as mediated by cortical or thalamic processes. Skin, as one of the body parts quickest to replace itself, can well be studied first.

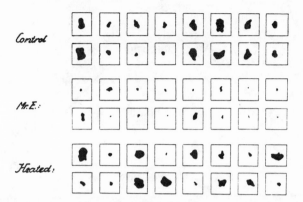

Control

Mr. E.:

Heated:

Figure 22: Fourteen Days After Wounding (from Grad, 1966).
Surface area of wounds fourteen days after wounds were
made. Obviously, the wounds in the mice treated by Mr.
E. are smaller than those of the other two groups, statistical analysis showing that the differences are significant beyond the .001 level. It is also obvious that there is no significant difference between the control group and the heated group.

Figure 23 becomes useful for suggested research into
healing. The triangle portrayed can offer a conceptual
framework, in part based on the thinking of men like Roland
Fischer (1971) and Colin Martindale (1975), for some of the
approaches that can be employed. The top of the triangle
represents ego strength, ego involvement, the balance point
for normal interactions with others.

The two legs are somewhat different. One leg points
toward lower levels of ego involvement and increased arousal
of the sympathetic nervous system around a positive set of
beliefs. This is the action or plus leg of the triangle. The
other is the opposite, representing the negative or inhibitory
leg, the area of rejection or inhibition, with increasing involvement of the parasympathetic nervous system (an inhibiting system).

The trigger of belief and set may well use the effect-
ing mechanisms of the hormonal chemicals, then in turn en-
ergize subtle bioelectrical charges. Much of this remains
to be explored in systematic, patient research into a complex series of processes.

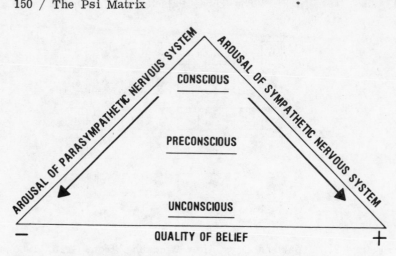

Figure 23: Inhibition and Arousal of PNS and SNS--Levels
of Consciousness vs. Quality of Belief

Aside from the key factor of the two different legs, with their quite different qualities of belief and rejection, inhibition and arousal, there is a constant between them: each leg represents the progressive loss of ego involvement, or weakness of central controls, if you like. These, significantly, permit suggestion process to operate so effectively, since the preconscious state is essentially uncritical and accepting of specially-defined situations. These can be self-defined or other-defined, as the circumstances dictate, but they do represent definitions frequently quite different from the normal conscious self.

Finally, professional healers from every culture deserve study--objective, preferably medical (provided the profession can face its own fears and doubts), but with an open rather than a cynical or hostile view of the problem. The recent study by William A. Nolen, Healing: A Doctor in Search of a Miracle (1974) is one very good start. More than this, however, healers everywhere should be studied and better understood: witch doctors, nature healers, psychich surgeons and surgeons with rusty or no knives. Something very good might come out of such study: a realization that there are many techniques of medicine, that ours is but one of these (one of the better, too), and that the relation between healer and healed, the caring person and the patient, is among the most important factors in working toward cures of illness. If a reorientation of some of our less sensitive physicians, nurses and ancillary medical personnel were to prove an ultimate result, all the work in this field of study will be worth the while.

Motor Automatisms

In our framework the automatist is caught in the interacting tension of two systems: empathic, with the potential threat to (or death of) a significant other, and motor, with motor stillness. The resultant vector is a sudden splitting away and autonomous activity of some aspect of body function. The usual non-psi expression of this, conversion hysteria, is a negation of function, such as paralysis, blindness or anesthesia on a psychological, but not a physiological, basis, so that the area affected is a functional, but not a neurological unit. The dynamic here would appear to be a form of immobilization or canceling that says: "This part must not continue functioning, since it is psychically dangerous to do so."

In psi process the old-fashioned form of the automatic writer is less seen today, although the planchette and the ouija board may still be found. Pendulums and rings hung by threads over the palm illustrate the same ability to tap the unconscious for answers to nagging personal questions. Today, tapes are handy for recording the autonomous personality expressions that may emerge. Styles change; psychological mechanisms do not.

The typical subject may be strongly suggestible. Some dissociation may be present and operative, especially for body parts and body action. The body may be seen as an instrument that can be manipulated by the self, or by other forces, to express beliefs.

Induction: Belief that the process is possible. Keeping the body, and especially the hands, extremely still. Tension buildup in the subject. Occasional reinforcement from other participating believers. A "surrender" to "other" forces external to the self (thereby building up the influence of unconscious forces and effects). Movement of the body part on an autonomous basis, as an altered state emerges.

Spontaneous Case: Although we have made it a rule to use cases since the Second World War, one of the English mediums of the First World War period, "Mrs. Willett, " provides a good case with process illustrations as well (Lodge, 1911):

> Mrs. Willett ... obtained a remarkable script, concerning the coming of which she makes the statement annexed:

> Statement by Mrs. Willett concerning her reception of the script of February 5th, a facsimile and a transcription of which follow.

> 5 Feb. , 1910
> Note about 6:10 p. m. I came downstairs from resting and suddenly felt I was getting very dazed and light-headed with a hot sort of feeling on the back of my neck--I was looking at the Times newspaper--I did not think of script until I felt my hands being as it were drawn together--I could not seem to keep them apart and the feeling got worse--and with a sort of rush I felt compelled to get writing materials and sit down, though (people) were in the room and I have never tried for Sc. [i. e. , script] except alone (with the exception of the time with Mrs. V.). The enclosed Sc. came--the most untidy Sc. I ever had--a long pause after the word "spell it. "

> After the sheet (1) I thought the Sc. was finished and began in a few minutes to copy it out when I felt my hands "going" again and took another sheet (2) when some more Sc. came.

> I am giving the original Script and this note to _____ now, as I do not feel a copy can be made of the writing, some of which is unlike any I ever had.

> I still feel very dazed and uncomfortable. The Sc. has no meaning whatever to me. I take the word in large letters to be

> Dorr,

> and this I know is the name of some man in America concerning whom Mrs. Verrall sent a message (to the Willett communicators) in the summer to

say his sittings (with Mrs. Piper, I think) had
brought good evidence--I know she has written a
paper about these sittings--but I know nothing whatever about them, nor about the person named
"Dorr," except that he exists, and is American.

Copy of Sc. of 5 February, 1910, ended 6:25 p. m.
    You felt the call it I it is I who write Myers.
I need urgently to say this tell Lodge this word
Myers Myers get the word I will spell it (scribbles)
Myers yes the word(?) is DORR
                     [end of sheet 1]

    We (?) H (scribbles, perhaps M)
    Myers the word is
    (Scribbles) D DORR
    Myers enough
          F   [end of sheet 2] [pp. 125-126].

Here Mrs. Willett has demonstrated the incoherence,
the problems involved in trying to use the muscles to express
deep-lying "messages." Current recording techniques for
mediums largely rely on verbal expressions, instead.

Experimental Case: Erickson (1969) has a last valuable instance of his remarkable work with Aldous Huxley that
is relevant here:

    There followed more deep trances by Huxley in
which, avoiding all personal significance, he was
asked to develop partial, selective and total post-
hypnotic amnesias (by partial is meant a part of
the total experience, by selective amnesia is meant
an amnesia for selected, perhaps interrelated items
of experience), a recovery of the amnestic material
and a loss of the recovered material. He developed
also catalepsy tested by "arranging" him comfort-
ably in a chair and then creating a situation constituting a direct command to rise from the chair
("take the book on that table there and place it on
the desk over there and do it now"). By this
means Huxley found himself, unexplicably to him,
unable to arise from the chair and unable to understand why this was so. (The comfortable arrangement of his body has resulted in a positioning that
would have to be corrected before he could arise
from the chair and no implied suggestions for such

correction were to be found in the instructions giv-
en. Hence, he sat helplessly unable to stand, unable to recognize why. This same measure has
been employed to demonstrate a saddle block anesthesia before medical groups. The subject in the
deep trance is carefully positioned, a casual conversation is then conducted, the subject is then
placed in rapport with another subject who is asked
to exchange seats with the first subject. The second subject steps over only to stand helplessly
while the first subject discovers that she is (a) unable to move, and (b) that shortly the loss of ability to stand results in a loss of orientation to the
lower part of her body and a resulting total anesthesia having been mentioned even in the preliminary discussion of hypnosis   (This unnoticed use
of catalepsy not recognized by the subject is a
most effective measure in deepening trance states.)
[p. 59].

Research Suggestions: What we need to know most in
motor automatisms are the psychophysiological concomitants
of anxiety, and the relation of tension systems to motor
functions, as they come together in the brain. Brain map-
ping studies are essential, but most particularly what happens
when tension levels build too high, so that some form of release or "snap" occurs. The switch occurs most likely
within the brain, and we should see the operative mechanisms
as systems of equivalence. Here is where the unconscious
and preconscious Freudian mechanisms need to be understood
better neurodynamically, for though they are symbolic and
abstract concepts, they may well have psychophysiological
concomitants. The work of the biofeedback researchers such
as Barbara Brown (1974) especially needs to be amplified and
related to this problem.

In the meantime, suggestion process and hypnosis can
help with simulation studies of the brain areas involved. In
this way some cues can be developed as to the actual dynamics of the mechanisms involved.

C. A FURTHER EXTENSION OF THE CONCEPT

There has just been presented a tentative matrix of psi phenomena, based on the possibility that psi processes are related, and may be specially grouped, as sympathetic and parasympathetic impulses surge through the unwary system exposed to stress and extremes of various sorts. At this point it may be worthwhile to sweep up a large group of psi and near-psi experiences that have been deliberately omitted heretofore, since they are even more speculative. Still, if a theory is worth anything, it should be able to assemble larger masses of data into a schema that helps the entire picture to make sense.

One additional area of mental functioning will be postulated: the definition of self in space and time, to fit alongside perception, empathy and motor/spatial body processes. At this point, then, the psi matrix widens considerably from nine up to sixteen elements, since it expands from a 3 x 3 web up to 4 x 4. More difficult, from a conceptual point of view, is the fact that some fairly controversial items are swept into the network, involving puzzling areas that have been avoided so far. These include all of the various phenomena around multiple expressions of personality as they emerge during trance experiences: possession; reincarnation claims; the confusion that arises during dreams and out-of-body experiences; the illusion of the déjà vu and its perceptual negative, false strangeness; cosmic consciousness; and finally, the most speculative area of all appears in precognitive claims for awareness of events yet to come.

Precognition

Here we need to step into a fourth dimension, the greatest mystery short of death itself--time. Perhaps we are like the fish in the bowl, destined never to fully understand the nature of the world outside the bowl, simply by virtue of its reflection in the glass. J. W. Dunne's two books on time (An Experiment with Time, 1927, and The Serial Universe, 1934) offer a good beginning discussion of the problem. In essence, we need a better reference point, from which we could perhaps perceive "eternity" at a glance. Perhaps.

Dreams have traditionally been the main medium through which precognitive perceptions occurred. A great problem with them is that most of them are not validated by recording prior to the event apparently perceived. They probably occur far more frequently than is currently accepted. Generally, they seem to relate to upcoming crises highly relevant to the personal sphere of the dreamer.

Figure 24 offers a model for precognition. The subject is moving between conscious and unconscious levels of mental functioning (e. g. just awakening), perceiving an external event or state of affairs. If an object is involved then we must face the problem of "encoded information" on matter. If it involves persons, then another personality takes the place of the external event. Probably in the real world it would involve both persons and objects. The channel shows noise, to interfere with the "message." Finally, there is a space-time "distorter" or compressor, which may be acting to "twist" time from one period to another. How such a process could operate is inconceivable at this time, but some physicists have suggested that there are microprocesses that theoretically could do this (e. g. tachyons supposedly travel faster than light, and hence could permit a reversal of time flow). The entry point for this information, as with other similar models, is at unknown levels, and the number of interactions upon the personality for the information obtained is unlimited. In any event here is a very crude model for study, examination and refinement, based on future experimentation.

Induction: A major event may loom up just ahead, significant to the life of the perceiver or those important to him or her. Less significantly, the person may face a trip with some new experiences out of the ordinary. Possibly disorientation for temporal factors takes place (e. g. during sleep, with conceivable right-brain dominance during REM dreaming). A sensory deprivation environment is very typical, usually occurring on the margins of REM sleep, with an altered state of consciousness operative, so characteristic of most psi processes.

Three More Pairs

Since we are constructing a matrix, we should continue listing the pairs, the arousing and quieting factors, so

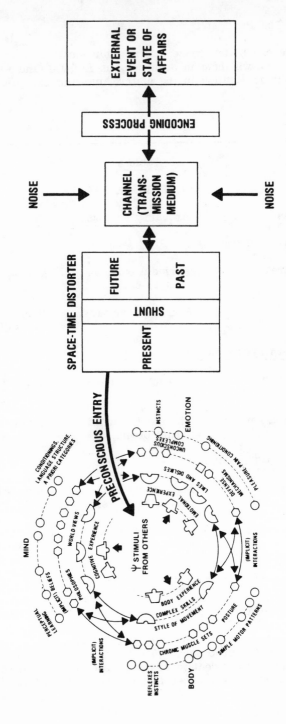

Figure 24: Model of Psi Process--Precognition (adapted from Tart, 1966, 1975)

that we can better conceptualize their location on the matrix. Table 7 shows them in sequence, as follows, and Figure 25 shows their addition to the matrix, omitting the prior items listed.

Table 7

THREE MORE PAIRS

Process	Arousing Factors	Quieting Factors
The Dream Pair		
REM dreaming	Periodic confusion as to self	Sensory deprivation
OBE's	Sensory overload	Clarification as to self
The Personation Pair		
Possession	Inadequately integrated ego	Suggestion process
Reincarnation	Threats to significant others	Clarification as to self
The Space-Time Pair		
Paramnesia	Momentary confusion as to self	Motor stillness
Cosmic consciousness	Motor excitation	Clarification as to self

The Dream Pair

Dreams and out-of-body experiences (OBE's) may be closely related processes. They both occur during sleep and they have a great deal in common, but they also have a few very important differences that can serve to differentiate the

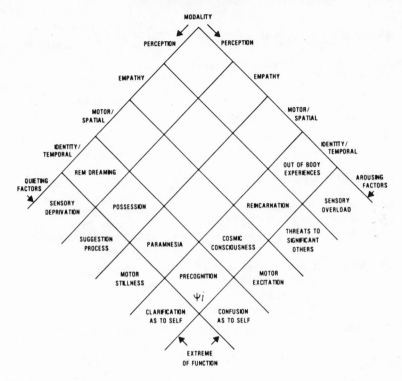

Figure 25: Seven Possible Additions to the Psi Matrix

two. For purposes of analysis let us match them, then, to see in detail the similarities and differences. The psycho-physical similarities are roughly as follows:

Claimed characteristics of OBE	Self-described characteristics of REM dreaming
A sense that the conscious self is separated from the physical body	Can occur
Ability to "move" anywhere	Can occur
Ability to "pass through" matter	Can occur
Loss of all sense of time and space	Can occur
Density of body can vary from solid to transparent	Can occur

Claimed characteristics of OBE	Self-described characteristics of REM dreaming
Can apparently "contact" physical matter	Can occur
Can communicate with others	Can occur
Can perceive extrasensorily	Can occur
Sense of "falling" just prior to end of experience	Can occur

The psychophysical <u>differences</u> are roughly as follows:

Continuity of consciousness and sense of acute identity with self.	Not usual. Sense of self may be blurred, masked, screened, diffused.
Frequently, there is a sense of being attached to one's physical body by means of a cord at the head or solar plexus.	No. Almost never occurs.
Self-reports indicate that movement of body during the experience tends to terminate the OBE.	No. Body movement, as viewed by observers, can take place at the beginning and end of REM dreaming.
Any expression of emotion during the experience promptly terminates it.	No. REM dreams can be highly emotional. Only at extremes do emotions cause termination.
Body feels "cold, clammy" upon "reentry."	No. Very unusual.
Experiences a "click," "snap," or "pop," in head, upon "reentry."	No. Does not occur.

To sum up, in dreaming there is a heavy confusion with regard to self, whereas in OBE self seems to be present. And, while both experiences may be dream processes, in REM dreaming sensory processes are heavily muted; in OBE the personality seems to be busy exploring the universe by sensory/extrasensory means. Finally, in OBE space/time functions are minimal, although there are apparently no barriers to space/time movement. Experiencing emotion or performing body functions tends to terminate the experience of OBE.

REM Dreaming

REM dreams may well be the source for most spontaneous psi experiences, since they are normal, natural and recurrent, even if mysterious in their presentation to the basic self. The moments just prior to sleep may constitute the most important area for psi research, since they seem to hold the key to that invisible door to psi in its multiple manifestations.

REM (rapid eye movement) dreaming, which takes place in roughly ninety-minute cycles, is apparently a universal phenomenon in humanity and most likely in all mammals, as well as some lower forms of life, such as birds. It may represent the primitive base out of which psi possibly originally evolved as an alternative parasensory scanning system for the protection of the organism while its defenses were at their lowest levels. The intermittent sympathetic surges may represent latent mobilization of the organism, when and if danger is perceived by sensory means. This concept has been spelled out by Ullman (1961). Significantly, REM dreams usually terminate in the awakening of the organism in the morning, as the last dreams help to puncture the delicate line between the preconscious and the conscious self.

Study of cats has suggested that it may not be the entire REM period that is so essential to sleep, but rather the much shorter pontine-geniculo-occipital (PGO) spiking in the midst of the REM period, that is a brain-wave process essential for the organism. Precisely what PGO spiking does for the brain is at present unknown. Perhaps it represents a rapid clearing of the computer; perhaps a resetting or recalibration that is under way.

The Hindus have long known of extrasensory phenomena, and consider them a kind of nuisance or distraction when one is learning to meditate properly and slides along the edges of preconsciousness similar to the process of falling asleep. The experiences are referred to as "siddhis" and those adepts who are misled into exhibiting this lower form of ability are pitied for straying from the path of meditation and the true purpose of their studies.

Induction: Sleep is marked by withdrawal from the normal world of intellectual and sensory stimuli as the "actor" of self is removed from the external stage of personality. The body relaxation of delta sleep (1-4 Hertz waves dominant) shifts into intermittent sympathetic surges; energy rises rapidly, as do respiration, body temperature, blood pressure, eye movements and norepinephrine levels. Only muscle tone drops, with parasympathetic paralysis of muscles. Unconscious functioning then begins to move upward, closer to the preconscious at theta wave levels (4-7 Hertz waves dominant). This process recurs through the night about every ninety minutes (although there are wide variations, with some persons only having sixty-minute cycles, others 120 minutes). With each recurrent dream period time spent in REM dreaming steadily lengthens through the night, from five to nine minutes for the first, to twenty to twenty-five minutes for the last pre-awakening dream period.

The dreaming self that participates varies widely with many different levels of awareness of participation in the dream process. The dreaming selves represent truly altered states of consciousness.

Out-of-Body Experiences (OBE's)

The fifties and sixties saw a host of studies and some serious research, most of it mildly suggestive rather than definitive in any way. Today we need a more precise definition of consciousness as it operates during the dreaming process. OBE's may be pure fantasy within a special variety of dream. Conversely, they may represent one of the more significant psi experiences. OBE's probably are a critical source of most beliefs in a soul that is detached (and/or detachable) from the physical self.

OBE's raise fundamental questions about the nature of consciousness itself. Can one be conscious and asleep, or is this a contradiction in terms? Or, restated, are lucid dreams real? Brain-wave studies conducted during sleep may be useful here. It may be possible ultimately to define asleepness or awakeness in terms of the total picture of brain-wave patterns. Then, we would have to pinpoint the experience of OBE and match it against any of several fundamental brain states. We may, in turn, discover it to be something different in quality and characteristics from any other state. Conceivably, OBE might be a variety of clairvoyance with occasional telepathy operative.

A common puzzle also exists: the dream of falling just prior to awakening. Is this the moment of "rejoining the astral self to the body" as Sylvan Muldoon asserts? Why is it so common in adolescence (along with eidetic imagery) only to fade upon psychosexual maturity?

Dozens of other questions follow. What is it that "travels"? How does perception then operate? What are the interrelations of this self with the body? Are the two interlinked at one, many or at all points?

Induction: Body immobility of the profoundest sort seems to be a sine qua non, since any movement whatever seems to shatter the experience. Sensory deprivation also appears to be essential, such as that during sleep. The onset of REM sleep is a typical time for many OBE's. One must lack fear of the consequences of "leaving" the body. Dissociation may occur, with the "externalization" of self from the body as an aspect of an emergent altered state of consciousness. Sometimes, there is subsequently a wish to leave the vicinity of the body and to move around.

The Personation Pair

In many societies around the world personation is a culturally acceptable form of incorporating various aspects of the troubling environment into an immature or personally uncertain ego. Anthropologists have written scores of PhD theses on the process. Unfortunately, we neglect a gold mine closer to home in our own society, particularly among the more fundamentalist sects for whom this is an acceptable mode of interpreting or neutralizing a confusing, dangerous or threatening world. Multiple personality is the more dramatic current non-psi version of the problem, seen as a psychiatric concern. Role theory and psychodrama are now beginning to cast a significant light on the varying aspects of personality that can be absorbed into a single personation or self.

Within psi, possession and reincarnation are cousin phenomena. In possession the suggestion aspects of the surrounding society are critical, and confusion re self is an important additional element. Possession implies a temporary process, with varying degrees of consciousness of the prior self during the experience. Reincarnation is different, implying that the young ego is in part an expression of a prior existing personality that had a task to fulfill in this life. A trauma to the prior personality is typical, but it is usually an uncompleted trauma, with some loose ends that needed tying together. The emergence of the prior personality seems to clarify many problems for the young ego, yet curiously enough, even before the passage through puberty, as a rule, the prior personality has faded away, under the impact of personal growth, definition and strength. Another puzzle here is: why do the well-structured memories of an earlier life fade away in the fluid memories of childhood? What is there in the inflow of current experiences that tends to wipe out a strong prior personality set?

Possession

Trance possession, or more simply "possession," is rather common in certain cultures and under certain forms of social influence. It appears in religions throughout the world, and is often used to help detect personalities with dissociative tendencies who can be turned into religious, shamanistic or medical leaders of the primitive community. In this discussion possession includes what is normally known as mediumship.

The suggestion process aspect of this phenomenon has been demonstrated widely since the novel and movie The Exorcist, but possession in reality takes milder, less dramatic forms. The wild exaggerations of the novelist once again drown out the simpler story of the truth.

What reinforces the barriers between aspects of the personality, so that these disparate elements can serve to play the part of complete players or actors of self? Role theory gives us a few clues, but not enough. In the course of a day all of us play many roles, and most of them are situation specific, so that persons who could observe us during a 24-hour period might be very surprised to discover the other aspects or sides to the self.

Tart (1975a) has given us a conceptual tool, with his concept of discrete states of consciousness, that implies use of different personality elements, in different settings and environments. But there is no dissociation that applies when we turn from our spouse to the children and a different approach emerges.

When we speak about self we are also speaking about a biophysical entity that is moving about and reacting to the outer world. The alternate selves that we see are also expressions in ways that are different from the expressions of the primary actor of self. These may be demonstrated by manner, gesture, physical movement, attitude, confidence or step--by each of the means of personal expression available to us in the wide repertory that lies latent, but is rarely used, except under unusual or free-flowing moments.

The physiological correlates for these personality expressions can be measured. In a particularly imaginative study Arnold Ludwig (1972) and his associates examined the EEG of one subject, discovering some surprising variations in brain functioning of the various personality expressions. A fifteen-minute sample of each personality, prime and alternates, revealed that Jonah, the primary, was in alpha 53 percent of the time and in theta 31 percent; one alternate personality was in alpha 20 percent of the time and in theta 75 percent of the time, which incidentally was roughly the same ratio for the subject under hypnotic trance. Apparently, different physical components and aspects came to the fore, as different personalities were mobilized for the special moments of the fray.

All aspects of personality need to be examined psychophysically, to see what is happening, how much of which element is being mobilized, for what purposes. We can expect more "integrity" of expression for each of the subordinate personalities than would normally be suspected.

But this is not enough. What precisely, in psychophysical terms, is repression? How is memory blocked? How are whole aspects of personality held back? We must assume physical mechanisms that parallel, derive from and help to express the psychological.

What is the mechanism that activates possession? Is it essentially socio-cultural? How much of it is internal and intrapsychic, incorporating such factors as cultural beliefs, family tendencies or simply acceptance of its possibility? How much may derive from or is related to "archetypes" in one's family or background? What are the immediate triggering factors for the initial expression or "conversion" by the "possessing" personality?

How much of what is expressed derives from the natural history of the earlier basic personality? From prior traumatic, repressed events? From other members of one's family? What is the natural history of a possession case? What about special talents such as music or mathematics? How does possession meet the basic psychic needs of the prior personality? What are the factors that result in mediumship, rather than in other forms of possession? Are they essentially cultural, or accidental? What is exorcism? What are the factors that make it effective? What is its relation to the end of a medium's trance?

Finally, we should not neglect the long-held theory that there are disembodied "spirits" that do the possessing, as well. What would it require to maintain such spirits external from a body? How would they relate to Carington's (1945) psychon system? How, or at what moments, could they enter the living personality? In a sense the concept should be transferred from the church to the laboratory for systematic study.

Induction: Personal belief in the phenomenon is typical but may not be essential. Social acceptability of some form of expression of possession may vary considerably, depending upon the cultural matrix. There may be confusion regarding the core of self and identification with and strengthening of one or more alternate personalities, with both internal and external components. Usually, we see repeated suggestion process, over a period of time. The presence of others to whom the concept is important and acceptable becomes a contributing element. The person may use a culturally conforming technique of dissociation that has local meaning. Finally, we may see an altered state of consciousness and the emergence of one or more "possessing" selves.

Reincarnation

In reincarnation study, the most definitive work is being done by Ian Stevenson, so that we should examine his cases as reference points for the process. At least two prime hypotheses are available to us, among many possibilities. The first is the traditional one, centering around a disembodied "spirit" or soul that exists separate from the body after death. Spirit obviously presents enormous difficulties to our current theories of existence. It posits (as does psi) other levels of energy unknown at present. It suggests "personality" surviving by unknown integrations and "takeovers" in the form of possession of living persons who may be experiencing an emotional or physical crisis, and hence may be in a relatively dissociated or ego-defenseless state.

An area too long neglected here is "need patterns." What needs in the deceased person's life called for completion, satisfaction or action demanding some form of return to this existence for a given event? Was there an event (or a related series of events) that was unfinished? Why does the personality have to be reconstructed, even if temporarily, and for what "assignment"? Is it the person alone, or the survivors and their needs, too? What is the relation to the "host" personality upon whom the reincarnation is visited? Who makes a good host in psychodynamic terms? Using this approach, it should be possible to get a better grasp of the process, so that we may be able to find a common ground for most of these forms of personation and assembly of personality characteristics.

Spirit can thus be an acceptable hypothesis in the psi framework, but a simpler alternative is available: personation, based on the assembled memories of the living, employing psi processes. Reincarnation has traditionally presumed the re-emergence of a prior personality in the mind of a young child, usually born after the prior person has died. In the concept being presented here, it may well be a process that emerges under telepathic experience in the unconscious young, sleeping (or gestating?) child, absorbing elements or simulating a personality that is now dead, from those still alive who knew the person.

The personation can be of a neighbor or a deceased friend or relative in an accepting milieu. The young child often insists on a prior existence, identifies with another person who has died, and only after the passage of seven to ten years as a rule (usually by puberty, if not sooner) is there an integration of the "former" self and the new self into a functioning whole. At that point the adolescent personality no longer refers to the earlier personality. Again, fraud, wishful thinking and other approaches that reject psi are also fully legitimate alternative frameworks.

Induction: Most usually, certainly in Stevenson's extensive studies, there is a cultural matrix accepting the phenomenon, impressed upon a young, unformed ego. There may be a specific incident with a local expression of need to

evoke a deceased personality (this may involve more than
one person). We frequently see a dream or an unconscious
psi process that incorporates elements of the deceased personality, as expressed by those wishing to see them evoked.
Finally, with this dissociation, there may occur the emergence of the "reincarnated" personation.

The Space-Time Pair

This pair represent space expanded and time ruptured,
broken by psychological means beyond their normal limits.
Paramnesia may be a fatigue phenomenon that coincides with
the ninety-minute intradiurnal cycle and the regular appearance of primary mental process in the daytime, corresponding to the night occurrence of REM dreaming (see pp. 186-
189).

Cosmic consciousness, however, is an extraordinary
experience that sometimes changes a person's life forever.
Those who experience it occasionally become religious mis-
sionaries, in a continual attempt to bring the awareness to
others (but it is so personal!). Experiences subsequent to
the initial one are often not as intense, but they are reinforcing, nevertheless. The person is initially a seeker, and
subsequently one who has found what was sought.

Cosmic Consciousness

Here the individuals are, in part, trying to find their
psychic coordinates in space. In a sense, they are disori-
ented and ask "Where am I?" More important, they may
also be looking for meaning in the universe. Upon entering
the state the boundaries of self seem to disappear, and a
sense of unity with the universe (or "oceanic" feeling) appears in the place of self. As dissociation occurs there is
the most astonishing revelation: everything is just where it
should be; so is the self. There is a profound release of
energy (frequently life-long), as the questions that bound up
so much energy and attention are answered. Many are thereby "born again."

Bucke (1901), in Cosmic Consciousness, implies the
divine touch in this experience. It is certainly unexpected,
but perhaps far more common than Bucke would concede.
It is unexpected in part because it requires the right set of

circumstances. In an experience of my own, I stepped from a narrow corridor into a vast college auditorium just as the opening chord of a Bach chorale began on the organ. I experienced an instantaneous surging feeling of unity with nature. I was as large as the auditorium, if not as large as the entire world. The experience was overwhelming, but not supernatural.

Cosmic consciousness may be typical of the psi experience in one regard: it demonstrates the extraordinary change that occurs when first compression and then release occurs in a given mode of psychic functioning. There is a sense of exhilaration that overwhelms the ego and in part produces the magnificent experience of unboundedness. It can be produced by either physical or psychological release, but the question we must wrestle with is whether this entire matter may be another of the ineffable experiences of the right brain that cannot be reduced to words and that may not actually "mean" anything at all.

Bucke, of course, is the authority on cosmic consciousness. However, his examples and definitions are simply too broad and loose to use in a research context. For him, many change experiences that alter personal behavior are also seen as examples of cosmic consciousness. In reality there may be dozens of forms of cosmic consciousness. They may range from a very brief emotional high that accompanies meditation or sex, through the "break-off" phenomena of the flier or the scuba diver, all the way to life-altering experiences that shatter the ego of the past, and produce the profoundest behavioral and character changes.

All of these need to be explored and categorized in something like a systematic manner. For those interested in a start Tart's (1975b) Transpersonal Psychologies can offer a very useful classification base. Some of these experiences are illusory, while others are real, and the line between them is often quite thin.

There may be a partial explanation for the ineffability aspect of cosmic consciousness in some of the findings of split-brain research. The experience of new, total insight could conceivably arise when there is a shift from left-brain dominance to right-brain dominance under pressure of any of the trophotropic mechanisms, such as sensory deprivation or body quiescence. When this first occurs a different view of the world may arise, as if a new set of glasses or screens have been applied. The new view is total, intuitive and certainly a strikingly different view of the cosmos. Later repetitions may be less profound, but still important.

A difficulty arises, since this alternate perceptual mode is also non-verbal, tending more toward mathematical, musical and artistic, but usually non-verbal expressions. As a result there emerges a profound sense of inability to explain or describe what one perceives, and it is a correct perception of self: one is <u>literally unable to describe the experience in verbal terms,</u> since the verbal mechanism does not share that particular set of perceptions. Then, when the shift back to left-brain dominance occurs, verbality returns, but alas the perception is no longer the same.

Arnold M. Ludwig (1968) has an amusing caution based on an experience that occurred when he took LSD experimentally:

> "... Sometime during the height of the reaction, I experienced an intense desire to urinate. Standing at the urinal, I noticed a sign above it which read, "Please Flush After Using!" As I weighed these words in my mind, I suddenly realized their profound meaning. Thrilled by this startling revelation, I rushed back to my colleague to share this universal truth with him. Unfortunately, being a mere mortal, he could not appreciate the world-shaking import of my communication and responded by laughing! [p. 80].

<u>Induction</u>: Withdrawal from the world of experience, or loss of self by "merging" into the world, is a common entry process. This can be accomplished by meditation, self-hypnosis, repetition of mantrams or similar techniques. Disorientation for space-time correlates or disturbance in sense of balance can be produced by use of the witches cradle. Very commonly the state can be induced by a sudden release that may be spatial, biochemical or psychological. Dissociation may result, so that the "actor of self" is not fully present on the external stage of personality. Finally, an altered state of awareness of self and existence comes into play and the experience is at a peak.

Paramnesia

Paramnesia includes both the déjà vu ("already seen") and the jamais vu ("never seen"), distortions or disturbances of remembering. The process appears to be an attempt to integrate the fleeting, distorted states of self that derive from a misperception of time.

For those unfamiliar with the déjà vu, it is a sensation that the experience one is living through has been experienced before, in exactly the same way. It is an illusion, because a careful check of memory usually reveals the fact that the same experience did not occur in just that way before. The jamais vu is a feeling of false strangeness with familiar materials.

The two are fairly widespread phenomena. In a survey of 100 persons more than thirty-five years ago (Leeds, 1944), roughly nine out of ten persons interviewed recognized the experience of the déjà vu. Andrew Greeley reports a somewhat lower percentage (under 60 percent) have experienced the déjà vu, roughly the same percentage as have experienced telepathy (Harris, 1976).

In his 1977 Presidential Address to the Parapsychological Association Charles Tart may have given us an important reason to include paramnesia among the psi processes. Basing his remarks on a series of laboratory experiments, he suggested that real-time hits significantly tend to inhibit hits before and after the immediate targets. But such a process proposes a time band in which we operate that is broader than the momentary now. It suggests that we can move precognitively as well as retrocognitively. Such a process, when functioning out of phase, could very easily produce a sense of "having been there before." If a double perception is taking place, one registering but a few microseconds ahead of the other, then déjà vu phenomena could be one logical consequence.

The neglect of research in this area is surprising, since much of reincarnation belief is built upon this very narrow ledge: a weird ephemeral psychic experience, an anomalous memory dysfunction that probably represents a highly complex process. One would assume that the experience would have been thoroughly researched by now, but like the nose on our face, it is simply taken for granted and thereafter ignored.

On the other hand poets and musicians seem to have caught the essence of the experience. For instance, the song "Where or When" discusses the ineffable experience of standing and talking and smiling and relating and laughing, and yet being unable to pinpoint the precise prior memory to which the experience seems to relate previously.

Richardson and Winokur (1967) have conducted some study of the problem, and have isolated a set of variables that may be useful for getting a better handle on it. Apparently it peaks in age ranges from twenty to thirty-five, and then begins to fade away steadily with age. It appears more frequently among those better educated. Students, professionals and clerical personnel seem to experience it more than others. Those who travel seem to experience it more than those who do not, the range for those who do travel reported at 25-44 percent, and only 11 percent for those who do not travel.

The higher reporting among travelers suggests that possibly the greater variability to which they are subjected could provide grist for the dreaming mill the night before travel takes place. Such was the suggestion of Dunne, in trying to report precognitive dreams: that the experimenters particularly record the dreams the night before they travel. In that way the highly unusual events that might occur in a strange city and a new setting might well become the subject of the preceding night's dreams.

In a parallel study Buck and Geers (1967) have indicated that the stronger correlations existed among daydreaming, déjà vu, depersonalization and hypnagogic and hypnopompic experiences, among all the varieties of consciousness they studied. Since these are essentially the primary process aspects of consciousness, that appear at the edges of waking and sleeping, they may well be interrelated. Thus a common altered state of consciousness may demonstrate some of these phenomena, at the 7-13 Hertz alpha states of brain functioning.

Studies of déjà vu occurrences are badly needed. How often? In whom? Do they in any way coincide with the ninety-minute intradiurnal cycle? Can one be trained by biofeedback to have them in the laboratory, so that they can be examined under the EEG? Do they also coincide in some persons with epileptiform seizures? Or with any other type of mental activity? Are there "double" perceptual-memory circuits involved (e.g. left-brain/right-brain)? Or memory filing defects? Or other critical factors, such as the biochemistry of memory?

What is the relation of the déjà vu to the experience of the jamais vu, the feeling of false strangeness? Are they inverse, related or unrelated processes of memory?

Induction: We should assume temporal dissociation or disturbance of some sort that produces some confusion as to time. Fatigue or drowsiness may be present, contributing to dissociation or disorientation, possibly based on the low points of the person's daytime ninety-minute cycle. There may be some elements of a prior experience present. This can include dream elements. The experience can also occur during REM dreaming.

Sometimes a highly repetitive sound, such as a single word, name or expression may be spoken over and over again. This frequently induces the jamais vu phenomenon, which may be a reaction to verbal fatigue and monotony, as a new integration occurs with the oft-repeated word. Finally, as dissociation proceeds more fully, an altered state emerges, in which the paramnesia experience is a part of the personality complex.

D.   THE COMPLETE PSI INDUCTION MATRIX

At this point, having completed the presentation of each of the matrix pairs, we can now present the complete matrix of psi modes (see Figure 26). Many questions immediately assert themselves. Aren't there other mental functions that could have been included in the matrix? Of course. Memory, for instance, very likely has psi manifestations. As with so many other psi phenomena, total recall is triggered by the threat of immediate death. And total recall is an astonishing personality-altering experience for anyone who has lived through it: the sudden, simultaneous discharge of thousands of programs and tapes of minor and major experiences. There are undoubtedly biochemical stress factors that help to trigger total recall. And there are certain settings that seem to be favored by this kind of memory discharge: a fall off a cliff, or drowning, parachute failure and similar brief, intense crises that seem to call for the instantaneous mobilization of every known experience in the attempt to find the answer to the ultimate personal crisis.

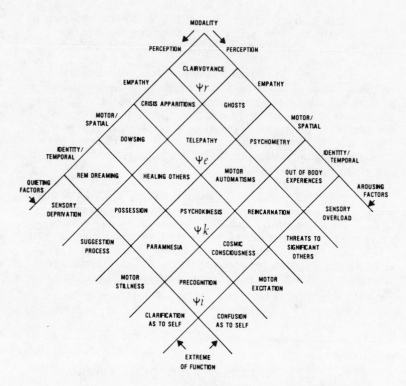

Figure 26: The Expanded Psi Matrix

However, we have chosen not to include such factors as memory, since the matrix would then have become unnecessarily complex, at a time when we have the greatest difficulty in sorting out the most basic elements of the psi process. Isn't a four-by-four matrix a bit simplistic? Of course. The only problem is our own limitation in introducing a scientific process into a difficult enough field, with but the fewest of reference points. It's a little like trying to learn chess when the chess master suddenly introduces three-dimensional chess into the discussion, and one is completely lost. In the real world, of course, the mind does not operate on one or two mental modes at a time. They figuratively cross, weave and involve each other like a basket of snakes. Most of us have seen the model for DNA molecules, two perfect helices circling neatly, endlessly around each other. In the real world, however, these

weave, break, lie flat, bend at right angles and twist every
which way. Mental functions, as non-dimensional processes,
can be assumed similarly to intertwine endlessly in the most
complex way possible. Only for purposes of analysis do we
separate functions out one by one or two by two, and then
theoretically assign characteristics to them.

Aren't there parts of the picture missing? Yes. We
do not have clear pictures of the neurophysical, the biochemical, the neuroelectrical and the various yet-to-be-identified
physical processes operating at the micromolecular level.
Despite all our growing knowledge of the electroencephalo-
graph, we still do not have good concurrent measures about
what is occurring at thirty or fifty or a hundred points within
the brain electrically, at various states of consciousness.
And this is but the smallest range of ignorance, compared
to what we shall come to know in time of the physiology of
the brain.

To summarize our assumptions: psi (assuming it
exists) is probably a unitary process, with many manifestations rooted in the normal personality. They are modified
by (among others) emotional, motor, perceptual, attitudinal,
stress, memory or ego factors. Psi, then, interlinks with
personality at thousands of points. Its particular expressions are essentially need (or goal) oriented. Psi-mediated
events are economical in the organism's terms, probably
moving along the shortest trajectories, if all the facts could
be known. Psi probably abounds during primary processes
and very likely is localized more in the right hemisphere.
Psi experiences hang on the margins of consciousness, in
the world of just awakening or falling asleep. Some of them
undoubtedly arise as a shift occurs from one state to another. Some persons can evoke more of the ability than others, probably because their particular personalities have
more of the factors that help to bring psi into being. Psi
seems to be universal and may be accepted in traditional
cultures, but tends to be ignored or repressed in the indus-
trial culture of today.

E. SPECULATIONS

The Psychological Makeup of the Psi Percipient

It should be possible to relate dominant personality characteristics to the form of psi that is individually experienced, per the theoretical formulations that have been spelled out heretofore. Thus, for instance, if certain subjects tended toward visual strengths, then conceivably we should expect them to experience clairvoyance as a characteristic form of psi-mediated instrumental response. Ingo Swann, an artist and psychic, comes to mind in this regard, since he demonstrates this clearly. So, if a psychic tends toward psychometry and dowsing, then theoretically he or she should demonstrate motor and muscular activity as a dominant mode of personality expression or response. Perhaps the perusal of a typical case can throw some light on this process, wherein (in this instance) the motor-perceptual aspects of the case insert themselves at every point.

Russell Felton, in the Prologue to Dykshoorn's (1974) autobiography, quotes from his personal experience in 1972 with James G. Bolton, a North Carolina businessman, as an additional witness to the remarkable apparent perceptions by Dykshoorn in a multiple-killing case. The material, somewhat compressed from the original, is as follows (emphasis supplied):

> We arrived in the small mountain town shortly after nine in the morning and were met by the sheriff, a deputy, and the local chief of police. The sheriff was a mountain himself, easily six-four and 280 pounds, a man as tough and rugged as the hills he policed. Leading us into a small back room, he gave the impression he could cross the room from door to window in a single, huge stride.

> At this point we--the clairvoyant, Jim Bolton, and I--knew nothing more about the case than we had read in the newspapers. Some months before,

the bodies of four people had been found in a house on the outskirts of town. They had been strangled.

This was all we knew, except that after months of investigation the police had made no arrests. Finally the sheriff had quietly sought the assistance of the clairvoyant, who had already worked on five similar cases in the South, with remarkable results. . . .

The clairvoyant moved from room to room busily, quickly, frowning over the spinning wire, pausing, hesitating, seeming to step around objects invisible to the rest of us. Suddenly, after stepping into the living room he halted. Then he lurched, stumbled, bent double, fell to his knees, gagging as though something had caught in his throat, coughing, choking, and gasping for breath. The veins leaped out of his neck and blood rushed to his face. His eyes bulged and his hands grasped at his throat. But just as the officers and I rushed to support him he straightened again as abruptly as he had slumped, and the face he turned on us was impassive, undistressed, even apologetic.

"It's all right," he said. "I'm sorry, I'm all right now." . . .

Then the clairvoyant announced the second phase of his psychic investigation. He would "follow, like a police dog," he said, the path each separate member of the killing party had taken from the house on the night of the murder, several months before.

"We will take each of them in turn," he said. "I will show you where they went." . . .

Following some instinctive "guidance system," always with the loop of wire spinning tirelessly in his hands, he led us right to the doors of houses and places of business, into the driveways and parking lots of gas stations, and once to a small hotel with an improbable back-street location. Where he believed a killer had walked on the night of the murders, he walked now.

Whenever he felt that a killer had driven a car, we climbed into the police car and drove with the clairvoyant giving directions. "Turn left ... slow down ... now faster ... slower, a little slower ... turn right here ... wait, stop. He stopped here ... back ... one got out here. There is another car waiting. A truck, a pick-up truck --five, six years old. Blue. It makes a lot of noise.... "

"There were three in the car. They stopped. Two got out. The first went on. Alone? Yes, alone. We'll follow him now, come back later for the others.... This hamburger place--is it open all night? I see a light inside.... "

It was broad daylight, but in his mind the clairvoyant had somehow gone back in time to a night months in the past. He was aware of us and of his real surroundings, but some part of his mind was in another car, and it was night.

"Slow down. Turn left. He stopped here. He was alone. The tall one. This is the killer. He went in this door. He went on? No, he stayed here. This is where he spent the night.... "

We were parked in the lot of a tire recapping business. A few bystanders watched us curiously. The clairvoyant was pointing directly at a doorway leading into the building. It was wide open, but he talked as if it were closed. "He had a key. He works here. He spent the night here. They know him. All these people know him. He works here in this place. His car was parked here all night.... "

Then we went back and followed the others-- from the house. We moved on foot through the woods. We rode in the police car. Once the clairvoyant made us stop at a green light because the other car, the one he saw in his mind, stopped when the light was red....

Then a truly astounding thing happened--an incident which, although comparatively unremarkable against the broader history of this clairvoyant's

achievements, still causes me to start in wonder
as I write about it.

Once again the clairvoyant led us from the
house, by way of a back route directly to a factory
in the town and through the open gate of its parking lot. The gateman peered at us in surprise
and suddenly it seemed strange, even slightly ri-
diculous, to be following the directions of a clairvoyant whose mind was in the past while around
us the world went blithely about its business.

But in an instant the mood changed. The dep-
uty, unable to hold down his dismay, blurted out
a revelation. Employed at this factory, he said,
is a prime suspect in the case--a man who might
have had a motive to kill. The suspect had argued with one of the victims over money. Threats
had been made.

Of all the buildings in town, the clairvoyant
had brought us to this one. And he had not only
brought us there, but brought us by the most direct route from the house--by a shortcut, in fact,
along an un-signposted back road which only local
people knew led to this part of town. And the
clairvoyant had never been in this county before.

Back in the sheriff's office, the clairvoyant invited the officers to ask him questions. "Ask me
anything, " he said. "I will try to work it out...."

Oddly enough, the more specific the questions,
the more detailed were the answers. The clairvoyant gave his replies exactly as if he had been
an eyewitness to the grim events of that earlier
day. The tension in the room heightened with the
dawning realization that a real case might gell
[sic] from this singular exercise in interrogation.

The clairvoyant paced back and forth across
the room, the loop of wire spinning in his hands.

"It was so, " he said. "Four went into the
house. One stayed outside in the car. He is the
short one, who went to his home. He is no killer.
He is very frightened...."

Then to the amazement of the officers, the
clairvoyant moved back a few paces. "Watch, "
he said. "This is the one. I'll imitate him. He
walks like this, see, with a limp. His left leg
is a little shorter than his right leg. He is shorter than I am, and I am five feet six. He went
to the house we went to, in the pick-up truck. "

While he spoke, the clairvoyant strode back and
forth in a limping gait. It was not the way he
usually walked.

Then abruptly, his manner of walking changed
again, drastically. He moved out with his shoul-
ders pulled back and his arms swinging in a rangy,
loose-limbed, athletic gait few short men can man-
age. Some gear seemed to have shifted in his
body, in his muscular and nervous systems. My
imagination might have been deceiving me, but he
seemed to be actually taller! He was the same
person, yet somehow we were watching a totally
different person.

"I'm imitating the tall one now, " he said.
"The killer. He is all right in his general health
but he suffers from hemorrhoids and they bother
him all the time. Also he spits a lot, every few
seconds. He is the one who works at the tire
place. He was in Vietnam and killed there, many
times, with the garrote. "

The officers exchanged glances. The sheriff
nodded to the chief of police and I was certain
they had given a name to this tall killer.

"You must understand I don't accuse anyone, "
the clairvoyant stated. "I am just a psychic and
can tell only what I see. You have to put it together your own way. "

Then he went on to describe--and imitate in
his fantastic way--each member of the killing party. Countless details of their lives flowed from
the seemingly bottomless well of information about
this months-old crime that was somehow contained
within his mind. He knew. He talked about ca-
reers, marriages and families, states of physical

and mental health, military service. He revealed
motives, plans, plots, meetings, arguments, con-
spiracies, and weaknesses. He described the relationships between the killers and between the
killers and the victims.

It went on and on. He described houses, vehicles, getaway routes, even the rooms in which he
envisioned principles [sic] of the case living. He
stated categorically that two of the killers were
seen and spoken to by outsiders who will remember them....

There was a momentary lull. Some confusion
over terms were cleared up. Then the clairvoyant
made a statement that lifted the sheriff right out
of his chair!

Shots were fired in the house, the clairvoyant
said. None of the victims had been shot, but he
insisted that shots were fired.

If a mountain of a man can be said to gape,
the sheriff gaped. "How many shots?" he de-
manded.

"Two," the clairvoyant replied. "It was so.
You found two bullets. One in the wall and the
other in the floor. Two shots were fired to scare
the people."

The sheriff slumped down into his chair again
like a wounded mammoth. He glanced at each of
his fellow officers, then returned his gaze to the
psychic. "Well, I don't know how you do it," he
said, "But you sure are right on that one. We
did find two bullets in the house."

Then, reluctantly, as though the feeling still
lingered that such impossible things should be left
in the realm of the impossible, the officers began
to admit the accuracy of other details pointed out
by the clairvoyant.

Some of them were minor but nonetheless significant: the arrangement of furniture in the now-
empty house; the positions of the bodies; the time
of the killings; the instrument of strangulation....

Then one detail more startling than the others was confirmed. The clairvoyant had said that one of the victims died not from strangulation but from heart failure brought on by sheer terror--and the sheriff revealed that the autopsy report agreed! Yet this clairvoyant had never seen the bodies, and the newspapers had reported that all the victims had been strangled!

The effect of all this on the officers may be imagined. Hardheaded and phlegmatic men as they were, married to their job with its tough, investigative methods and welded into their rugged mountain environment, they scratched their heads in bemusement at the scenes they witnessed and the statements they heard. But as the confirmable facts were confirmed, they took a hard look at their case and the new countenance it had suddenly assumed.

They had reached an impasse. They had had no real lead or theory, but now, out of the blue and out of the mind of a man who had been hundreds of miles away the night the murders were committed, they suddenly found themselves not only with dozens of leads and clues but--if they could prove it--the whole story....

Then, as we were preparing to leave, an incident took place that seemed to add a point of punctuation to the whole remarkable exercise. The officers, talking among themselves, mentioned a name. It was the name of a man--a local lawyer--we had not seen or met that day.

The clairvoyant turned, set himself, and strode across the room in yet another totally different manner of walking--ducking his head and coughing into his cupped hand.

"Is this the fellow?" he asked, smiling. "A fat fellow? Cigar smoker? Coughs a lot, like this?"

The officers--startled this time into laughter, shook their heads one last time in bewilderment.

"Yes sir. That's the one, all right" [pp. 12-20].

If nothing else, Dykshoorn uses motor and muscle process to convey his perceptions, sensory and/or extrasensory.

The Problem of Consciousness

An additional framework for a range of states of consciousness may be provided, as follows (see Figure 27):

3 1/4 /Sec.

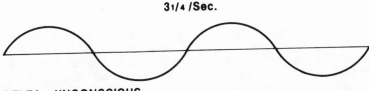

DELTA - UNCONSCIOUS

6 1/2 /Sec.

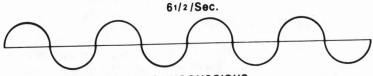

THETA - PRECONSCIOUS + UNCONSCIOUS

13/Sec.

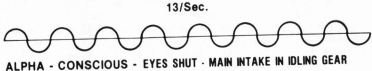

ALPHA - CONSCIOUS - EYES SHUT - MAIN INTAKE IN IDLING GEAR

26/Sec.

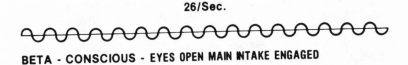

BETA - CONSCIOUS - EYES OPEN MAIN INTAKE ENGAGED

Figure 27: A Harmonic Concept of Consciousness

Let us assume a basic brain rhythm or cycle, at a beat of $3\frac{1}{4}$ per second, a working rate for basic functioning at the slowest level; sleep and physical rest. A first harmonic of this may be established at $6\frac{1}{2}$ beats per second, or double the initial rate. This rate serves interim vigilance for the sleeping self, masks a clearing and tuning function that keeps the organism in top condition, and guards the edge of awakeness in the event of trouble threatening from the outside.

The second harmonic, doubled again, operates at 13 beats per second. This stage also serves as a resting stage, in which the organism is still and peaceful, eyes closed, but other senses alert. The third harmonic doubles again at 26 beats per second. Here the organism is completely alert, fully awake, aware of itself and its surroundings. It functions well at this level, with all its higher functions in good order, assuming its lower functions perform correctly and well.

The basic rhythm ($3\frac{1}{4}$ sec.) may be called delta; the first harmonic ($6\frac{1}{2}$ sec.), theta; the second harmonic (13 sec.), alpha; the third harmonic (26 sec.), beta.

There is an important problem buried in this matter of Hertz brain waves. There are a number of clues in the literature that suggest that psi motor phenomena seem to occur in young persons with 4-5 Hz cycles predominant in their EEG's. Other clues from a variety of sources suggest that 6-9 Hz, or roughly high-theta and low-alpha ranges, seem to accompany many of the perceptual empathic phenomena. Certainly this range of Hz vibration rates seems to accompany the shift through preconscious functioning, whether upward into awakeness or downward into sleep. The problem is complicated by the fact that all waves are present in the brain at all times, to greater or lesser degree. However, certain forms and aspects of consciousness seem to be accompanied by wave-trains of a given frequency, that seem to become a characteristic of a given state of consciousness, in given areas of the brain. Computer work that assembles the average processes out may be of great assistance here. The EEG studies of E. Roy John (1975) with multiple monitoring points, though not specifically related to psi, seem to point the way for instrumentation studies that could be very fruitful in the future. The process is simply too complex to be derived without the assistance of computer technique.

In any event a suggested way of arraying some of these factors has been assembled into a single diagram (see Figure 28). While hardly definitive, it is intended to suggest additional conceptions for study and research.

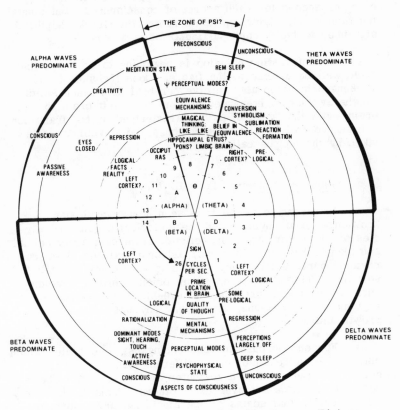

Figure 28: The Zone of Psi in the Larger Picture of Mental Functioning

The figure combines and suggestively relates a multitude of elements into a single figure, around the theme of conscious, preconscious and unconscious elements of personality functioning. The outer ring states level of consciousness; the next ring, characteristics of the psychophysical state, such as sleep or awakeness; the next ring, perceptual modes that tend to come into play or are turned off at the various levels; the fourth ring, the typical mental mechanisms that operate at these levels, such as conversion, symbolism and regression; the fifth ring, the quality of thought, especially logical and pre-logical aspects; the sixth ring, the apparent triggering location in the brain, based on best current research; the seventh ring, the predominant Hertz cycles per second for each aspect of consciousness and mental functioning; the eighth and ninth rings, the Greek shorthand sign used to typify each particular state.

An interesting question is beginning to be asked that could well be applied to the figure: does the shift from awakeness to sleep also involve cerebral dominance shifts (in the average right-handed person) from left brain to right brain, with the "zone of psi" characterized by the transition between control by either hemisphere and a dominant role taken by the corpus callosum?

Physical Aspects: Body Rhythms

In recent years we have seen a near-explosion in knowledge about rhythms and the biological organism. Cycles of every sort are being elicited from data about animal and plant behavior. Chemical, astronomical and electrical rhythms pervade the living system in a complex difficult to sort out. These may range from brief, familiar rhythms, such as heartbeat, breathing or eye-blink, to the year-long rhythms of the seasons, or lifelong rhythms of emergence, growth and decay.

For our purpose in researching psi, one cycle, which may well be a result of many different forces, weaves together like the work of a computer of average transience, a vector that stands out over many others. This is the ninety-minute cycle, that seems to operate in humans, more or less, throughout the day and night. Daniel F. Kripke's term for this is the "paradoxycle," and it may well serve as one of the most basic ultradian (less than twenty-four hour) cycles. It is clearly demonstrated during sleep, when after the first hour of sleep, the REM stage of dreaming begins. However, there also appear to be daytime correlates of this, during which one may become hungry, start to daydream or have sexual fantasies.

Richard M. Jones (1970) has diagrammed this, extrapolating outward from what is known about the nighttime rhythms into the daytime, as well. An adaptation of his chart is seen as Figure 29.

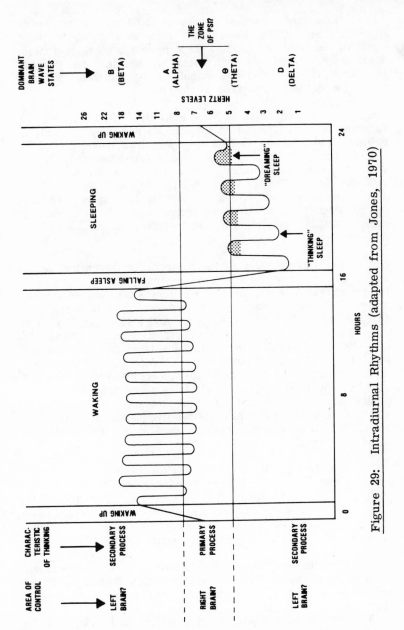

Figure 29: Intradiurnal Rhythms (adapted from Jones, 1970)

Generally, the first dream period tends to last about nine minutes. Then, about ninety minutes after the initial onset of the dreams, another REM period begins, this time a bit longer. The last such period of the night can last as long as thirty or thirty-five minutes. By the time this is over, the dreamer has fully awakened.

My own experiences, for what little they are worth, have tended to fall into this pattern. I normally fall asleep between midnight and 12:15 a.m. My first dream period begins about 1:15 a.m., or perhaps a few minutes earlier. When I awaken on command at that time, my dreams are full and vivid. The next period tends to begin about 2:45 a.m., the next about 4:15 a.m. and the last about 5:45 a.m. Again, when I awaken at these times (per suggestion just prior to falling asleep), I am in the midst of very active dreams.

The waking parts of the same cycle (assuming they exist, and I suspect that they do) seem to show a heavier fatigue or restlessness beat at the three-hour marks (every other cycle), which for me are subsequently 8:45 a.m., 11:45 a.m., 2:45 p.m., 5:45 p.m. and 8:45 p.m. By 11:45 p.m. I become very irritable and tired, ready for bed. The cycle is fairly regular, but with some variation, depending in part on the time of going to bed. Altering bedtime, in turn, may shift the first and subsequent dreaming periods a bit back and forth. Characteristic of these fatigue cycle points during the day are yawning, sleepiness and lack of ability to concentrate. After about five to ten minutes or so, ability to concentrate returns, and mental functioning returns to normal.

Incidentally, there is nothing mechanical about the ninety-minute period. Rather, it serves as a kind of template that has consistency, but still varies, depending on the actual events of each day and hour. Interesting events elevate a sag; activity, too, may shorten or obliterate it; boredom or quiet activity lengthens its period and depth even more.

What is the potential significance of the ninety-minute cycle for psi research? The periodic dips toward the preconscious (or rise, in the case of sleep) represent a brief time when psi can possibly be tested, to help overcome one of its greatest mysteries, its unreliability and undependability for repetition in laboratory experiment.

Subjects should be carefully charted to discover the timing of their personal ultradian cycles, and then tested when psi is most likely in operation, at the ninety-minute dips or rises. Biofeedback training can probably help to extend the subject's dip, thereby extending the usefulness of the psi-research period.

Physical Aspects: Neurophysical Concepts

If the assumption can be made that psi process is lawful, and is a part of mental functioning, then there should also be neurological correlates that accompany the process. The simplest aspect of this should be localization of brain function. So, for instance, if the process involved is telepathy, then we should carefully study the interaction between the cortex and the limbic system or visceral brain, as areas that are most likely to be involved in emotional and empathic effects. If the function is motor, then brain motor areas should be studied. Clairvoyance should logically call for the examination of the perceptual areas, and more narrowly, if visualization is apparently occurring, then the occiput should be studied.

Much of psi is a subtle process, not easily duplicated in the laboratory or under experimental control conditions. Still, repetitions or simulations can occur. By suggestion process, or more narrowly, hypnosis, we can reconstruct or relive experiences such as cosmic consciousness or precognitive dreams. Then, in the laboratory, EEG leads can be applied to relevant areas, to determine whether they are involved, and if so, in what way, and with what inner effects.

The induction process should be studied similarly, to determine precisely (and this implies down to the cellular level) what is occurring as dissociation begins, or the ASC emerges, and the psi process begins. Much of what takes place seems to begin in a small circle at the center of the brain, as Figure 30 would seem to suggest. It certainly merits further study, since this is a focal area for alterations of consciousness, as well.

The center of the brain, particularly the medulla and the limbic structures, also represents the old brain, the animal brain, since the cortex is the "new" brain, the brain of humans that thinks and makes them different from the

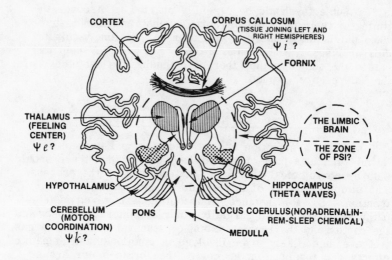

Figure 30:   The Brain--Frontal Cross-Section

animals.   Psi may have been a function of the limbic brain,
somewhere between the mammalian and simian brain structures, but gradually by-passed in the evolutionary process.
Then, as the greater refinements of perception and thinking
succeeded in humans, the more primitive system that psi
represented may have simply become less important.   This
could also suggest that the function may still exist in certain
animals, particularly those mammals like cats and dogs,
closer to humans.   Jule Eisenbud (1976) and Sir Alister
Hardy (1965) discuss the possible role of psi in intergroup
function and as an evolutionary modifier in two brilliant discussions that are well worth exploring for additional theoretical ideas.

The Bridge of Psi

More than a quarter of a century ago, Gardner
Murphy (1949) observed:

> I will suggest that [a] clue to the paranormal
> lies beyond the realm of needs and barriers, in-
> deed that it does not lie inside of human personal-
> ity at all, whether in its generic or in its indi-

vidualized aspects. I believe, on the contrary, that it is strictly interpersonal; that it lies in the relations between persons and not in the persons as such. If it be objected immediately that it must be personal if it is to be interpersonal, then let me plead that there is all the difference in the world between our stretching the conception of the personal to the breaking-point and on the other hand, our burning all our individualistic bridges behind us, and saying that the world of interpersonal phenomena is a world which must be faced on its own terms; pursued in its own right; its laws made clear and recognized to be essentially different from those laws which apply to individuals. I would plead for the direct empirical study of the laws of the interpersonal; the functions of an interpersonal field. I suggest that it is not within the individual psychic structures, but within certain specific relations between the psychic structure of one individual and the psychic structure of another that our clue lies; or if you like, that the phenomena are, so to speak, trans-personal, just as they are, indeed, trans-spatial and trans-temporal [pp. 11-12].

This can be extrapolated outward significantly. If we bother to arrange the various elements of existence in a sequence, ranging from the creation of the universe upward through life to humanity and consciousness, we find a curious process being illustrated at the same time (see Figure 31). Joining the extremes of these elements is the frequent presence of psi function, which seems to serve as a functional glue, operating as it were in the interstices of the universe. For instance, in the area of time, between the momentary "now" and the "eternal" record of all time, retrocognition and precognition seem to range most frequently during our sleep. The Siamese twin of time, space, seems to have its ranges of "here" and "there" joined by psychokinetic functioning. The postulated ranges of matter (the third of the basic elements of existence), extending "our" matter to "antimatter" appear to be bridged at the moment of annihilation by the world of irrational numbers, the world of "i," the square root of minus one (which may or may not have psi characteristics).

As we move upward on the scale of existence from matter to organic matter, the bridge between life and death

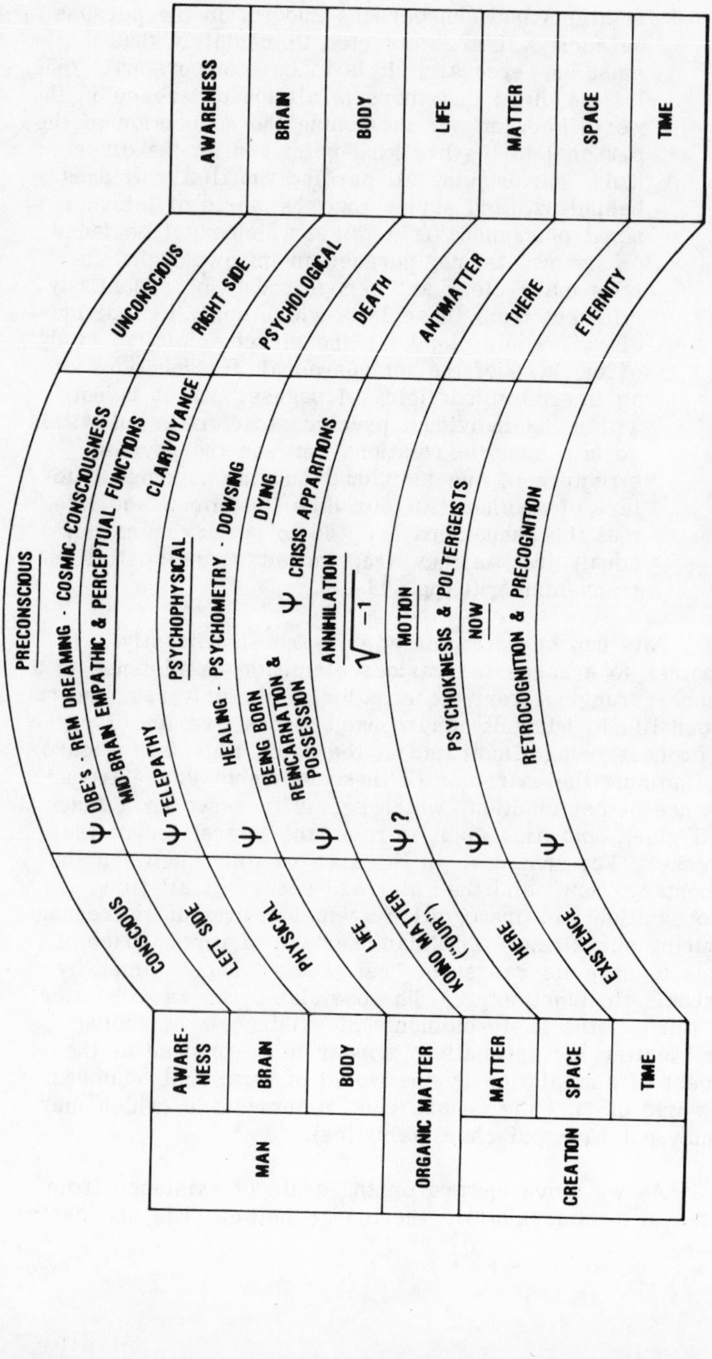

Figure 31: The Bridge of Psi

seems to be occupied by reincarnation and possession processes at the beginning of life and by crisis apparitions at
the end, just at the moment of death. Continuing on the
trip upward, to the human physical body, the physical and
psychological seem to be bridged by psychophysical functioning in the form of healing, psychometry and dowsing. The
brain, the crown of humanity's physical existence, seems to
center its psi functions in the mid-brain area, the corpus
callosum perhaps, very likely the limbic areas of thalamus
and hypothalamus, bridging the left and right brain. Finally, in the area most characteristic of humanity, awareness,
we see telepathy, REM dreaming and possibly out-of-the-
body experiences apparently functioning in the zone of the
preconscious, between conscious and unconscious functions.

The "bridge," if it may be called that, is suggestive,
more than anything else. Still, it is curious, somewhat like
Bode's law concerning planetary distances: no special reason as presently understood, but there is. It is inserted
as an irritating and stimulating artifact for philosophic mus-
ing; those of meditative bent may be able to develop this
concept, or group of concepts, further.

Part V

Some Final Words

A. IMPLICATIONS OF THE THESIS

What can we expect, if some of the concepts that have been sketched out heretofore are validated over the next few years? Many changes in our thinking, to say the least. In historical terms we should anticipate a gradual merger of the ideas of East and West, of modern science and the older wisdom of the self. Just as the industrialism of the West is rapidly overtaking the mass of peoples of the East, in turn the concepts of self and of existence, of the continuity of living and non-living processes, of the implications of altered perceptions of the world--all these can begin to take their place in the scientific perception of reality.

Psi will very likely continue to be studied by the military carefully, especially for long-distance, closed-channel communication possibilities. Alas for their ambitions: standard techniques of communication will continue to prevail for a very long time to come, since psi can be expected to be weak, uncertain, unpredictable and essentially unreliable in a world of beta consciousness.

We should expect a great deal of study of death, with less fear and repression and more willingness to accept it as a normal part of the process of living. Conceivably, physical death may come to be seen as an interim step in a far more complex process of being than we can currently conceive. Ghosts can be accepted and not feared, but rather studied for why they appear, and then properly "exorcised" and removed.

Medicine can be expected to change, certainly for the better. To the extent that we see the person as a whole, and to the extent that that physician is better trained to react to the whole person, to that extent will we see better medicine in the long run. Conceivably, persons with "healing" powers may be called upon to assist the nurse and the physician. In the more distant future we may possibly search out such persons and give them medical training for various roles in the healing arts. The personal role of attitude, set, prayer and meditation in healing may be better understood and very likely harnessed as a part of the curative process.

In the future psi may come to be casually accepted, just as evolution has been. There is certainly more acceptance today of our evolutionary forebears, and of our place in the natural order of things. An acceptance of psi may also further the sense of wholeness of our experience, may strengthen our ties with each other and with the universe at large. The curiously Western approach that each individual is a separate sack of walking sea water may give way to an awareness that we may occasionally, perhaps in critical moments, interjoin in our life spaces, communicate, relay some form of message, pass a torch or concept on to a waiting other. The relay may even go from one generation to another in ways that we have difficulty envisioning today. There may perhaps arise some better understanding of why there is such a strong persistent wish to push toward freer, primal thinking processes, away from secondary, more rigid approaches. There may well result better ways of coping with drug addiction and alcoholism. Conceivably, we could come to a greater understanding of the role of dreaming and could better utilize it in our daily lives, toward balance and more sanity.

All in all, we should anticipate a somewhat changed picture of the world, broader, more complex, with less and less mysteriousness ... and yet, with some important mystery still present.

B.   THE SKEPTICAL PARAPSYCHOLOGIST

So here we stand in the last quarter of the twentieth century, almost as puzzled as were the founders of the SPR a century ago. We deal with a phenomenon that still challenges the rigid canons of science, but there seems to be a relaxing of the dogma. The physical scientist may be upset, but a change is in the wind. We have spent more than two centuries concerned with thingness. Now we must also begin to discuss wholeness, completeness, the larger picture of the self in the universe.

More than a century and a half ago, members of the French Academy were openly ridiculing those who discussed "stones from the sky." Now scientists ridicule those who deal with phenomena even more evanescent, since psi leaves no hard residues behind, only memories of curious experiences that cannot be explained by a constricting "scientific" framework.

We may be fortunate that there are successions of generations, so that old ideas, too, can slowly die off, and the young can inherit a new world view. The young are curious to hear about the comet that returns every seventy-five years or so, and in-between is known only by memory and an occasional flickery picture. They are now beginning to reconsider the nature of personal and physical reality. "State-specific sciences" do not disturb them, if they have sampled (as so many have) mind-altering substances.

Our discussion has come full circle. We began with a history and a philosophy of the study of psi. We have pointed out the circumstances in which it appears to occur, however unreliable those circumstances may turn out to be. We seem to be dealing with a historical process somewhat similar to the eighteenth-century study of electricity, that showed countless manifestations, but the points of reference were few. What we understand about electricity today would certainly stagger people of the eighteenth century, no matter how sophisticated they might have been. And we do not know all about it, even now.

We have suggested that marginal states of mental functioning tend to lead to the operation of psi. Psi, when it does function, apparently can take any one of a hundred forms, utilizing the more commonly understood channels of the mind as vehicles. It operates in the interstices of certain preferred modes. For analysis purposes we have created little pigeonholes, but psi refuses to be pigeonholed. Its quicksilver process evades our analysis, as we reach for and desperately try to grasp it. Like the chain that bound the Norse god Loki, it is invisible, yet a bond of steel. And in its grip we are as baffled as he.

Thus, we have in our discussion tried to suggest that there is yet another aspect to mental functioning. Precisely what the physical and physiological components of this process are, we cannot pretend to know at this time. We have, however, tried to show its embeddedness in the makeup of human personality. Telepathy is not photography, just as the mind is not a clear mirror. Psi intermingles with every element of personal functioning, as much as perception, motor function, emotion and thinking. It is evanescent only because, like the hypnotized subjects who have been told not to see persons standing before them, we have banished it from our perceptual field. Similarly, psi is there, but we must learn not to believe everything we are told. We should instead continue to believe that answers to this master puzzle can be found, in the future, if necessary, but they can be worked out, on a scientific, thoughtful, studied basis.

The devout churchmen who feared the emergence of evolutionary thinking were no less fearful than some of the most respected of modern scientists who are afraid to consider a larger scope to their science. This is not a plea for woolly-mindedness. Rather, it is a plea for a lack of fear, and for an open-mindedness to facts, lead where they may. The larger view of humanity in the universe has steadily taken over the world of understanding and learning. We have transcended the geocentric universe and the heliocentric universe. Perhaps we can transcend the anthropocentric universe as well. We do not know the outer limits of all the forces that operate in the physical world. Nor do we know all the physical laws of existence. Each decade in our lifetimes has brought an increasing flood of information and knowledge that now has begun to shift the very anchor of our beliefs. But we can assume that the newer picture yet to emerge will tend to reassemble the entire structure again, even if the later picture is an unfamiliar or strange one. The Nature that emerged after evolution was far more complex than the paternal, authoritarian God that preceded Darwin and Wallace. Perhaps the universe will turn out to be similarly far more complex than our simplistic minds can conceive of, at present, with the limited data at hand. Space and time puzzle us, as well they should: we are tiny creatures, all in all, and our history has just begun. Creation, life and its laws puzzle us, as well. If we could but learn to place a part of our fears and beliefs on a shelf, and say simply: this we do not understand as yet--at that moment much of our problem would be put to rest. For then we could proceed into the future with less bickering and an easier conscience, as we together dismantle the Chinese walls of our ignorance.

C. A NOTE ON THE ISSUE OF SURVIVAL

While anyone seriously interested in psychical research in 1900 would have taken for granted the relation of survival issues to some of our foregoing materials, almost no modern reader would respond in this way. The problems of the survival hypothesis seem to have become less and less real to the generation trained in experimental and quantitative parapsychology.

The era of the great mediums, roughly from 1880 to 1925, has passed. Why have the great mediums moved on, and why have we failed by search and training to replace them? Perhaps there is a circular relationship: doubt inhibiting the development of mediumship and the failure of mediumship adding to doubt.

So, what then can we offer you? Do we expect you to take seriously, in the midst of modern skepticism and hostility to "outrageous hypotheses," first that a soul could exist independently of its material body, and secondly that this soul could communicate with the living? The data on survival were collected within a framework of such beliefs, and therefore they have a prima-facie reason to be studied in their cultural context and offered as serious hypotheses with reference to such evidence as can be marshaled. A case has been offered for communication from the deceased, and in this modern empirical era no theological or philosophical argument will any longer be taken seriously without empirical evidence.

Can the evidence be considered "convincing"? First, as the biological evidence comes in, decade after decade, year by year, it becomes increasingly difficult to find a way to conceive of a soul, a spiritual entity independent of the living system known to biology, psychiatry and psychology. Difficulties that were already serious three centuries ago as the physiology of the brain began to be understood, have become more and more serious. The intimate unity of psychological and physiological processes known to us through anatomy, physiology and psychopathology, even biochemistry and histology, makes the conception of an independent soul recede more and more into the land of the utterly incredible and unimaginable. As a modern psychologist, I find myself forced, as most psychologists find themselves forced, into this never-never land in which theoretical objections are so enormous that no empirical material can stand up against them. There is so far as I know no survival evidence that is completely unambiguous, complete in itself and free of all competing or alternative explanations. The theory offered by Mrs. Sidgwick (1900-01)--according to which secondary personalities are dissociated fragments of sensitives or mediums acting under the influence of suggestion, vividly impersonating the personalities of the deceased--can be maintained if one gives it a very great capacity to use telepathic information from the living, or telepathic and clairvoyant information combined. It is true that it takes forcing, but this can be done and will always be preferred when the alternative is an utterly incredible hypothesis.

But is that the only honest way of looking at the survival hypothesis? No; in all candor, there are several kinds of evidence that still remain essentially as they have remained all through psychical research, and that so far as I know cannot be swept aside or essentially weakened. There is the patent fact in the case of many apparitions, some dreams and many mediumistic performances, that the initiative--the directing force, the plan, the purpose of the communication--seems pretty plainly to come from no living individual, however fragmentary, dissociated or subconscious the vehicle appears to be. At the time of death, or some time after death, there seems to be a will to communicate. It appears to be autonomous, self-contained, completely and humanly purposive. In the best cases the intent is didactic, clear, sure of itself and shows initiative. It is the autonomy, the purposiveness, the cogency, above all the individuality, of the source of the messages, that cannot be bypassed. Though I have struggled as a psychologist for forty-five years to try to find a "naturalistic" and "normal" way of handling this material, I cannot do this even when using all the information we have about human chicanery and all we have about the far-flung telepathic and clairvoyant abilities of some gifted sensitives. The case looks like communication with the deceased.

Where, then, do I stand? Well, what happens when an irresistible force strikes an immovable object? To me, the evidence cannot be by-passed, nor on the other hand can conviction be achieved. It is trivial and childish to ask whether I believe fifty-five--forty-five or forty-five--fifty-five. Trained as a psychologist and now in my sixties, * I do not actually anticipate finding myself in existence after physical death. If this is the answer you want, you can have it. But this does not mean that in a serious philosophical argument I would oppose the survival case. I linger because I cannot cross the stream. We need far more evidence; we need new perspectives; perhaps we need more courageous minds.

Some recent work in this field has begun to explore the OBE connected with the moment of death. A paradigm of the experience has been drawn up, consistent with our general approach, as follows (Moody, 1975):

> A man is dying and, as he reaches the point of greatest physical distress, he hears himself pronounced dead by his doctor. He begins to hear an uncomfortable noise, a loud ringing or buzzing, and at the same time feels himself moving very rapidly through a long dark tunnel. After this, he suddenly finds himself outside of his own physical body, but still in the immediate physical environment, and he sees his own body from a distance, as though he is a spectator. He watches the resuscitation attempt from this unusual vantage point and is in a state of emotional upheaval.

> After a while, he collects himself and becomes accustomed to his odd condition. He notices that he still has a "body, " but one of a very different nature and with very different powers from the physical body he has left behind. Soon other things begin to happen. Others come to meet and to help him. He glimpses the spirits of relatives and friends who have already died, and a loving, warm spirit of a kind he has never encountered before-- a being of light--appears before him. This being asks him a question, nonverbally, to make him evaluate his life and helps him along by showing

*Before he died, G. M. added: "In my eighties I see no reason to change these views. "

him a panoramic, instantaneous playback of the
major events of his life. At some point he finds
himself approaching some sort of barrier or border, apparently representing the limit between
earthly life and the next life. Yet, he finds that
he must go back to the earth, that the time for
his death has not yet come. At this point, he re-
sists, for by now he is taken up with his experiences in the afterlife and does not want to return.
He is overwhelmed by intense feelings of joy,
love, and peace. Despite his attitude, though, he
somehow reunites with his physical body and lives.

Later he tries to tell others, but he has trouble
doing so. In the first place, he can find no human words adequate to describe these unearthly
episodes. He also finds that others scoff, so he
stops telling other people. Still, the experience
affects his life profoundly, especially his views
about death and its relationship to life [pp. 23-24].

Utilizing the foregoing framework, it should be possible to design research, picking up on the work of Osis
(1961). In addition, further systematic case materials need
to be assembled to test and reinforce the model, or to
modify it, as research and case study demand.

Finally, at the risk of appearing overwhelmed by a
single vein of evidence, we are adding our profound impression that survival states seem to be immensely bettered by
the work of Ian Stevenson, especially his impressively docu-
mented cases of reincarnation, which may not be properly
summarized, but which must be carefully studied, thought
through and studied again.

(Incidentally, nothing in this book is offered as implying a solution to the ancient mind-body problem, or even
implying that it is soluble. We are trying to think in modern scientific and philosophical terms. Ours is not an effort to show the ultimate relation of mind and body.)

D. POSTSCRIPT: ADVICE TO THE RESEARCHER

We must learn how to disarm our own defenses, learn how to minimize the massive forces in our society and in our own individual character that make us unwilling to confront psi, even unwilling to confront the very signals by which the presence of psi might be hinted. The existentialist, the psychoanalyst and the physiologist will join hands with new workers from unguessed future psychological schools to enrich our understanding of that vast system of the here-and-now that has been so unwilling to come to terms with the there-and-faraway, the displaced in time that is a special preoccupation of parapsychologists.

It is important to emphasize the problem of pattern or system, the problem of interrelated aspects of our life and of the deep reciprocities between our inner life and the social world of physical and cultural ecology, beyond which lies the world of energies not yet guessed, the world of cosmic relations, which unconsciously pushes up like a suboceanic volcano to break into the world of experience, whether of cosmic consciousness or of telepathy, clairvoyance and precognition or of other functions for which we have no names. I would specially emphasize also the conception of interaction in R. A. Fisher's (1942) sense, that no single variable will turn out to have exclusive control of the mainsprings from which psi makes its entrance, but rather the more delicate problem of interactions in which major cues, as yet unguessed, may still cooperate with essential minor cues of many sorts, of which we have preliminary and fragmentary knowledge.

What a lot of work lies ahead! Yet, look back to the physics of 1600 in which Gilbert did his experiments in magnetism and Francis Bacon wrote about inductive methods, a world even before Harvey, and long before Newton. That world of 1600 is about where we stand with regard to any real systematic understanding of psi. Even when the laws begin to line up in an orderly way, they will still, like all things biological and psychological, display staggering and bewildering individual differences that lie partly in the depths of molecular biology and genetics, and party in unique ecological relations between persons and certain fields as yet unknown.

Repeatability, then, depends upon the identifiability of components and of the requisite interactions considered systematically. Very broad generalizations--for example, about relaxation and motivation--are probably just barely worthy of being mentioned again, but most of the needed work will probably be of a more specific and refined type. It is certainly clear that the gross psi phenomenon does not ordinarily appear just by providing large quantities of the obvious variables--motivation, emotion, relaxation, dissociation and the rest. It is not that easy. Vast numbers of unsuccessful experiments lie cluttering the desks and files of many psi researchers. Repeating the experiments of A, B, C in the hope of getting the results M, N, O reminds me of Crumbaugh's (1959) heroic attempts with the help of two of his graduate students, to replicate the fine series of studies of psi in the classroom carried out by Anderson and White (1958). Using a very adequate method and with very adequate groups, a clear confirmation was obtained in one of the Crumbaugh replications and no results at all in the other. If this is true of our best studies, what shall we say of our ordinary studies? We will say that the psi processes have not been analyzed in anything like sufficient detail to permit real replication. Perhaps there were differences in subject talent; perhaps in experimenter attitudes; perhaps in the interactions among students and experimenters. At present we do not know.

Good psi performances just won't be replicated without the series of steps, the analytical work for which we have pleaded, both at the phenomenological and at the physiological level, and at the mathematical level of a careful study of factors and particularly of interactions. One experimenter with both genius and patience may replicate his or her own work, but it is very much more than this that we must demand.

I will agree with any critic who would interject at this point the fact that a computer of average transients (CAT) could probably comb out some slight generic factor that is usually present in successful psi experiments. That is, one might find a way to shortcut with modern techniques the enormous mountain range of complexities that we have suggested. Let us, however, think twice about this. If it is really true that some slight effect can be teased out by a CAT, we will still have the problem of finding out what it is in the organism or in the organism-environment relations that made that particular effect appear. If we knew what

particular parameter in our experimental procedure is caus-
ing this positive result, we would be more than half way to
our goal, but that is exactly what we do not know. We shall
have to do the hard psychophysiological work to find out
and give a name to a particular aspect of our procedure,
expression of which will then appear through the CAT.

We might as well, indeed, be looking for such major
components right now as we use sensitive equipment. In
fact, the CAT will be a wonderful cane to assist us in walking, but a very poor crutch if we expect to swing along with
its unaided support. In other words, the computer will help
us only if we are already marching along.

But what can we do to prepare ourselves for what is
needed at this juncture? What are our practical strategic
possibilities? They appear to be two:

The first strategy might be as follows. Just try patiently and energetically to replicate exactly whatever experiments have been most successful. When you get the
thing running smoothly, then drag in tough but cooperative
scientific collaborators if you can find them, saying, "If you
do exactly the following in the necessary order you will get
confirmatory results." Then you could go after funding on
the assumption that a hard-bitten scientific collaborator who
has gotten results somewhat like your own will be an active,
or at least a passive, support to you with NIMH, NSF, or
any other alphabetic support to which hard-nosed investigators
can appeal. This is mostly what we have been doing and
the results have not been exactly spectacular. In fact, it
has been the maverick individual, not the foundations and
not the federal agencies, who has had the sensitivity of ear,
the far-flung imagination, the tender heart or some combination of all these, to support us in the pinch. Maybe it is
only the rare maverick who can ever be expected to support
our efforts.

But there is another strategy involving three major
steps: (a) Disentangle the fact, the psi phenomenon, by all
the phenomenological and other methods described above,
getting the picture reasonably full and clear as to what the
components in the successful method actually are; then replicate, bit by bit, and all the bits together, with a full,
complex multivariate design to see the component and inter-
active aspects of the replicated successful outcome. (b)
Then, as you replicate over and over again, disentangle some

factors for specially close study, distinguishing between generic results that call for human subjects in general and on
the other hand individual results that relate to the biology
and ecology of a single individual who is nevertheless capable
of replicated positive work in a given context month after
month. (c) Then systematically separate out and also combine two or three or more factors that appear to be responsible for your success, until you get something that is ra-
tional in the sense that it can be conceptualized both for itself and in its relation to other scientific conceptualizable
principles, something that hangs together and can be described so as to keep your colleagues informed and motivated
to attempt replications from one research center to another,
using not only grossly similar methods but a comparable
design. What is replicable, then, in the narrow sense becomes replicable in the broader sense, not limited to particular times, places and persons.

Go after your funding for your broad support by serious scientific bodies, insofar as something has actually met
the replicability test. Then, with a very, very deep breath,
ask for the kinds of support that will be offered to anyone
who, after this running of the marathon, this running of the
gauntlet, accepts this ordeal by staff and study sections, in-
terdisciplinary committees, editors of AAAS and APA journals, official and unofficial spokespeople of the whole array
of pundits, who will determine what science can and cannot
allow to exist, and who will be ready to acknowledge that
you have reached the goal. By that time you will have gone
through all the steps requisite to build a model, i. e. , a
general theory of psi. You will have done what Conant
(1951) and Kuhn (1962) have asked us to do. You will have
marshaled not only a brilliant little jewel of a fact that you
want everybody to acknowledge, but you will have done the
hard work in putting together a new system of observations
and concepts in which your jewel, like any self-respecting
jewel, is properly set and can shine to advantage. Replication will not come your way as a prize for ingeniously copy-
ing some new experimental technique. It won't copy, won't
replicate, it won't even know itself when next you try to
show it to your skeptical colleagues. Replication will come
when the context of the event is well understood; and when
it comes it will be a fulfillment of a long series of immature, fragmentary, incomplete replications, none of which
was ready to become the authentic fulfillment of our hope,
until the phenomenon was so well understood that it created
for itself a context in which it could live.

References

Anderson, M., and R. A. White. A survey of ESP and teacher-pupil attitudes. Journal of Parapsychology, 1958, 22, 246-268.

Barrett, W. F. Address by the President. Proceedings of the Society for Psychical Research, 1903-04, 18, 323-350.

Bateson, G., and M. Mead. Balinese Customs. New York: New York Academy of Sciences, 1942. 2 vols.

Beloff, J. (Ed.). New Directions in Parapsychology. London: Paul Elek, 1974.

Braud, W. Allobiofeedback: Immediate Feedback for a Psychokinetic Influence Upon Another Person's Physiology; in Roll, W. (Ed.), Research in Parapsychology, 1977, pp. 123-134.

Broad, C. D. The Mind and Its Place in Nature. New York: Harcourt, Brace, 1925.

Brown, B. B. New Mind, New Body. New York: Harper and Row, 1974.

Browning, N. L. The Psychic World of Peter Hurkos. New York: Doubleday, 1970 (reprinted by Signet, 1972).

Brugmans, H. I. F. W. A communication on the telepathy experiments in the Psychological Laboratory at Groningen.... Proceedings of the First International Congress of Psychical Research, Copenhagen, 1922. Pp. 396-408.

Buck, L., and M. Geers. Varieties of consciousness: I. Intercorrelations. Journal of Clinical Psychology, 1967, 23, 151-152.

Bucke, R. M. Cosmic Consciousness. Philadelphia: Innes, 1901 (reprinted by Causeway, 1974).

Capra, F. The Tao of Physics. Berkeley: Shambhala, 1975.

Carington, W. Experiments on the paranormal cognition of drawings. III. Steps in the development of a repeatable technique. Proceedings of the American Society for Psychical Research, 1944, 24, 31-107.

_____. Telepathy: An Outline of Its Facts, Theory and Implications. London: Methuen, 1945 (reprinted by Creative Age Press, 1946, as Thought Transference).

Cobb, S. Foundations of Neuropsychiatry. Baltimore: Williams and Wilkins, 1944.

Conant, J. B. On Understanding Science. New Haven: Yale University Press, 1951.

Coover, J. E. Experiments in Psychical Research. Palo Alto, Calif.: Stanford University Press, 1917.

Dale, L. A., et al. Dowsing: A field experiment in water divining. Journal of the American Society for Psychical Research, 1951, 45, 31-16.

Desguisne, A.; G. Goldstone; and J. C. Crumbaugh. Two repetitions of the Anderson-White investigation of teacher-pupil attitudes and clairvoyance test results. Journal of Parapsychology, 1959, 23, 196-214.

Dodds, E. R. Gilbert Murray's last experiments. Proceedings of the Society for Psychical Research, 1972, 55, 371-402.

Dunne, J. W. An Experiment with Time. New York: Macmillan, 1927.

_____. The Serial Universe. London: Faber and Faber, 1934.

Dykshoorn, M. B. (as told to R. B. Felton). My Passport Says Clairvoyant. New York: Hawthorn, 1974.

Eddington, A. S. The Philosophy of Physical Science. New York: Macmillan, 1939.

Eisenbud, J. Evolution and psi. Journal of the American Society for Psychical Research, 1976, 70, 35-53.

Erickson, M. H. A special inquiry with Aldous Huxley into the nature and character of various states of consciousness. American Journal of Clinical Hypnosis, 1965, 8, 17-33.

Esdaile, J. Mesmerism in India and its practical application in surgery and medicine. London: Longman, Brown, Green and Longmans, 1846.

Estabrooks, G. H. A contribution to experimental telepathy. Bulletin of the Boston Society for Psychic Research, 1927, 5, 1-30.

Fischer, R. A cartography of the ecstatic and meditative states. Science, 26 November 1971, 174, 897-904.

Fisher, R. A. The Design of Experiments. London: Oliver and Boyd, 1942.

Gibson, J. J. The Perception of the Visual World. Boston: Houghton Mifflin, 1966.

Grad, B. Some biological effects of the "laying on of hands": A review of experiments with animals and plants. Journal of the American Society for Psychical Research, 1965, 59, 95-129.

Green, E. and A. Beyond Biofeedback. New York: Dell, 1977.

Grof, S., and J. Halifax. The Human Encounter with Death. New York: Dutton, 1978.

Gurney, E.; F. W. H. Myers; and F. Podmore. Phantasms of the Living. London: Trübner, 1886. 2 vols.

Hardy, A. The Living Stream: Evolution and Man. New York: Harper and Row, 1965.

Harris, T. G. Catholics prosper, while the Church crumbles. Psychology Today, 1976, 10, 44-51, 82.

Hart, H., and E. B. Hart. Visions and apparitions collectively and reciprocally perceived. Proceedings of the Society for Psychical Research, 1933, 41, 205-249.

Henny, J. H. Possession trance. In F. D. Goodman, J. H. Henny, and E. Pressel, Trance, Healing, and Hallucination: Three Studies in Religious Experience. New York: Wiley, 1974. Ch. 7, Pt. 1.

Hilgard, E. R. Divided Consciousness: Multiple Controls in Human Thought and Action. New York: Wiley, 1977.

Hintze, N. A., and J. G. Pratt. The Psychic Realm: What Can You Believe? New York: Random House, 1975.

Honorton, C., and S. Harper. Psi-mediated imagery and ideation in an experimental procedure for regulating perceptual input. Journal of the American Society for Psychical Research, 1974, 68, 156-168.

James, W. Report on Mrs. Piper's Hodgson-control. Proceedings of the Society for Psychical Research, 1909, 23, 2-121.

John, E. R. How the brain works--a new theory. Psychology Today, 1975, 9, 48-52.

Jones, R. M. The New Psychology of Dreaming. New York: Grune and Stratton, 1970.

Kennedy, J. E., and J. L. Taddonio. Experimenter effects in parapsychology. Journal of Parapsychology, 1976, 40, 1-33.

Kuhn, T. S. The Structure of Scientific Revolutions. Chicago: University of Chicago Press, 1962.

Leeds, M. One form of paramnesia: The illusion of déjà vu. Journal of the American Society for Psychical Research, 1944, 38, 24-42.

LeShan, L. The Medium, the Mystic, and the Physicist. New York: Viking, 1974.

Lodge, O. Evidence of classical scholarship and of cross-correspondence in some new automatic writings. Proceedings of the Society for Psychical Research, 1911, 25, 113-175.

Long, J. K. (Ed.). Extrasensory Ecology: Parapsychology and Anthropology. Metuchen, N. J.: Scarecrow, 1977.

Ludwig, A. M. Altered states of consciousness. In R. M.
Prince (Ed.), Trance and Possession States. Montreal:
R. M. Bucke Memorial Society, 1968.

_____. The objective study of multiple personality.
Archives of General Psychiatry, 1972, 26, 298-331.

McDougall, W. Body and Mind. London: Methuen, 1911.

Maher, M. , and G. R. Schmeidler. Quantitative investigation of a recurrent apparition. Journal of the American
Society for Psychical Research, 1975, 69, 341-352.

Mangan, G. L. A Review of Published Research on the Relationship of Some Personality Variables to ESP Scoring
Level. New York: Parapsychology Foundation, 1958.

Margenau, H. ESP in the framework of modern science.
Journal of the American Society for Psychical Research,
1966, 60, 214-227.

Martindale, C. What makes creative people different. Psychology Today, 1975, 9, 44-50.

Monroe, R. A. Journeys out of the Body. Garden City,
N. Y.: Anchor/Doubleday, 1973.

Moody, R. A. Life After Life. Covington, Ga.: Mocking-
bird, 1975.

Morris, J. D. , et al. (Eds.). Research in Parapsychology,
1974. Metuchen, N. J.: Scarecrow, 1975.

Muldoon, S. , and H. Carrington. The Projection of the
Astral Body. London: Rider, 1929 (reprinted by Weiser
in 1973).

Murphy, G. Are there any solid facts in psychical research?
Journal of the American Society for Psychical Research,
1970, 64, 3-17.

_____. Body-mind theory as a factor guiding survival
research. Journal of the American Society for Psychical
Research, 1965, 59, 148-156.

_____. A Caringtonian approach to Ian Stevenson's Twenty
Cases Suggestive of Reincarnation. Journal of the American
Society for Psychical Research, 1973, 67, 117-129.

Murphy, G. (cont.)
_____. Challenge of Psychical Research: A Primer of Parapsychology (with Laura A. Dale). New York: Harper, 1961.

_____. Concentration versus relaxation in relation to telepathy. Journal of the American Society for Psychical Research, 1943, 37, 2-15 (with Laura Dale).

_____. Frederic Myers and the subliminal self. Journal of the American Society for Psychical Research, 1971, 65, 130-143.

_____. The natural, the mystical and the paranormal. Journal of the American Society for Psychical Research, 1952, 46, 125-142.

_____. On psychical research. Journal of Communications, 1975, 25, 98-102.

_____. The problem of repeatability in psychical research. Journal of the American Society for Psychical Research, 1971, 65, 3-16.

_____. Psychical phenomena and human needs. Journal of the American Society for Psychical Research, 1943, 37, 163-191.

_____. Psychical research and personality. Proceedings of the Society for Psychical Research, 1949, 49, 1-15.

_____. Psychical research and the mind-body relation. Journal of the American Society for Psychical Research, 1946, 40, 189-207.

_____. Removal of impediments to the paranormal. Journal of the American Society for Psychical Research, 1944, 38, 2-23.

_____. Research in creativeness: What can it tell us about extrasensory perception? Journal of the American Society for Psychical Research, 1966, 60, 8-22.

_____. Unfinished business. Journal of the American Society for Psychical Research, 1966, 60, 306-320 (with Herbert Klemme).

_____. W. Whately Carington: In memoriam. _Journal of the American Society for Psychical Research_, 1947, 41, 123-135.

_____. _William James on Psychical Research_ (with Robert O. Ballou). New York: Viking Compass, 1960.

Myers, F. W. H. _Human Personality and Its Survival of Bodily Death_. London: Longmans, Green, 1903. 2 vols. (reprinted, with an introduction by G. Murphy, by Longmans, Green/Garrett Publications, 1955).

_____. The subliminal consciousness. _Proceedings of the Society for Psychical Research_, 1891-92, 7, 298-355.

Nash, C. B. _Science of Psi: ESP and PK_. Springfield, Ill.: Charles C Thomas, 1978.

Nolen, W. A. _Healing: A Doctor in Search of a Miracle_. New York: Random House, 1974.

Osis, K. _Deathbed Observations by Physicians and Nurses_. New York: Parapsychology Foundation, 1961.

_____, and E. Haraldsson. _At the Hour of Death_. New York: Avon, 1977.

_____, and M. E. Turner, Jr. Distance and ESP: A transatlantic experiment. _Proceedings of the American Society for Psychical Research_, 1968, 27, 1-48.

Palmer, J. Scoring in ESP tests as a function of belief in ESP. Part I. The sheep-goat effect. _Journal of the American Society for Psychical Research_, 1971, 65, 373-408.

Panati, C. _Supersenses_. New York: Quadrangle, 1974.

Pearce, J. C. _Exploring the Crack in the Cosmic Egg_. New York: Julian Press, 1974.

Pierce, H. W. RSPK phenomena observed independently by two families. _Journal of the American Society for Psychical Research_, 1973, 67, 86-101.

Pratt, J. G. Clairvoyant blind matching. _Journal of Parapsychology_, 1937, 1, 10-17.

Pratt, J. G. (cont.)
_____. ESP Research Today: A Study of Developments in Parapsychology Since 1960. Metuchen, N. J.: Scarecrow, 1973.

Price, H. H. Presidential address. Proceedings of the Society for Psychical Research, 1939, 45, 307-343.

Puthoff, H., and R. Targ. Psychic research and modern physics. In E. D. Mitchell, et al., Psychic Exploration: A Challenge for Science. New York: Putnam's, 1974. Pp. 524-542.

Randall, J. L. Parapsychology and the Nature of Life. New York: Harper and Row, 1976.

Rhine, J. B. Extrasensory Perception. Boston: Boston Society for Psychic Research, 1934 (reprinted by Branden Press, 1964).

Rhine, L. E. ESP in Life and Lab: Tracing Hidden Channels. New York: Macmillan, 1967.

_____. Frequency of types of experience in spontaneous precognition. Journal of Parapsychology, 1954, 18, 93-123.

Richardson, T. F., and G. Winokur. Déjà vu in psychiatric and neurosurgery patients. Archives of General Psychiatry, 1967, 17, 622-625.

Roll, W. G. The Poltergeist. New York: New American Library, 1973.

_____ (Ed.). Research in Parapsychology, 1977. Metuchen, N. J.: Scarecrow, 1978.

_____; D. S. Burdick; and W. T. Joines. Radial and tangential forces in the Miami poltergeist. Journal of the American Society for Psychical Research, 1973, 67, 267-281.

_____, and J. G. Pratt. The Miami disturbances. Journal of the American Society for Psychical Research, 1971, 65, 409-454.

Rose, R. Living Magic. Chicago: Rand McNally, 1956.

Ryzl, M. Some observations bearing upon the mental impregnation hypothesis. Proceedings of the Parapsychological Association, 5, 44-46.

_____. Parapsychology: A Scientific Approach. New York: Hawthorn, 1970.

Saltmarsh, H. F. Report on cases of apparent precognition. Proceedings of the Society for Psychical Research, 1934, 42, 49-103.

Schmeidler, G. R. Predicting good and bad scores in a clairvoyance experiment: A preliminary report. Journal of the American Society for Psychical Research, 1943, 37, 103-110; a final report, ibid., 210-221.

_____ (Ed.). Parapsychology: Its Relation to Physics, Biology, Psychology, and Psychiatry. Metuchen, N. J.: Scarecrow, 1976.

_____, and McConnell, R. A. ESP and Personality Patterns. New Haven: Yale University Press, 1958 (reprinted by Greenwood Press, 1973).

Schmidt, H. Toward a mathematical theory of psi. Journal of the American Society for Psychical Research, 1975, 69, 301-319.

Shevrin, H., and L. Luborsky. The rebus technique: A method for studying primary process transformations of briefly exposed pictures. Journal of Mental and Nervous Disease, 1961, 133, 479-488.

Sidgwick, E. M. Discussion of the trance phenomena of Mrs. Piper. Proceedings of the Society for Psychical Research, 1900-01, 15, 16-38.

_____. On hindrances and complications in telepathic communication. Proceedings of the Society for Psychical Research, 1924, 34, 28-69.

_____. On the evidence for clairvoyance. Proceedings of the Society for Psychical Research, 1891-92, 7, 30-99.

Sidgwick, H. The Methods of Ethics. London: 1874.

_____, and Committee. Report on the Census of Hallucinations. Proceedings of the Society for Psychical Research, 1894, 10, 25-422.

Stanford, R. G. An experimentally testable model for spontaneous psi events. I. Extrasensory events. Journal of the American Society for Psychical Research, 1974, 68, 34-57; II. Psychokinetic events, ibid., 321-356.

_____. Toward Reinterpreting Psi Events. Journal of the American Society for Psychical Research, 1978, 72, 197-214.

Stevenson, I. Cases of the Reincarnation Type. Volume I. Ten Cases in India. Charlottesville: University Press of Virginia, 1975.

_____. Twenty Cases Suggestive of Reincarnation (2nd ed., rev. and enlarged). Charlottesville: University Press of Virginia, 1974. (First published in 1966 as Vol. 26 of the Proceedings of the American Society for Psychical Research.) (a).

_____. Xenoglossy: A Review and Report of a Case. Charlottesville: University Press of Virginia, 1974. (Also published in 1974 as Vol. 31 of the Proceedings of the American Society for Psychical Research.) (b).

Stevenson, R. L. Across the Plains. New York: Scribner's, 1892.

Tanner, A. Studies in Spiritism. New York: Appleton, 1910.

Targ, R., and H. Puthoff. Mind-Reach: Scientists Look at Psychic Ability. New York: Delacorte, 1977.

Tart, C. T. (Ed.). Altered States of Consciousness. New York: Wiley, 1969.

_____. Learning to Use Extrasensory Perception. Chicago: University of Chicago Press, 1976.

_____. Psi: Scientific Studies of the Psychic Realm. New York: Dutton, 1977.

_____. States of Consciousness. New York: Dutton, 1975.

_____ (Ed.). Transpersonal Psychologies. New York: Harper & Row, 1975.

Taves, E.; L. A. Dale; and G. Murphy. A further report on the Midas touch. Journal of the American Society for Psychical Research, 1943, 37, 111-118.

Thouless, R. H., and B. P. Wiesner. The psi processes in normal and "paranormal" psychology. Proceedings of the Society for Psychical Research, 1947, 48, 177-196. (Digested in the Journal of Parapsychology, 1948, 12, 192-212.)

Tyrrell, G. N. M. Apparitions (rev. ed.). London: Duckworth, 1953 (reprinted by Collier, 1970).

Ullman, M., and S. Krippner with A. Vaughan. Dream Telepathy. New York: Macmillan, 1973.

Warcollier, R. Experimental Telepathy. (Trans. by J. Gridley; ed. and foreword by G. Murphy.) Boston: Boston Society for Psychic Research, 1938.

Wheatley, J. M. O., and H. L. Edge. Philosophical Dimensions of Parapsychology. Springfield, Ill.: Charles C Thomas, 1976.

White, R. A. The influence of persons other than the experimenter on the subject's scores in psi experiments. Journal of the American Society for Psychical Research, 1976, 70, 133-166.

_____. The limits of experimenter influence on psi test results: Can any be set? Journal of the American Society for Psychical Research, 1976, 70, 333-369.

_____, and L. A. Dale. Parapsychology: Sources of Information. Metuchen, N. J.: Scarecrow, 1973.

Wilhelm, J. L. The Search for Superman. New York: Pocket Books, 1976.

Wilkins, H., and H. Sherman. Thoughts Through Space. New York: Creative Age Press, 1942 (reprinted by Fawcett, 1973).

Wolman, B. B. (Ed.). Handbook of Parapsychology. New York: Van Nostrand, Reinhold, 1977.

Glossary

alpha: the most common brain-wave form of the EEG from the adult cortex when the subject is resting and the eyes are closed; the resultant waves are smooth and regular at a rate of 8-12 per second.

altered state of consciousness (ASC): a state of mind in which an individual feels a qualitative shift in the pattern of mental functioning, from the normal state; this may include one or more shifts of quantitative functioning as well; a typical example is the shift from dreaming sleep to awakening.

ASPR: The American Society for Psychical Research.

automatism: generally, refers to muscle movements or acts beyond the conscious awareness of the person; automatic writing is one form of automatism, reflexes and tics are others.

beta: the normal brain-wave form of those conscious and functioning in the outer world of sensory-perceptual and intellectual awareness; it usually is defined in terms of oscillations of 13-26 per second.

biofeedback: a process of learning to detect small differences in internal perception of functioning that successively refines the perception, so that what were formerly imperceptible unconscious processes come under conscious or partly conscious control.

clairvoyance: the ability to perceive objects or events without using the conventional sensory-perceptual modes.

communication: a message of varying length spoken or written down by a medium and purporting to come from discarnate minds or to be otherwise paranormally derived.

220

computer of average transients (CAT): a computer that produces a visual screen wave averaging all relevant factors
into a single mode.

conscious: the zone or sector of personality that is aware
of its functioning self; in terms of usual EEG brain waves,
it generally covers the Hertz levels 8-26, or alpha and
beta.

conversion (or conversion hysteria): an unconscious mechanism or process that turns psychic conflict into bodily
symptoms, including anesthesia, paralysis and similar
dissociated dysfunctions.

cortex: the outer, or evolutionarily newest, layer of the
brain, the so-called grey matter, in which most thinking,
memory, perception and certain motor functions are controlled and coordinated.

cosmic consciousness: a dissociated state of mind, in which
the boundaries of the self seem to disappear and a sense
of unity with the universe, or a part of it, appears.

crisis apparition: a visual hallucination by one person of
another person experiencing a critical moment, such as
death or threat of death.

cross-correspondences: communications obtained by different
mediums who are not in normal contact with each other,
the material making no sense individually, but conveying
an intelligible message or meaning when put together.

delta: an EEG brain wave, ranging from .5-4 Hertz; tends
to occur most frequently during non-REM sleep, with few
dreams; those that occur tend to be essentially realistic.

dissociation: a preconscious state, in which the subsystems
of personality maintain or increase their internal organization, while they begin to lose coherence with the rest
of personality.

dowsing: the clairvoyant ability to perceive water, minerals
or other natural elements below ground, without using the
normal sensory-perceptual means; may involve use of a
wand, forked stick or other instrument held in the hands
that points downward when the dowser is over the material being sought (syn.: water-witching).

dualism: the philosophy that mind and body are qualitatively different.

eidetic: a person with the ability to reproduce mentally prior perceptions with almost literal accuracy (syn.: one with a photographic memory).

emergence: the monistic philosophy that the properties of a compound or of complex processes transcend the properties of the single elements that make up the compound or process.

ESP: extrasensory perception; a general term used to describe the perceptual aspect of psi process.

Ganzfeld screen: two pingpong ball halves, usually tinted pink, taped in place over the eyes; white light then provides sensory deprivation to the open eyes, frequently resulting in visual hallucinations; if the ball plastic is left white, pink light will serve the same purpose.

ghost: the hallucination of a past event or person by another person.

goat: one who does not believe in the possibility of the phenomena categorized as psi.

gyrus: a convolution or fold of the surface of the cerebral cortex.

hallucination: a sensory illusion that appears to exteriorize an internal creation or experience.

Hertz: electromagnetic wave measurements, as defined in beats or waves per second; named after the nineteenth-century German physicist Heinrich Hertz.

hippocampus: a lobe of the brain cortex partly wrapped below and around the hypothalamus; it is apparently the site of slow-train theta waves during REM-sleep.

hypnagogic: the drowsy moments just prior to sleep.

hypnopompic: the drowsy moments just upon awakening.

hypnosis: one aspect of suggestion process, in which one is responsive in varying degrees to suggestions, generally

of other persons who have induced the state, and who
have thereby partly shaped the definition of the state.

hypothalamus: a lobe of the older brain that hangs below
and toward the back of the thalamus; it is at the base of
the brain.

idealism: the monistic philosophy that physical matters are
illusory and that the only reality is mind, its functions
and perceptions.

interactionism: the dualistic philosophy that the mind and
the body are distinct entities that act upon and influence
each other.

JASPR: the Journal of the American Society for Psychical
Research.

K-object: (Carington) a set of common facts or items, shared
by sender and percipient, that tend to serve as a carrier, channel or mirror (depending on the model used) for
the psi experience.

locus coeruleus: two small groups of cells high in the pons
of the brain, that produce noradrenalin, which results in
REM sleep.

mandala: a pattern, usually circular and symmetrical, which
draws the visual attention of the meditator, and keeps it
focused increasingly inward, until dissociation is achieved.

mantra or mantram: an auditory pattern, usually embodying
resonant sounds, that is repeated to produce auditory deprivation and monotony, leading to dissociation; in Asia
the sounds are held to have an influential power in themselves apart from meaning.

mechanism: the monistic philosophy that the mind consists
only of the functions carried out by the body, especially
the brain.

meditation: any one of several techniques for turning the
attention, perception and thinking inward and away from
the outer world, in the attempt to achieve dissociation initially, and a state of non-self-awareness ultimately.

medium: a person who is able to dissociate easily, and by
any one of several expressive means can allegedly "com-

municate" with other "personalities" on other "planes of existence"; voice and writing are favored means of expression.

medulla oblongata: the top part of the spinal cord, just below the pons, where the cord joins the brain.

MOBIA: mental or behavioral influence of an agent.

monism: the philosophy that the mind is the body at work, or that mind and body are different ways of perceiving the same reality.

multiple personality: the organization of several selves within the same person, alternately expressed.

noise: meaningless or distracting material that helps distort the message in any communication sequence.

OBE: out-of-body experience; a sensation that one is conscious while asleep and dreaming, with an alternate, greatly thinned body that is able to move around relatively freely (syn.: astral travel).

occiput: two paired lobes at the back of the cerebral cortex, the organizing center for most visual impressions.

panpsychism: the monistic philosophy that all matter shares elements of consciousness, at higher or lower levels.

parallelism: the dualistic philosophy that mind and body operate interactively in lockstep and can never get out of step with each other.

paranormal: sensory phenomena or physical events not explicable by present concepts of perception and motor capacities.

parapsychology: the scientific study of psi or psychical phenomena by psychologists, biologists and physicists.

parasympathetic nervous system: essentially the cranial and sacral parts of the nervous system that serve to relax and quiet the organism.

percipient: one who "receives" or tries to receive a telepathic image or message.

PMIR: psi-mediated instrumental response; some action by the person (conscious or not) in response to a psi stimulus.

poltergeist: the movement of physical objects by unknown forces or means, usually in the presence of a young person (syn.: troubled spirit or ghost).

pons: the part of the brain stem, enlarged somewhat like a bulb, that joins the brain and the spinal cord.

possession: the apparent occupying of one person's mind by another person's personality, living or dead.

precognition: the act of becoming aware of an event by psi processes before it occurs.

preconscious: the zone or aspect of personality (including much of accessible memory) that lies between the conscious and unconscious selves; it is most apparent just prior to and after sleeping, in hypnotic and suggestive states, in dissociation and altered states of consciousness.

psi: the abbreviation for all psychical phenomena; the research object of parapsychologists.

psychic mechanisms: the unconscious mechanisms, including sublimation, regression, repression, reaction formation and similar dream and preconscious processes; these are largely mechanisms of equivalence, wherein tension, energy or anxiety are transmuted into other forms of behavior or symptomatology.

psychokinesis: the movement or influencing of matter by psi means or mechanisms (abbr.: PK; syn.: psi kappa).

psychometry: the clairvoyant ability to read off prior events that have taken place in the presence of an object, by holding or touching the object.

psychon: (Carington) a disembodied memory or group of memories; a conscious element, or consciousness.

reaction formation: one of the unconscious psychic defense mechanisms that compensates for an unconscious wish or fear by compelling the adoption of negating or canceling behavior (e.g. handwashing for a guilty person).

regression: another of the unconscious psychic defense mechanisms, manifested by a return to earlier forms of behavior, under stress or other forms of personal difficulty
or failure.

reincarnation: the concept that human personality consists
of a physical body and a mind, spirit or some non-physical aspect that survives the death of the physical body
and later becomes associated with a new physical body,
thus developing a new personality that is to some extent
continuous with the first one.

REM sleep: rapid eye movement sleep; a level of light
sleep in which most dreams occur, accompanied by the
quick movement of the eyes behind the closed eyelids;
theta brain waves ranging from 4-8 Hertz commonly occur at the same time; REM sleep tends to recur in 60-90
minute cycles, beginning about an hour after the person
falls asleep (syn.: paradoxical sleep).

repression: another of the unconscious psychic defense mechanisms that involves the forgetting of painful material
or events.

reticulo articulating system: white nerve cells that reach
up through the medulla and the pons into the cortex; they
serve to assist in wakening and alerting the organism
(abbr.: RAS).

retrocognition: the perception of past events in the present
by psi processes.

scrying: a method for stimulating clairvoyance using a
blurry, unformed background on which to project the impressions; more narrowly, refers to use of a crystal
ball for this purpose.

sender: one who "sends" or tries to send a telepathic image
or message.

sensory deprivation: the cutting down of sensory processes
and stimuli, so that dissociation sets in and preconscious
processes come to dominate the personality.

SPR: the Society for Psychical Research, a London-based
research group.

sheep: one who believes in or tends toward accepting the possibility of the existence of psi phenomena.

stigmata: the appearance of meaningful symbols or markings on the body through suggestion and imitation.

subception: subconscious perception.

sublimation: another of the unconscious psychic defense mechanisms, in which energy or tension is creatively changed into useful or socially acceptable activity.

subliminal: below conscious levels of perceptual experience.

suggestion process: the entire range of empathetically-induced mutually reinforcing belief systems; hypnosis is one aspect or part of this larger range.

symbolism: another of the unconscious psychic defense mechanisms, wherein the tension or anxiety process emerges into consciousness in a condensed or simplified form disguised as a symbol or sign.

sympathetic nervous system: largely, the thoracolumbar division of the nervous system that heightens tension and preparation for activity; its effects are countered by the parasympathetic nervous system.

telepathy: the passage or sharing of information between two personalities by extrasensory processes.

temporal lobes: parts of the cerebral cortex inside the temples, at the sides of the brain.

thalamus: a brain lobe close to the center of the brain, involved with control of the emotions and relaying information between various sensory organs and the cortex.

theta: EEG brain waves ranging from 4-8 Hertz, common in preconscious and upper unconscious brain functioning especially during REM sleep; may accompany some psi phenomena.

trance: a mental state in which the usual actor of self is partly or wholly submerged and unconscious or preconscious mechanisms come into play (syn.: dissociation).

<u>unconscious</u>: the aspect of personality deeper than the conscious and preconscious levels; part of it may constitute the memory filing system for every experience to which the organism has been exposed (those readily recallable are preconscious); non-REM sleep can also occur while the person is unconscious.

<u>white sound</u>: a blurry, "shshing" form of sound, used to mask pain, similar to the sound of a seashell; it can provide auditory sensory deprivation, frequently resulting in auditory hallucinations.

<u>witches cradle</u>: a triangular platform, so rigged that the person standing on it with eyes closed rapidly becomes spatially disoriented, since every movement produces successively correlated additional swaying and rocking; it is one of the more effective forms of inducing motor dissociation, ranking with the Ganzfeld screen and white sound; it was adapted and perfected by the team of Robert Masters and Jean Houston (syn.: ASCID, Altered State of Consciousness Induction Device).

<u>Zeigarnik phenomenon</u>: the urge to completion of an incompleted action; first studied by Bela Zeigarnik.

Two Personal Notes

Gardner Murphy:
Most books have a history or story behind them, and this one is no exception. I grew up in an atmosphere of interest in psychic matters. In Concord, Massachusetts, my home base, not far from Harvard, the influence of William James was strong, and James was deeply concerned with the subject. My grandfather's library included a book by Sir William Barrett, Psychical Research, which I read excitedly at the age of 16. A few years later, the fall of 1916 saw me a graduate student at Harvard with an opportunity to combine psychology and psychic research; Troland helped to guide me through the literature. This whetted my appetite for further work in the field. Later, an invitation to accept the Richard Hodgson Fellowship in Psychic Research from 1922 to 1925 gave me a chance for more intensive study. In the summers of 1921 and '22, while exploring work in parapsychology abroad, I became acquainted with the British leaders and the French chemist, Warcollier, with whom I carried out long-distance experiments. One result of my British experience was election to the presidency of the Society for Psychical Research in London for one year.

In New York, as president of the American Society for Psychical Research (ASPR) for ten years, I worked with Laura Dale and others to raise the scientific standards of the Society. Subjects and experimenters were not hard to recruit at Columbia University. The summer of 1942 found me teaching a class in psychic research at Harvard; this brought the gifted Gertrude Schmeidler into the field and also led to collaborative research with J. G. Pratt, Ernest Taves and J. L. Woodruff. Later, at the Menninger Foundation, Alice Moriarty and I carried out study of the relation of extrasensory perception to creativity.

Through these years I had been writing theoretical, critical and research papers, most of which were published in the

237

Journal of the ASPR. A book, Challenge of Psychical Research, attempted to present a sample of the most important scientific work in the field in a readable form.

My main professional life from 1920 on was teaching and research in psychology. At that time established psychologists and scientists in general were not only skeptical of the worth of research in parapsychology--they ridiculed and attacked it. There was no way to earn a living in the field, taboo as it then was. After sixty years many scientists have now become interested, partly as a result of new work in physics, neurology, and the impact of Eastern thought. Dozens of courses and a few degrees in parapsychology are offered at good universities. Although the rigid taboo has noticeably softened, ridicule and closed minds have not vanished.

Morton Leeds:
As a teenager during the late thirties I became deeply interested in the problem of time anomalies. The first book I ever reviewed in print was Henry James Forman's The Story of Prophecy, for a science fantasy magazine, Unknown. The experience of déjà vu was common to me, and one day in the early forties I brought the problem to Gardner Murphy, then a psychology professor of mine at City College. He recited a list of excellent resources with which to study the problem and then suggested that I begin to examine it seriously. Eventually the work became my honors project, and for a two-year period I examined more than a hundred instances of it in myself, while conducting interviews for a hundred employees at work, regarding their familiarity with the experience (an article derived from this was ultimately published in the Journal of the ASPR). At about the same time I was recruited as a potential psi subject at the ASPR, panning out as essentially average, except for one wildly exciting run (four or five in a row) that followed the sudden announcement of a major Russian victory over the Nazis in the midst of a soothing music program on the radio. During the Second World War I was a psi subject for G. M. (who was in New York) while in Calcutta, where I was stationed for a year (the Sherman study with Wilkins in Alaska was very fresh in G. M.'s mind at the time). After the War I joined G. M. as a research assistant on a Hyslop-Prince Fellowship at the ASPR, assisting him with the appendix to his book Personality: A Biosocial Approach. At the ASPR I learned the vocabulary of psi and the broad range of its apparent expression. However, the War had changed me and

I turned away from psychology after a stint in psychiatric social work, going into social administration, social gerontology, writing and teaching.

G. M. and I continued in communication all during the years he was at Menningers. Then in the late sixties, when he came to Washington (where I had been since 1962), we resumed a working partnership, planning to review and condense all of his publications on psi. For two years we interrupted this to bring out his book on insight, <u>Outgrowing Self-Deception</u>, but then we returned to these labors, gradually evolving this MS. His fall in Florida a few years ago slowed down the work, but did not stop it. In weekly discussions over a seven-year period, we thrashed out questions regarding the content, with Lois Murphy as an active participant after the fall. At any rate, the work is now done.

It should be noted that G. M. died in March 1979, at the age of 83, while the MS was being prepared by the publisher.